AT HOME IN TWO COUNTRIES

CITIZENSHIP AND MIGRATION IN THE AMERICAS

General Editor: Ediberto Román

# At Home in Two Countries

*The Past and Future of Dual Citizenship*

Peter J. Spiro

NEW YORK UNIVERSITY PRESS

*New York*

NEW YORK UNIVERSITY PRESS

New York

www.nyupress.org

References to Internet websites (URLs) were accurate at the time of writing. Neither the author nor New York University Press is responsible for URLs that may have expired or changed since the manuscript was prepared.

Library of Congress Cataloging-in-Publication Data
Names: Spiro, Peter J., author.
Title: At home in two countries : the past and future of dual citizenship / Peter J. Spiro.
Other titles: Citizenship and migration in the Americas.
Description: New York ; London : New York University Press, [2016] | "2016 |
Series: Citizenship and migration in the Americas |
Includes bibliographical references and index.
Identifiers: LCCN 2015047797 | ISBN 9780814785829 (cl : alk. paper) |
ISBN 0814785824 (cl : alk. paper)
Subjects: LCSH: Dual nationality—United States—History. | Dual nationality—History.
Classification: LCC KF4719 .S65 2016 | DDC 342.7308/3—dc23
LC record available at http://lccn.loc.gov/2015047797

New York University Press books are printed on acid-free paper, and their binding materials are chosen for strength and durability. We strive to use environmentally responsible suppliers and materials to the greatest extent possible in publishing our books.

Manufactured in the United States of America

10 9 8 7 6 5 4 3 2 1

Also available as an ebook

*For Liana and Julian*

# CONTENTS

# Introduction

In March 2013, my two children and I walked into the German consulate on the East Side of Manhattan without an appointment. We were there to collect our German citizenship. We took a number, deli style, and sat in airport-mode black-plastic seating in the small, spare waiting area of the services department on the consulate's fourth floor, accessible through a separate entrance on 49th Street. It was mid-morning and not very crowded. In turn a cordial consular officer behind thick security glass, a woman with shoulder-length blond hair, located our file, called out the surname, checked our IDs, and had us sign some papers. We left with naturalization certificates. We were German citizens now.

My kids have never been to Germany and don't speak a word of German. I haven't been there in years. All three of us are native-born U.S. citizens. We were eligible for German citizenship through my father, who had fled his hometown, Hamburg, as a boy in November 1939. He had lost his German citizenship in 1941 pursuant to the Eleventh Decree to the Law on the Citizenship of the Reich, which stripped all Jews of their German nationality. Decades later, Germany made it possible for those targeted by the law—and their immediate descendants—to have their German citizenship "restored." My father never got around to claiming his before he died in 2010.

The process was simple, a matter of establishing the lineage on a two-page form. I had most of the birth certificates, marriage licenses, and U.S. naturalization certificates that were required as documentation, and I suspect famously efficient German record keeping filled in any gaps, going back to my grandparents and other ancestors who had lived in Hamburg since the eighteenth century. (The name Spiro derives from the medieval Jewish community in Speyer—Spira in Latin.) Notarizing copies of historical documents in a foreign language had proven a challenge; three notaries refused flat-out to have anything to do with them. It took me a couple of years to complete the file and submit it.

There was no rush. I had long known of the eligibility without acting on it. The immediate impetus for applying came out of a teaching stint in Rome in the summer of 2008. Museums in Italy can be expensive, and there is no discount for children—at least not for non-EU-citizen children. Never again was I going to dig so deeply into my wallet with my German-passport-toting son and daughter. I was also beginning to have some vague sense that my children might be able to exploit EU citizenship in less trivial ways, on bigger ticket items like graduate school. With an EU passport, you can work anywhere in the European Union. That might come in handy for them some day.

So my motivation was instrumental. That jibed with my academic take on dual citizenship, a subject I had been studying for almost twenty years. Picking up the issue on the first wave of globalization, I had been an early exponent of the view that dual citizenship isn't really a problem anymore, in part because citizenship itself had been degraded. Academics who find themselves alone in a position—especially a normative one—often take it up with the fervor of an evangelist. That was me on the subject of dual citizenship. Naturalizing as a German took on an analytical element, an exercise I could use to prove the rectitude of my scholarly theorizing.

It turned out a little more complicated than that. In the process of gathering documentation, the prospect of becoming German took on an emotional valence. It generated a family riff, a running joke the punch line of which would be along the lines of "like the good German you are." My father, not uniquely among German Jewish refugees, had been a Germanophile. Robbed of his future, a comfortable, assimilated, bourgeois life in a cosmopolitan European port, he had returned to Germany later in life, as a political scientist at the Free University of Berlin. Though it didn't turn out to his liking, he blamed that not on Germany but on Berlin. One of his last trips to Europe was for a reunion at his private elementary school, a *Gymnasium*, several classmates from which he had stayed in regular contact over the decades. I had stayed in his Berlin apartment during a sabbatical of his in the early 1980s, during which I had taken an introductory language course at the Goethe Institute.

In other words, I had some German in my blood, of a kind. It is part of my identity. Tying the citizenship knot accented the relationship. I have some idea of picking up the language from the rudimentary level at which I left it thirty years ago, and to make it part of a family vacation, someday.

But I can hardly call myself a German in any real way. My mother is a Main Line WASP, so no help there. I can locate only a handful of cities on the map. Beyond the prime minister, I don't know the name of a single government official. I have the outlines of German history only because I studied European history in college, but I have none of the national myths to back it up (the German equivalent of George Washington chopping down the cherry tree). I know little of German social customs, though some might feel familiar in an attenuated kind of way. (For the record, I am extremely punctual.) I would never identify myself as German, or even as German American, though now I am German and American.

* * *

This kind of story is an increasingly common one. Though no one keeps a master list, there are millions of U.S. citizens who also hold the citizenship of another country. Some, like me, have acquired the nationality of their ancestors—Irish, Greek, Italian. Many others have retained their birth citizenship at the same time that they have naturalized as Americans, and will pass that other citizenship on to their U.S.-born children. The progeny of "mixed marriages"—spouses of different nationalities—will also have dual citizenship at birth. Dual citizenship has become a commonplace of globalization.

The rise of dual citizenship could hardly have been imaginable to a time traveler from a hundred or even fifty years ago. Dual nationality was once considered an offense to nature, an abomination on the order of bigamy. It was the stuff of titanic battles between the United States and European sovereigns. As those conflicts dissipated, dual citizenship continued to be an oddity, a condition that, if not quite freakish, was nonetheless vaguely disreputable, a status one could hold but not advertise. The mantle of loyalty and allegiance that has historically hung so heavily over citizenship continued to cloud popular perceptions of the status. Even today, some Americans mistakenly understand dual citizenship to somehow be "illegal," when in fact it is completely tolerated. Only recently has the status largely shed the opprobrium to which it was once attached.

This book charts this history from strong disfavor to general acceptance. It is a story the broad sweep of which no one else has told. There have been millions of dual citizens through decades in which it was considered offensive, then ill-advised, and now benign. The status has touched many; there are few Americans who do not have someone in their past or present who has held the status, if only unknowingly. The history reflects on the course of the state as an institution at the level of the individual. The state was once a jealous institution, justifiably demanding an exclusive relationship with its members. Today, the state lacks both the capacity and the incentive to suppress the status as citizenship becomes more like other forms of membership. This book explains why dual citizenship was once so reviled and why it should be embraced today.

The history necessarily focuses on the United States. Dual nationality is a byproduct of migration. The United States was by far the most important immigrant destination during the nineteenth and twentieth centuries; most dual nationals shared another nationality with U.S. nationality. Chapter 1 describes how the feudal approach to nationality set the stage for major diplomatic disputes between the United States and European governments. In the medieval world most people were born and died in the same place; the incidence of dual nationality was near zero, to the point that it was not understood even as a concept. Before modern migration, nationality itself was epiphenomenal. The great international law commentators of the sixteenth and seventeenth centuries devoted few pages to the subject because there were few disputes relating to nationality. Consistent with the sedentary context— and with the prevailing view of the natural order of things, a hierarchy that put all in their place, from God to peasant—individuals were considered bound to the sovereign in whose lands they were born on a permanent basis.

This regime of "perpetual allegiance" was a poor match for American independence and the emerging era of trans-Atlantic migration. At the same time that large numbers resettled in the United States, European sovereigns refused to recognize any transfer of allegiance. Those who naturalized as U.S. citizens were saddled with their birth allegiance, with dual nationality the result. States clashed in their claims over people. These claims sparked public outcry when European states treated naturalized Americans on return visits home for various purposes as if they had never left, including for purposes of military service. In the face of sustained U.S. pressure, important European states moved to recognize transfers of nationality through the mechanism of expatriation, extinguishing original nationality upon naturalization in the United States.

But that hardly took care of the problem. Chapter 2 describes how individuals attempted to exploit dual nationality to their advantage, playing one state of nationality off the other. This was tolerable to U.S. authorities where an individual remained a genuine American; the United States was willing to defend those who were its own in name and in fact against European overreach. But the price was unacceptably high where a citizen had relocated permanently to another country, often the country of birth, in which he also held nationality. In those cases, the United States sought to shed nominal citizens by forcing an election between the two. The policy emerged through the accumulated, sometimes inconsistent practice of State Department officials. After a series of presidential-level entreaties, Congress finally enacted an expatriation measure in 1907 to address cases in which naturalized citizens moved back home—the surprisingly common phenomenon, even in steamship days, of circular migration. Where official policies left off, social norms kicked in; it was during this period that virulent condemnations of the status were internalized. As Teddy Roosevelt asserted, dual nationality was a "self-evident absurdity."

But it wasn't until the mid-twentieth century that Congress took a hard line on dual nationality. As detailed in chapter 3, the nationality acts of 1940 and 1952 made it almost impossible under U.S. law to actively maintain another nationality without forfeiting one's U.S. citizenship. Many were born in the United States with dual nationality, inheriting the nationality of immigrant parents while acquiring U.S. citizenship under the Fourteenth Amendment. As state competition reached the bloody zenith of the world wars, it became imperative to keep lines neatly drawn among them. Hair-trigger expatriation rules were the result, under which individuals were stripped of their citizenship for any conduct evidencing ongoing ties to another state. These rules were consistently upheld by the Supreme Court against constitutional challenges so long as the expatriating conduct was undertaken voluntarily, for instance, the mere act of voting in a foreign political election.

Chapter 4 documents the shift toward toleration of the status, beginning with the Supreme Court's 1967 decision in *Afroyim v. Rusk*. The
Warren Court came to see citizenship as a right, raising the bar for its
dispossession. Justice Black's categorical rejection of Congress's power to
"take away an American citizen's citizenship without his assent" was not
meant to protect dual citizenship, but it set in motion a series of judicial
and administrative decisions that reached that destination. These moves
were enabled by a shift in global relations. It was no longer imperative
to maintain clear boundaries of human community. Competing claims
became less incendiary as the human rights revolution constrained the
ways in which states could mistreat any individual, regardless of nationality. Manpower became less important to establishing state power in the
wake of military mechanization. The ideological and bipolar orientation
of the Cold War helped break down old-world notions of loyalty to the
sovereign.

The international community, meanwhile, attempted to manage dual
nationality and the threat it posed to peaceful relations between states.
Although ambitious undertakings to eradicate the status fell short as
states refused to cede discretion over their nationality practices, international tribunals adopted their own kind of election mechanism under
which only the more dominant nationality would be effective for purposes of international disputes as well as for military service obligations.
Dual citizenship was accepted as international fact but also understood
to be an international problem, avoided where possible, managed where
not. By the end of the twentieth century, U.S. citizenship could not be
terminated without an individual's cooperation; Americans were free
to keep other citizenships acquired at birth or by naturalization. An increasing number of those who naturalized in the United States were able
to keep their original citizenship through changes in home country law
and U.S. practice.

Mexico's acceptance of dual citizenship in 1998 put a punctuation
mark on the new indifference to dual citizenship, at least from a U.S.
perspective. The change in Mexican law meant that almost all of the
more than a million Mexican nationals who have naturalized after 1998
are dual Mexican-U.S. citizens. Notwithstanding the heavy political
contestation surrounding Mexicans and immigration policy, there was
hardly a murmur about the emergence of this large population of dual

citizens. Dual citizenship is an issue that has cut across powerful political constituencies—it implicates not just Mexicans and other recent immigrants, but also Irish, Italian, and Jewish communities, all of which have a high incidence of dual citizenship on the basis of ancestry. Dual citizenship is here to stay. That's a matter of political fact.

As described in chapter 5, dual citizenship serves the American national interest. Dual citizenship presents no significant societal costs. The trope of dual citizens as a fifth column never conformed with realities on the ground. The non-state nature of contemporary conflict makes the security threat more implausible still. Dual citizens are capable of political engagement in more than one polity, and they are no more likely than non-citizens to do the bidding of their home country governments. There is an upside to the status, from the state's perspective. Dual citizenship facilitates naturalization, which facilitates immigrant integration. In the American context, dual citizens are positioned to put newly assimilated political knowledge to work back home.

Dual citizenship also serves the interests of other states. Chapter 6 describes the dramatic change in global attitudes toward the status. During the late twentieth century, other countries also relaxed their position on dual citizenship. Developing states once equated emigration with abandonment, forsaking those who left by terminating their nationality. Today, developing countries seek to harness emigrant communities as diasporas for economic and other purposes. Citizenship is part of the toolbox for keeping diasporas connected to the homeland. These "sending" states have moved from merely tolerating dual citizenship to actively embracing it. This is partly in response to the demands of the diaspora members themselves, who have used their economic and political muscle to win acceptance of the status by their countries of origin. Other countries, including most European states, have also come to appreciate ethnic kin outside the homeland. Because citizenship no longer provokes turf battles between states, many states have abandoned previous restrictions on the status. With a few major holdouts, a clear majority of countries now permits dual citizenship, and the trend is unidirectional. The more pressing question today is not so much whether dual citizenship is acceptable but rather how citizens residing outside the homeland should be politically accommodated, especially with respect to voting rights. This chapter addresses novel issues of diaspora citizenship rights, arguing for the extension of full political rights to external citizens. Those who have relocated elsewhere and acquired another citizenship will still have interests in homeland governance that should be reflected in institutionalized voice.

Chapter 7 builds on the growing global acceptance of dual citizenship to suggest that it may rise to the level of a right. Where an individual is eligible for dual citizenship (that is, where an individual would otherwise qualify for citizenship in each of two or more states), states should be constrained from standing in the way. Dual citizenship is often a matter of actuating individual identity and reflects associational urges. This is clear in the case of the child who inherits citizenship from each of two parents. Why should the child be forced to choose between the two? Other associational memberships are protected, absent a compelling interest on the government's part to intervene. There were once good reasons to limit multiple state memberships, which explains the historical disfavor attached to the status. Now that dual citizenship no longer threatens world order in any concrete way, an individual's interest in retaining or acquiring the status should be vindicated as a human right.

Dual citizenship also advances political rights insofar as rejecting the status denies an individual the capacity to participate politically in one or the other of states in which she has political interests. Sacrificing citizenship in one state shouldn't be the price of full political rights in another. Protecting dual citizenship would bar states from requiring new citizens to renounce their original citizenship, terminating the citizenship of those who naturalize elsewhere, or forcing those born with dual citizenship to choose one at majority. Recent developments point to emerging norms protective of the status. When Germany recently backed down from a principled stance against dual citizenship, for example, international rights–framed pressure was an important part of the story. An emerging right to dual citizenship is also suggested by an increasingly critical perspective on policies that discriminate against dual citizens.

Chapter 8 describes how dual citizenship will over the long term nonetheless undermine solidarities located in the state. States may try to put dual citizenship to work as a strategy for cementing diaspora ties, but that doesn't mean the strategy will be successful. On the contrary, dual citizenship will tend to undermine the intensity of national identities defined by citizenship status. Exclusive memberships extract a higher membership price. Institutions that demand exclusive membership are inherently more jealous and intensely felt. Allowing dual or even multiple citizenship lowers the barriers to entry. In the U.S. context, it has spawned a population of "second choicers." If one can add a citizenship without giving up another, the cost of retaining each is reduced. In a world that frowned on dual citizenship, individuals had a strong incentive to opt for the citizenship of the country to which they had the strongest attachment.

Many dual citizens maintain citizenship in countries with which they have nominal socio-cultural connections. That inevitably dilutes citizenship as a proxy for social solidarity. This chapter describes two new forms of instrumental citizenship: Olympic citizenship and investor citizenship. Individuals are gaming citizenship rules to secure eligibility in international sporting competitions. Others are simply buying it. In both cases, formal membership is detached from social connection. Neither would exist without broadened acceptance of dual citizenship. Dual citizenship tends to hollow out citizenship as defining meaningful community on the ground. That has led some to call for policing the status. But it is too late to reverse the material forces that have resulted in its growing frequency and acceptance. Dual citizenship has become a fact of globalization.

There is a clear arc to this story. The place of dual citizenship in world society has been dramatically transformed. It was once the bane of statesmen, a threat to international stability. In some countries it remains an important policy concern, in battles that have a legacy feel to them as the status comes to be recognized as innocuous, even beneficial. As its acceptance among states has grown, it has become more important to individuals as so many more look to acquire and hold the status. As a sociological fact, dual citizenship has never been as important as it is today.

The shift reflects on changed meanings of citizenship itself. As Rainer Bauböck observes, "The rules which govern individual entries or exits and the transmission of citizenship from one generation to the next are themselves deeply embedded in specific concepts of political community."[1] A change in even one element of these rules signifies a fundamental shift in the nature of the relationship of the individual to the state.

Nationality first established a kind of parent-child relationship between sovereign and subject, a product of nature and hence indissoluble. The succeeding regime of exclusivity more resembled marriage—voluntary and terminable, but also singular. We may be moving toward a paradigm in which citizenship is more like membership in a club or civic association, in a class of affiliation that does not necessarily constrain other attachments, a part of our identity but not the sort of trumping presence that it once enjoyed. Dual citizenship vindicates individual autonomy at the same time that it demotes the state from its historical primacy. Dual citizenship shows the continuing salience of the state at the same time that it suggests new dimensions of how humans organize themselves on a changing global landscape.

1

# The Feudal Roots and Modern Emergence of Dual Nationality

John Warren stood in the dock in Dublin in March 1867 to hear his indictment on treason charges for "feloniously and wickedly" seeking to depose Queen Victoria from her imperial rule. Warren had been implicated as a gun runner in the Fenian uprising, an attempt to overthrow British rule in Ireland. But what occupied the court in intense legal arguments at the trial's opening had nothing to do with the inflammatory nature of his activities in an era of heavy-handed monarchical rule. Warren's first defense was to plead citizenship in and allegiance to the United States of America. Warren was looking to secure the procedural benefit of a jury *de medietate linguae*, composed one half of subjects of the British crown, one half of foreigners. The mixed jury was a product of the Middle Ages, used mostly in cases involving foreign merchants. It was available only to foreigners. Warren claimed that as a citizen of the United States he was no longer a British subject and thus qualified for the special procedure.[1]

Warren had been born in County Cork to Irish parents. After immigrating to the United States, he became a journalist and a leader in the substantial Boston Irish community of Charlestown. He served as a captain of the 63rd New York Infantry for the Union during the Civil War, part of the so-called Irish Brigade, and was the Massachusetts representative of the Fenian Brotherhood of America. Warren had naturalized as an American on October 1, 1866. In April 1867 he sailed on the brigantine *Jacmel Packet* with forty other American Fenians as part of an "implausibly farcical" expedition to join an uprising that had already failed.[2]

In the Dublin courtroom, the Queen's attorney general fervently denied the possibility that a person born in the realm to British subjects could have the status of an "alien" entitled to the mixed jury. The prosecution found the request so objectionable that they argued against it even being entered into the record. The presiding judge, Chief Baron

Pigot, had no trouble rejecting Warren's claim of alienage out of hand. "I cannot allow that proposition to be put forward without meeting it with a prompt and unhesitating denial," Pigot intoned. Claiming it "was really almost pedantry to cite authorities . . . familiar to every lawyer," he proceeded to recount the many jurists, including American treatise writers "of the greatest weight and highest reputation," holding that those born in British territory owed perpetual allegiance to the crown. "Natural born subjects owe an allegiance," Pigot quoted the American legal giant Chancellor James Kent, "which is intrinsic and perpetual, and which cannot be divested by any act of their own."[3]

In other words, even though Warren had naturalized as an American, in the process expressly renouncing allegiance to Queen Victoria, this was ineffective to cut the tie to his birth sovereign. The chief baron denied the request for the mixed jury. A jury of British subjects went on to find Warren guilty of levying war against the Queen. An unrepentant Warren was sentenced to fifteen years' hard labor and rendered to the jailer at Millbank Prison.[4]

Warren wasn't the only naturalized American who found himself facing British justice for complicity in the Fenian uprisings. In all cases, Britain refused to recognize the effectiveness of their U.S. naturalization. The prosecution of the U.S. citizens (and the rough justice that followed their convictions) put the United States and Great Britain at loggerheads, not the least because of the intense popular interest in the controversy in the United States. Britain's arrest of the Americans provoked national outrage, in Secretary of State William Seward's description, "throughout the whole country, from Portland to San Francisco and from St. Paul to Pensacola."[5] Several state legislatures and city councils passed resolutions demanding federal legislation to declare a right to shed nationality.[6] The Wisconsin state legislature, for example, resolved that "the principle derived from the feudal system . . . 'once a subject always a subject,' is repugnant to the dictates of enlightened civilization, and opposed to the rights and best interests of mankind[, and] that expatriation is one of the inalienable rights of man," in demanding federal action to protect the rights of naturalized citizens "temporarily sojourning in foreign countries."[7]

U.S. actors were thus focused on establishing a right to expatriation. But the ill to be addressed was dual nationality. John Warren and his counterparts were saddled with allegiance to more than one sovereign. They were not alone. For every European sovereign that refused to recognize the effect of naturalization in the United States, every immigrant acquiring U.S. citizenship also continued to hold nationality of his country of origin. The upshot was a continuing series of disputes as states purported to lay exclusive claim to their nationals, the human equivalent of turf contests among sovereigns. Dual nationality destabilized the fragile constellation of states.

## "Once a Subject, Always a Subject"

Instances of dual nationality are almost as old as the concept of nationality itself, and the phenomenon has been deplored for just as long. The incidence of dual nationality is the inevitable result of the failure to develop a universal rule of nationality. States have historically been more or less unfettered in devising their own nationality rules.[8] "There can be no doubt that nationality questions must be regarded as problems which are exclusively subject to the internal legislation of individual States," the Polish jurist Szymon Rundstein observed in 1926. "It is, indeed, the sphere in which the principles of sovereignty find their most definite application."[9] The interplay of different approaches coupled with migration gave rise to cases in which individuals held nationality in more than one state. But it was the historically anarchical context of the state system, one in which no superior authority imposed order and in which each nation's fortune faced constant threat from other states in a zero-sum world, that made dual nationality so threatening.

Neither states nor sovereigns were a part of the medieval world. Individuals were identified not by nationality but rather by personal allegiances tied to natural law. As Sir Edward Coke asserted in the first major judicial articulation of the doctrine of perpetual allegiance, "Ligeance or Obedience of the Subject to the Sovereign is due by the law of nature."[10] The notion of personal allegiances persisted as Europe divided into distinct territorial units, each ruled by an individual sovereign. Early models of nationality worked from the putatively personal relationship between the individual and the sovereign. Because it was natural, it was also perpetual and immutable, something that the laws of men had no power to trump.[11]

This posture reflected prevailing notions of the individual's relationship to the state. One finds the words "subject" and "claim" at the center of the language of perpetual allegiance, as opposed to "citizen" or "right."[12] Individual consent—of citizenship as part of a social compact—played no part in this system. The sovereign did owe certain obligations to his subjects, including a duty of minimal protection, for which he was answerable only to God.[13] Notions of a representative connection between the state and society did not exist before the French Revolution and advanced thereafter only in fits. The individual figured primarily as an instrument of the person of the sovereign.

The common law followed the rule of *nemo potest exuere patriam*: no man may abjure his country. The individual lacked the legal capacity to forsake his sovereign. As Blackstone characterized it, obligations to one's sovereign represented "a debt of gratitude, which cannot be forfeited, canceled, or altered, by any change of time place or circumstances."[14] In this world, the law did not recognize dual nationality as a legitimate status; it was not merely a problem, it was an offense to law and nature. Regimes adhering to perpetual allegiance prohibited naturalization before other sovereigns. As Lord Grenville wrote to the American minister in London in 1797, "a declaration of renunciation made by any of the King's subjects would, instead of operating as a protection to them, be considered an act highly criminal on their part."[15] It was "not in the power of any private subject to shake off his allegiance, and to transfer it to a foreign prince," held the House of Lords in 1747. "Nor is it in the power of any prince by naturalizing and employing a subject of Great Britain, to dissolve the bond of allegiance between the subject and crown."[16] Russia punished naturalization with perpetual banishment, or, in the case of unauthorized return, with deportation to Siberia.[17] During the War of 1812, the British Prince Regent threatened to execute as a traitor any naturalized Englishman captured from American forces, a threat from which he backed down only upon President Madison's own threat to take the same action against British prisoners on a two-for-one basis.[18]

## Nationality as Battleground

But perpetual allegiance could not change the fact of greater global mobility. Although the doctrine itself did not recognize the possibility of dual nationality, perpetual allegiance generated a huge population of dual nationals. All migrants from the many states following perpetual allegiance held two nationalities after naturalizing in their new state of residence. Two sovereigns demanded their allegiance. Reflecting migration between the two countries in the late eighteenth and early nineteenth centuries, this resulted in a significant number of dual British and American nationals. A British subject who emigrated to and naturalized in the United States became a dual national in the sense that he was claimed by both.

Such dual nationals posed a threat not because they sought to divide allegiances but rather because they sought to transfer them. Subjects were useful as instruments only in the competition with other sovereigns. They were to be put to work as resources. Actual sentiments of allegiance counted for little. The British crown would not have cared particularly whether a seaman had in fact transferred his affections to the American flag; if reclaimed by his former master, he either accepted his lot or faced the yardarm. As "population came to be perceived as a scarce resource," in Aristide Zolberg's formulation,[19] expatriation represented an intolerable loss of strength to the birth sovereign, a human version of mercantilist competition. As a United Nations report later put it, the main historical obstacle to eliminating dual nationality was the refusal of states to "los[e] a potential soldier."[20] Competition for subjects was like competition over territory. If not in one sovereign's tally, a subject was in his enemy's. Nationality was a zero-sum proposition.

Britain aggressively asserted perpetual allegiance at the beginning of the nineteenth century against subjects who emigrated to and naturalized in the United States. It refused to allow individuals to terminate their British nationality; there was no right of expatriation. Rejecting the legal fact of naturalization as diminishing obligations to the crown, the King proclaimed in November 1807 that "no such letters of naturalization, or certificates of citizenship, do, or can, divest our natural-born subjects of the allegiance, or in any degree alter the duty which they owe to us, their lawful Sovereign."[21] The English navy impressed naturalized Americans at sea into its service on the grounds that they had never been released from their obligations to their country of birth. British naval vessels took to stopping U.S. flag ships and seizing those crew members thought to be (former) British subjects. As Henry Adams observed, "The measure, as the British navy regarded it, was one of self-protection."[22] At the same time as Britain sought to stem a loss of man-power through attempted expatriations, the United States saw a threat not only to the strength of its own forces but to its sovereignty.[23] The problem festered through the first decade of the century. British impressment policy was an important contributing factor in the outbreak of the War of 1812.[24]

In the wake of that conflict, Britain stood back from efforts to return would-be former subjects by force. But it did not abandon perpetual allegiance within Britain itself. Naturalized Americans returned to Britain at risk of having to fulfill putative duties as British subjects, including military service. In this sense, the impressment controversy was more an issue of enforcement jurisdiction—sovereigns could continue to claim subjects indefinitely, but could enforce that claim only on their home turf.[25] Other states recognized a qualified right of expatriation, accepting the validity of naturalization elsewhere only upon satisfaction by the expatriating individual of home-country military service obligations. France, Prussia, and Spain, among other states, attempted to extract military service from naturalized Americans on mere visits to their countries of birth.[26]

The United States wavered through the mid-nineteenth century in its willingness to protect naturalized citizens who returned to the grasping clutches of their homeland sovereigns. The United States was thirsty for immigrants. As Attorney General Jeremiah Black observed in 1859, it was upon the principle of voluntary expatriation that "this country was populated. We owe to it our existence as a nation."[27] Not surprisingly, perhaps, the United States extended full legal equality (with the small exception of presidential eligibility) to naturalized citizens. As the Supreme Court observed in 1824, the naturalized citizen "becomes a member of the society, possessing all the rights of a native citizen, and standing, in the view of the constitution, on the footing of a native. The constitution does not authorize Congress to enlarge or abridge those rights."[28] Those rights included the right to diplomatic protection by U.S. authorities outside the United States. As Secretary of State James Buchanan advised a naturalized citizen looking to visit his homeland, "The fact of your having become a citizen of the United States has the effect of entitling you to the same protection from this government that a native citizen would receive."[29] That pointed to American defiance of any limits on the recognition of expatriation and naturalization. The United States would stick up for naturalized citizens against European sovereigns who refused to let them go.

On the other hand, there was an understanding that the right of expatriation would always remain constrained at some level. The United States could hardly argue that expatriation be effective as cover for desertion from another sovereign's armed forces—although in practice, U.S. authorities may often have been too quick to accept deserters as fit for naturalization. "A little perjury, in no wise unsafe," Henry Adams later recounted, "was alone required to transform British seamen into American citizens." Desertion, Adams noted, "received no discouragement from the United States Government; on the contrary, deserters, known to be such, were received at once into the national service."[30] As the United States grew stronger, it had to consider how unrestrained expatriation by its own citizens might undermine U.S. interests. The United States had difficulty, for example, securing the return of U.S. citizens who fled to their countries of birth to avoid service during the Civil War.[31] U.S. law itself later prohibited expatriation by U.S. citizens during wartime.[32] Nor could expatriation insulate other criminal acts from punishment. Although the United States never adhered to the doctrine of perpetual allegiance, at points it limited the right of Americans to expatriate.[33] U.S. authorities had to be mindful of their own interests in limiting expatriation at the same time that they considered pressing it against other states.[34]

Some waffling resulted. To the extent that other countries reasserted claims to their native-born subjects (now naturalized U.S. citizens) only on their own territory, it posed much less of a threat than did British-type impressment on the high seas. It was, in fact, the assertion of American diplomatic protection on behalf of the naturalized citizen that could be taken as the greater interference in another's internal affairs. As Secretary of State Edward Everett observed in 1853, Prussia's military service requirement, even as applied against naturalized U.S. citizens, "is purely a matter of domestic policy, in which no foreign government has the right to interfere."[35]

U.S. policy at times demanded that foreign governments release naturalized U.S. citizens from service obligations. In 1859, for example, Attorney General Black rejected the position that "naturalized citizens ought to be protected by the government of his adopted country everywhere except the country of his birth," proclaiming that a "native and a naturalized American may, therefore, go forth with equal security over every sea and through every land under heaven, including the country in which the latter was born." He denied a German principality's right to conscript a naturalized American on a temporary visit to country of birth.[36]

In other cases, the United States refused to intercede on behalf of naturalized citizens. In one 1840 episode, the U.S. minister to Prussia refused to protest compelled military service of a naturalized U.S. citizen who had returned there; "having returned to the country of your birth, your native domicil and national character revert (so long as you remain in Prussian dominions), and you are bound in all respects to obey the laws exactly as if you had never emigrated."[37] The U.S. government sometimes warned individuals that even the temporary return to home countries could result in the imposition of military service or other obligations of nationality. As Secretary of State Daniel Webster cautioned a naturalized American born in France in 1852, "If . . . the Government of France does not acknowledge the right of natives of that country to renounce their allegiance, it may lawfully claim their services when found within French jurisdiction."[38]

## Perpetual Allegiance in Decline

The Fenian controversy brought the issue to a head. John Warren's case and the British denial of his U.S. citizenship attracted intense public attention to the issue. Warren was one among many prosecuted as British subjects notwithstanding their naturalization as Americans. In the Capitol, members excoriated the continued British adherence to perpetual allegiance. The right of expatriation, trumpeted Representative Nathaniel P. Banks, "stands upon the same ground as the right of free speech, the right to see, the right to hear, the right to think, the right of locomotion."[39] The influential *North American Review* characterized the expatriation issue as "the last weighty question of international law, assum[ing] the form of a conflict between the New and Old World, between new and old ideas, between the doctrine of progress and the belief in precedent."[40] In his annual message to Congress in late 1867,

President Andrew Johnson urged Congress to act on the question. It responded with the Expatriation Act of 1868, which categorically affirmed expatriation as "a natural and inherent right of all people, indispensable to the enjoyment of the rights of life, liberty, and the pursuit of happiness."[41] The law declared any prior U.S. pronouncements to the contrary to be "inconsistent with the fundamental principles of this government," and directed the president to employ all means short of war to secure the release of U.S. citizens, naturalized or native-born, from unjust imprisonment by any foreign government.[42]

The Expatriation Act had its intended effect. British editorialists condemned the doctrine of perpetual allegiance. As one letter to *The Times* submitted under the pseudonym "Historicus" exhaled, the "great and never-ceasing tide of emigration" was a phenomenon for which a feudal legal regime made no provision. "The consequence is that we find ourselves in the presence of political facts which are wholly irreconcilable with our legal theory."[43] (The letter was written by the barrister William Vernon Harcourt, who later served as Whewell Professor of International Law at Cambridge.)[44] The new U.S. minister in London pressed the issue as "the most important question" requiring his attention.[45] In March 1869, John Warren was released from prison. Following on the recommendations of a royal commission, Parliament adopted the Naturalisation Act of 1870, recognizing the right of British subjects to expatriate.[46] Section 6 of the act provided that "[a]ny British subject who has . . . become naturalized in [any foreign state] shall from and after the time of his so having become naturalized in such foreign state, be deemed to have ceased to be a British subject." The act had retroactive effect to those who had naturalized before its passage. Parallel to the legislation, Britain and the United States negotiated a bilateral convention accepting the legitimacy of U.S. naturalization.

The United States had in the meantime negotiated treaties first with the North German Confederation (including powerhouse Prussia), and thereafter with Belgium, Austria-Hungary, Sweden, Norway, Denmark, Ecuador, and other German states by which they would reciprocally recognize naturalization upon five years' residency in the other state. These agreements, known as the Bancroft treaties (after U.S. negotiator George Bancroft), paved the way to more general recognition of the right of expatriation. As the historian Mark De Wolfe Howe would write in 1908,

"The importance of these treaties, which have been said to mark a new epoch in international law, can hardly be overrated."[47] As Bancroft observed in his valedictory letter to Washington from his post as minister to Berlin, "You in Washington can hardy conceive the degree of comfort secured to our German fellow-citizens by the peaceful security which they obtain for their visits in Germany by the treaty of naturalisation." The prior refusal to recognize naturalization had weighed heavily on immigrants returning for homeland visits. "From 10,000 to 15,000 of them come yearly from America to their mother country and now without suffering the least anxiety," wrote Bancroft, "where before many of them in order to see their friends were obliged to remain on the other side of the frontier or come into Germany stealthily, running the risk of arrest every hour."[48] Bismarck himself took an active role in the negotiations.

The spate of activity surrounding the 1868 act marked perpetual allegiance for inevitable decline. It took many more years for it to be universally abandoned. As late as 1931, Yale Law School's Edwin Borchard was complaining that "many countries have seen no reason to surrender the claims of indelible allegiance."[49] Benito Mussolini reportedly contended that "[o]nce an Italian, always an Italian, to the seventh generation."[50] A few powers (Russia and Turkey, for instance) continued to adhere to perpetual allegiance. Several more continued for some time to condition expatriation on satisfaction of military obligations, as was the case with France until 1928.[51] Such conditions on expatriation continued to present a matter of international controversy.[52] But perpetual allegiance could not over the long run withstand the "diversity of opinions and practice,"[53] for such diversity unavoidably led to competing claims of allegiance that threatened the peaceful relations of states. By the beginning of the twentieth century, the right to terminate nationality was increasingly prevalent in state practice.[54] The right to expatriation was later enshrined in the Universal Declaration of Human Rights as well as international and regional conventions.[55] Citizenship came to be founded, at least in part, on notions of individual consent.[56] Dual nationality was an important driver, for it was dual nationality and the resulting irreconcilable state claims that the right of expatriation was meant to correct.

The right to expatriation reduced the incidence of dual nationality. Individuals were now free to transfer allegiance from one state to another through naturalization. Cases of dual nationality no longer primarily arose by one state's refusal to release subjects from its claim. The common law doctrine of perpetual allegiance, a last legal vestige of feudal conceptions of the relationship between sovereign and subject, could not survive modernity and increasingly global mobility. Expatriation was normalized. That reestablished a rough equilibrium in how states laid claim to individuals, reducing what had become a major source of diplomatic conflict.

But all this did nothing to address cases in which individuals sought affirmatively to maintain ties to more than one state. Loyalty and allegiance replaced the natural order as an orienting principle for how states related to individuals. The new framing implicitly acknowledged individual agency. Individuals could now choose their sovereign. But loyalty also implied exclusivity, not just as a preferred default position but as a moral imperative. Failing to eliminate dual nationality through harmonization of nationality laws, states fell back on powerful social norms to combat the status. Those norms continue to loom large in how we process membership in the state even today.

2

International Threat, Moral Disgrace


Writing post-presidency in *Metropolitan Magazine* in 1916, Theodore Roosevelt described the case of one P. A. Lelong, a New Orleans native and life-long resident who considered himself "as much an American citizen as President Wilson or any members of his cabinet." Lelong wished to visit France on business but had been informed by the French consul at New Orleans that upon arrival he "could be either impressed into the French service or punished for not having reported for military duty, and also for having served in the State Militia of Louisiana without permission from the French Government." The French considered Lelong a national by birth to a French citizen father, even though Lelong himself had never set foot outside the United States. He sought some assurance from the State Department in advance that it would protect him from being "molested" by French military authorities.[1]

No such luck. Noting Lelong's apparent dual nationality, counselor (later secretary of state) Robert Lansing rejected Lelong's request. Roosevelt deplored the policy as "dangerously close to treason." The former president called on U.S. authorities to champion the rights of Lelong and the many similarly situated "against any foreign power that interferes with them," failing which it was "the clear duty of the American people immediately to repudiate the doctrine thus laid down by the Wilson Administration."[2]

Lelong's case demonstrated the long tail of state claims on manpower. (France allowed expatriation, but only upon satisfaction of military service obligations, a policy it did not change until 1928.) But Roosevelt was not bellowing out of solicitude for the individual. He emphatically rejected the possibility that immigrants could retain their nationality of origin after naturalizing to American citizenship, the duties of which "were necessarily exclusive of and inconsistent with the profession of citizenship in or allegiance to any other nation." In Roosevelt's view, the "theory" of dual nationality was a "self-evident absurdity."[3]

Expatriation may have been framed as a right. But for Roosevelt and others it was not a right to be exercised at individual option. From the individual's perspective, the right was more in the way of a duty. The individual naturalizing before a new sovereign could not choose to retain the nationality of his birth sovereign. As George Bancroft observed in 1849, states should "as soon tolerate a man with two wives as a man with two countries; as soon bear with polygamy as that state of double allegiance which common sense so repudiates that it has not even coined a word to express it."[4] Attorney General Black noted ten years later that "[n]o government would allow one of its subjects to divide its allegiance between it and another sovereign, for they all know that no man can serve two masters. . . . [T]he allegiance demanded of the naturalized resident must have always been understood as exclusive."[5] In other words, dual nationality was an offense to nature. The notion of voluntary attachment to more than one state was alien to that era, so much so that the term "dual nationality" did not enter the lexicon until the beginning of the twentieth century. In his important digest of international practice, the jurist John Bassett Moore spoke rather of "the doctrine of double allegiance," while noting (perhaps more tactfully than Roosevelt) that it was "often criticised as unphilosophical."[6]

In a world of state competition and national interests, divided loyalties could not be sustained, at least not from the state's perspective. Where states once sought to maintain their formal claim to emigrants, they now cast them off. States attacked dual nationality with two weapons. First, loss of nationality was the price of naturalization in a foreign state. Expatriation became the remedy for the abandoned state, as divorce for the cuckold. Second, those born with dual nationality (through the interplay of different mechanisms of citizenship by descent and by place of birth) would have to choose between the two or have that choice made for them through a required "election." Even with the decline of perpetual allegiance, dual nationality was considered no less a threat to the stability of international relations. States moved aggressively to root out the status.

Reflecting a conception of citizenship (indeed of the entire social order) in which individual will played its part, these approaches took account of the mutual obligation between citizen and state. No longer was the individual a mere pawn in a contest of sovereigns, to be fought over as chattel. The new regime worked from a mutuality of obligation between the state (no longer simply the sovereign) and the citizen (no longer simply the subject). For the state, this translated into a protective function. The citizen could expect the assistance of his state where he faced individual mistreatment at the hands of another state. He expected the state as well to manage its international relations so as to minimize and defend the national community against foreign encroachments. In return for this protection, the state exacted certain obligations of its citizens.

In the face of those obligations, many birthright dual nationals had an evident self-interest in election—namely, those who faced conflicting, duplicative, or merely undesirable burdens as a result of the status, especially with respect to military service. As a UN report later observed, dual nationality could have "serious consequences" for individuals.[7] The right of expatriation enabled individuals to avoid conflicting or cumulative obligations, as they were now free to rid themselves of one or the other set of burdens. Beyond the duplicative obligations of dual nationality, the perception of divided loyalty could also weigh heavily against the status. To the extent that opprobrium imbued social norms regarding the status, holding dual citizenship could no doubt result in "mental conflicts" and "psychological difficulties," "inconveniences and hardships."[8] In the face of such material and cognitive challenges, in many cases the "problem" of dual nationality was self-correcting.

## Exploiting Dual Nationality

For others, dual nationality represented a strategic advantage. As part of the bargain between individual members and the state, citizens could look to the state for protection against mistreatment by foreign governments. This practice—formally known as "diplomatic protection"—stood at the core of nineteenth-century international law and relations.[9] In a world that had few brake points on the way to war, diplomatic protection was a dangerous proposition. Where the wrong done a citizen went without remedy, his state could pursue retaliation up to and in some circumstances including armed force.[10]

Dual nationals posed peculiar risks in the diplomatic protection regime. On the one hand, the treatment of aliens was a matter clearly limited by international law. "When the citizen leaves the national territory he enters the domain of international law," noted Edwin Borchard in his magisterial treatise on diplomatic protection.[11] On the other, international law posed no restraints on a state's treatment of its own nationals. Those two premises came into conflict with the dual national. When within its territorial jurisdiction, State 1 would claim the right to treat its national as it pleased while State 2 could assert international law constraints by way of diplomatic protection with respect to the same individual.[12] The conflicting principles led inevitably to the conflict of states. Dual nationality did not compute. It was "a contradictory element in the divine work that was the nation."[13]

There were cases in which this conflict resulted from one country's refusal to recognize an individual's transfer of allegiance. Where the status resulted from a foreign state's claim of perpetual allegiance, the United States typically interceded on its national's behalf, diplomatic complications notwithstanding.

But there were exceptions and policies wavered from one administration to the next, as with the Wilson administration's failure to go to bat for P. A. Lelong. Authorities were more consistently skeptical of protection claims from those with tenuous continuing attachments to the United States. The availability of diplomatic protection allowed for exploitation by dual nationals. A dual national could, for example, invoke the protection of the United States against a military service obligation in his homeland even if he maintained few connections to the United States. Individuals started to game the system, asserting a paper nationality against a real one. In those cases, the United States found itself out on a limb, risking the interests of the polity for someone who was not really a part of it. No less than President Grant decried the phenomenon, in his 1874 annual message to Congress, of

> persons claiming the benefit of citizenship, while living in a foreign country, contributing in no manner to the performance of the duties of a citizen of the United States, and without intention at any time to return and undertake those duties, to use the claims to citizenship of the United States simply as a shield from the performance of the obligations of a citizen elsewhere.[14]

Similar laments were expressed by U.S. policymakers for decades thereafter. A 1906 State Department study asserted that "none of us desire that some foreigner who does not intend to cast his lot permanently with us should endeavor to avail himself of the flag as a fraudulent protection."[15] As late as 1940, one member of Congress lamented that some nominal citizens "have gotten awfully patriotic along about the time that they have had trouble abroad. They rush to the State Department, waving the American flag in one hand and holding out the other to be pulled into the United States, just as soon as there is trouble."[16]

Some countries resolved this difficulty by categorically refusing to protect their nationals from mistreatment by another state in which they also held nationality, even if they had transferred identity as a matter of social fact. The rule was adopted, for example, as a matter of domestic law in the United Kingdom. British naturalization certificates and passports of naturalized citizens included special endorsements indicating their lack of effect in the holder's country of birth.[17] There were efforts to adopt the rule as a matter of international law. The undersubscribed 1930 Hague Convention on nationality law provided that "[a] State may not afford diplomatic protection to one of its nationals against a State whose nationality such person also possesses."[18] The United States was less inclined to accept this approach, which would have precluded the protection of those who had genuinely transferred allegiances but whose countries of origin refused to allow their release. Instead, the United States moved to pursue each case on its "particular facts and circumstances."[19] Without a bright line, dual nationals incurred high diplomatic transaction costs. They represented a threat to national interests and indeed to world public order. States had strong incentives to develop mechanisms by which to eliminate or at least reduce the incidence of dual nationality itself.

## Forcing Choices

The first targets in these efforts were those who naturalized in other countries. If permitted to maintain their original nationality, they would become dual citizens by acquiring another. That had been the problem with perpetual allegiance and its refusal to recognize the fact of naturalization. But as states abandoned perpetual allegiance, they moved from denying individuals the right to expatriate to requiring it. The result could not be universally achieved by treaty to the extent states were unwilling to cede sovereign control. What they could not achieve by mutual agreement, they could achieve on their own.

Most states came to terminate the nationality of individuals who naturalized elsewhere. When one secured citizenship in another state, it was extinguished at home. As Borchard observed, "Among the modes of expatriation, naturalization in a foreign country is the one most universally recognized."[20] When, for instance, Great Britain finally relented in acknowledging the legal effect of naturalization in other states, naturalization automatically resulted in termination of British nationality.

Under U.S. practice, naturalization in another country was understood by late-nineteenth-century executive branch officials, the courts, and commentators as effecting the loss of U.S. citizenship. As Chief Justice John Marshall observed in the 1806 decision *The Charming Betsy*, "the situation of an American citizen is completely changed where, by his own act, he has made himself the subject of a foreign power."[21] Attorney General George Henry Williams concluded in an 1873 opinion that naturalization is "the highest evidence of expatriation."[22] The Department of State "frequently declared" that when a citizen of the United States naturalized in another country he was "regarded as having lost his rights as a citizen of the United States."[23] This was compounded where naturalization involved an oath of allegiance to the other sovereign, as was typically the case. As Secretary of State Walter Gresham instructed the U.S. minister in Hawaii with respect to the case of a Mr. Bowler, in rejecting his request for the protection of U.S. authorities: "He manifested his intention of abandoning his American citizenship by taking the oath to support the constitution and laws of Hawaii and bear true allegiance to the King. . . . That oath is inconsistent with his allegiance to the United States. . . . He could not bear true allegiance to both Governments at the same time."[24]

So much for Americans naturalizing in other countries. With respect to immigrants to the United States, all naturalization applicants for U.S. citizenship had been required by law since 1795 "to renounce forever all allegiance and fidelity to any foreign prince, potentate, state or sovereignty whatever."[25] (The now archaic language remains substantially the same today.) As a practical matter, this oath could not be enforced so long as other states adhered to perpetual allegiance, at least not to the extent that the nation sought new immigrants. The United States could not require new citizens to terminate original citizenship without the cooperation of the home country. As one federal judge noted, at the time of naturalization "[w]e do not inquire what [the applicant's] relation is to his own country; we have not the means of knowing, and the inquiry would be delicate."[26] American authorities nonetheless asserted the naturalization oath to be effective as against the country of origin. As Attorney General Black declaimed in 1859, if the oath of renunciation "did not work a dissolution of every political tie which bound him to his native country, then our naturalization laws are a bitter mockery, and the oath we administer to foreigners is a delusion and a snare."[27] As scholar-diplomat David Jayne Hill wrote in a 1914 editorial in the *American Journal of International Law*,

> By every canon of sound judgment, when a person becomes an American citizen he ceases to be a German. The whole meaning and value of nationality turn upon that distinction. A German-American is a political impossibility. A choice, free from all ambiguity, must be made, or citizenship does not exist at all. To profess to be both German and American is an act of equivocation that obscures the claim to be an American citizen in any acceptable sense.[28]

The United States clearly thought naturalization to be effective as against the individual. In the throes of the expatriation debate, pronouncements on the subject left no doubt as to the consequence of naturalization. "The moment the foreigner becomes naturalized his allegiance to his native country is severed forever," wrote Secretary of State Lewis Cass in an 1859 circular. "He experiences a new political birth."[29]

As other states relented from perpetual allegiance, they moved to terminate the nationality of their subjects/citizens who naturalized in the United States. That was the premise of the Bancroft treaties, which worked to address nationality conflicts on a bilateral basis.[30] In the wake of the 1868 treaty between the United States and the North German Confederation, for example, a German immigrant would be treated as a U.S. citizen only by both parties after naturalization and five years' residence in the United States.

Otherwise, U.S. authorities in effect took it on faith that the naturalizing citizen was transferring his true and exclusive allegiance to the

United States. That created a kind of insecurity on the part of American authorities, who could never be quite sure enough that the migration of loyalty was complete. David Hill, for example, fretted about a 1913 German citizenship law that seemed in theory to allow for the retention of German nationality upon naturalization in the United States, the Bancroft treaty notwithstanding. "[T]he door is open to a secret divided allegiance that may be extremely dangerous to the United States."[31] That created incentives to police new citizens and any continuing relationship with their former sovereigns. Where there was evidence of reversion to original affiliation, expatriation could be put to work post-naturalization. Any active association with the homeland state would result in the loss of U.S. nationality.

## Testing Attachments

State Department practice applied a balancing test under which an individual would be expatriated for showing more attachment to the other country than to the United States. With respect to native-born Americans, protracted foreign residence alone (in most cases) did not present a sufficient basis for expatriation. Carl Gottlieb Rau, a native-born American of a naturalized German father, moved to Switzerland as a minor but did not acquire Swiss or other nationality. Rau was found entitled to a U.S. passport.[32] As Secretary of State William M. Evarts advised the U.S. chargé d'affaires in Switzerland on the matter, "The Department holds that for a native American to put off his national character he should put on another. . . . Continued residence of a native American abroad is not expatriation, unless he performs acts inconsistent with his American nationality and consistent only with the formal acquirement of another nationality."[33]

But where such residence was not accompanied by "some acts of allegiance [to the United States], and the discharge of some duties of citizenship," it could "raise a presumption of renunciation of citizenship."[34] The absence of a definite intent to return to the United States at one time could also result in loss of citizenship, as evidenced, for example, by the purchase and cultivation of land abroad.[35] A 1910 State Department circular softened that presumption, in recognition of the "vast improvement in facilities for communication and transportation between the various nations of the earth, and a corresponding increase in international travel and trade" and the direct or indirect contribution that permanent foreign residence might make to "the wealth and strength, the prestige and the general welfare" of the United States.[36] The upshot was a circumstances test, under which U.S. officials continued to consider property ties to the country but also such factors as "the original nationality of the individual's wife and the mode of raising the children, and finally, the general conduct of the person in question."[37] Participation in the politics of the country of foreign residence could also be taken into account, although voting in foreign elections was not taken as a categoric act of expatriation. Use of a foreign passport could result in at least temporary forfeiture of the right "to recognition and protection" as a U.S. citizen.[38]

While applicable in theory to all citizens, these sorts of lifestyle inquiries left the dual national at much greater risk than the mono-national. As an assistant secretary of state cabled the U.S. ambassador to China in 1936, "any person who wishes to enjoy the benefits of one citizenship should refrain from any statement or action which might indicate that he wishes to enjoy the benefits of the other."[39] In 1929, Secretary of State Henry Stimson admonished the U.S. legation in Peiping to undertake diplomatic protection for dual nationals only where they "have done nothing to emphasize their Chinese citizenship."[40] Naturalized citizens who returned to their homelands prompted the most vocal demands for clearer expatriation protocols. Diplomats came to presume expatriation where a naturalized citizen reestablished residence in his country of origin for a certain period of time. The Bancroft treaties took this approach. A German-born immigrant, for example, would be held to have renounced U.S. naturalization two years after returning home pursuant to the U.S. accord with the North German Confederation.[41]

## Birthright Dual Nationals and "Election"

The United States had a tougher time policing dual citizenship acquired at birth, almost literally a "next generation" problem to that posed by the immigrants themselves. Starting in the late Middle Ages (one scholar pegs the date to 1290 in Great Britain) through the modern era, many European states extended birthright citizenship on a territorial basis,[42] so that any child born within the state's territorial jurisdiction was by that fact counted as among the subjects of the realm. This was the so-called rule of jus soli, Latin for "right of the soil." That rule worked in an era of extreme geographical rootedness, for it could be assumed that those born within national borders were part of the national community, and that those born without were not. As one jurist noted, "The rule was the natural outcome of the intimate connexion in feudalism between the individual and the soil upon which he lived."[43] As mobility increased, however, it became necessary to confront the problem of children born to subjects located in foreign countries. This the law answered with jus sanguinis ("right of the blood"), by which citizenship was extended on the basis of parentage. By the beginning of the nineteenth century, countries typically (and automatically) extended nationality to the children born abroad to parents who were themselves nationals. In its first session, in 1790, Congress enacted a measure extending citizenship to children born to U.S.-citizen fathers abroad, so long as the father had resided at some point in the United States.[44] At the same time as most states adopted a jus sanguinis basis for citizenship for out-of-jurisdiction births, many continued to apply the rule of jus soli in more or less pure form to those born within their territories.

The interplay of these two regimes—jus soli and jus sanguinis—inevitably resulted in a large number of dual nationals in immigrant communities in the United States. The child born to nationals of a country allowing citizenship on the basis of parentage in a country extending it on the basis of territorial birth would hold nationality in both states. As Europe turned to jus sanguinis and the United States applied an almost absolute rule of jus soli—almost all persons born on U.S. territory counted as citizens at birth[45]—a large population of birthright dual nationals followed in the natural wake of the great migrations to America, hence the focus on birthright dual nationals in much of the commentary on dual nationality from the turn of the century onward.[46] One commentator, writing in 1920, feared that as many as nearly half of all Americans were "subject . . . to a dual nationality and a double allegiance" by virtue of the foreign birth of one or both parents.[47]

States sought to defeat birthright dual citizenship through the mechanism of "election," by which individuals were compelled to choose a single allegiance at or early in one's majority, failing which one state or the other stood ready compel expatriation. In the abstract, election could have resolved all cases of birthright dual nationality. A blue-ribbon Harvard research project's draft convention on the laws of nationality called for mandatory election among those born with dual nationality.[48] Many states have at times strictly enforced a formal election requirement.[49]

For the United States, such strict enforcement was both impractical and unnecessary. It would have been a huge task for U.S. authorities to determine who had dual nationality. For most, the formal status of dual national was essentially inchoate. It reflected neither loyalties actually divided nor a necessary dilution in the performance of obligations or in the citizen's genuine attachment to the American community. Many were surely not even aware of their dual nationality. Most birthright dual nationals were thus not required to make formal election (most of those born in the United States to foreign parents), and might "carry such dual nationality with them from birth to the grave."[50]

It was (once again) in the context of diplomatic protection that dual nationality sparked bilateral conflict. Many were born abroad to U.S. citizens, had U.S. citizenship at birth, and continued to live outside the United States. Dual nationals born in the United States would in many cases find themselves located in their other country of nationality. With respect to these populations, the United States imposed what amounted to an informal election requirement. As Acting Secretary of State James D. Porter instructed the U.S. minister to Switzerland in 1885, "Of this election, two things are to be observed; when once made it is final, and requires no formal act, but may be inferred from the conduct of the party from whom election is required."[51] In the late nineteenth century, native-born American dual nationals residing abroad, as well as those born abroad to U.S. citizens, could retain their U.S. citizenship only upon election at majority, as indicated not by formal action on the individual's part but rather by intended place of residence.

Friedrich de Bourry was born with dual nationality in New York in 1862 and resided there until at the age of five his parents returned with him to Austria. He continued to live there into adulthood, working for the Austrian railway service. Secretary of State Thomas Bayard denied his request in 1886 for diplomatic protection, given his failure to record an election of U.S. citizenship upon coming of age formally or signified with acts "plainly expressive of intention, such as immediate preparations to return to the elected country."[52] Bayard elsewhere held that election by birth dual nationals was "evidenced by placing themselves in the country they elect."[53] The practice made sense for an era in which residence would ordinarily reflect a person's political and social identification, and was consistent with the practice of other states.[54] It also explains why the United States appears to have tolerated the nominal dual citizenship of the millions of second-generation immigrants who never formally renounced their "alleged technical allegiance" to other states.[55] Most immigrants and their children stayed put in the United States, in which case the question never arose; their continued residence would have signified election of U.S. citizenship.

## Looking to Congress

Nineteenth-century U.S. efforts to minimize conflicts arising from dual nationality were accomplished almost entirely through executive branch interpretations, a combination of State Department practice and Justice Department legal opinions. Both expatriation and election were devised on the administrative fly, and there were deviations from one administration to the next. Executive branch officials made repeated entreaties for legislation on the subject. Calls for statutory standards to set forth grounds for denationalization came quickly on the heels of the 1868 legislation codifying the principle of voluntary expatriation. In two successive annual messages (the forerunner to State of the Union addresses), President Grant implored Congress to act on the subject. "The United States, who led the way in the overthrow of the doctrine of perpetual allegiance," he wrote in 1873, "are among the last to indicate how their own citizens may elect another nationality," asserting the following year that the importance of the question was "obvious."[56] Such calls had dated back to the early years of the United States.[57]

Decades later, Congress finally responded with the Expatriation Act of 1907. First, the legislation provided for the expatriation of American citizens who naturalized in or took an oath of allegiance to a foreign state.[58] Second, addressing a perennial lament of American envoys, the act included a special rule for naturalized citizens that presumed loss of citizenship after two years' residence in their country of first nationality or five years in any other foreign state.[59] Lastly, the 1907 act required children born and thereafter residing outside the United States "to record at an American consulate their intention to become residents and remain citizens of the United States" upon reaching the age of eighteen. In other words, the measure mandated an election requirement in at least some cases of individuals born with dual citizenship.[60] The election requirement was fortified with a 1934 statute requiring those born with citizenship abroad to one citizen and one non-citizen parent to reside in the United States continuously for five years before reaching the age of eighteen.[61]

The 1907 act ostensibly resolved these three core questions but left other important ones unsettled. The State Department continued in some cases, for example, to expatriate citizens born in the United States with dual nationality who relocated to another state of nationality, a circumstance not covered by the law. The act did not address nagging issues relating to diplomatic protection, and of course it could not by itself change the practice of other states. Naturalized citizens who returned to their homelands were only presumed to have expatriated; the presumption could be overcome by returning to the United States, at any time.[62] Meanwhile, the many persons born within the United States with dual nationality were subject to no statutory election requirement, and other mechanisms for suppressing the status were leaky.

## Marrying Out

The 1907 law also provided for the expatriation of women upon marriage to foreign men. The nineteenth-century practice had been variable on the point, a strand in larger ambiguities surrounding the State Department's approach to expatriation and diplomatic protection. In the totality of the circumstances, it was understood that the woman who married a foreigner and resided abroad was not eligible for protection nor considered a citizen for other purposes (such as tax obligations). By the middle of the nineteenth century, most countries (including the United States) automatically naturalized a non-citizen woman upon marriage to a citizen man. When an American woman married a foreigner, she thus became a citizen of her husband's country of nationality. It was assumed that termination of the marriage and return to the United States would revive U.S. citizenship; in that sense, citizenship was held in abeyance during the time of the marriage.

Nellie Grant, the daughter of Ulysses S. Grant, provided one high-profile example. In 1874 she married a British subject, Algernon Sartoris, Jr., in a White House ceremony. She became a British national under British law by virtue of the marriage, and she and her husband resided in England. Although Nellie Sartoris was hardly at the center of any controversy (quite the contrary—she was beloved by the American public), her U.S. citizenship was held in suspense during the marriage. After her husband's death in 1896, she returned to the United States. Although it may not have been necessary under the administrative practice, Congress passed a special act under which Sartoris was "unconditionally readmitted to the character and privileges of a citizen of the United States."[63] In another case, a federal court found a native-born American beyond the reach of U.S. tax authorities, ruling that she had lost her citizenship by marrying a Frenchman and living continuously thereafter in France.[64]

It had not been U.S. practice, however, to terminate the citizenship of women who married foreign men and continued to reside in the United States.[65] That was consistent with the tolerance for birthright dual nationals living in the United States; so long as they remained in the United States, diplomatic complications from dual nationality were unlikely to arise. They were unlikely to be a problem, even if they acquired their husband's nationality at the same time that they retained U.S. citizenship.

The 1907 measure abandoned this balance by taking a blanket, bright-line approach to the question. The act mandated the loss of citizenship for any American woman who married a foreigner, regardless of location. The woman's desire to retain citizenship was irrelevant to the statutory mechanism; the measure resulted in forced expatriation that obviously discriminated on the basis of sex. Upon termination of the marriage, the woman could "resume" her U.S. citizenship by registering with an American consul, or by returning to reside or continuing to reside in the United States. The measure was effective at suppressing a growing source of dual nationality. But it was also infected by the legacy of coverture, under which a wife's legal identity was subsumed in her husband's, and clearly reflected a patriarchal conception of family that was already under assault by a budding women's rights movement.

The overreach proved unsustainable. Many women, some prominent, lost their U.S. citizenship under the act, which was applied on a retroactive basis to strip women who had married foreign men before 1907 as well as after. As non-citizens, women expatriated under the measure were disqualified from a range of professions. One New York woman who had "carefully built up a remunerative practice of law," hardly a common thing in the early twentieth century, had it all taken away after marrying a Dutch citizen.[66] As a non-citizen, she was ineligible to practice law under New York statutes. During the First World War, women who married nationals of the Central Powers were not only expatriated but designated as enemy aliens under U.S. law. As such, these former Americans were subjected to property confiscations and could have been (at least in theory) interned and deported.

The 1907 regime also threatened to snatch defeat from the jaws of victory as women secured political rights. Women were winning the vote on a state-by-state basis. California adopted women's suffrage in 1911. But when San Francisco suffragette Ethel Mackenzie attempted to register to vote in 1913, her application was rejected on the grounds that she was not a citizen of the United States. Mackenzie had married a British citizen in 1909 (the Scottish tenor Gordon Mackenzie) and was thus expatriated under the 1907 statute, even as she continued to live in San Francisco.[67] The discriminatory nationality regime became a major target of the women's movement, especially after adoption of the Nineteenth Amendment in 1920, which guaranteed women equal voting rights nationwide. The result of a major lobbying campaign, the 1922 Marital Women's Independent Citizenship Act (also known as the Cable Act, for sponsoring GOP Ohio congressman John L. Cable) rolled back the expatriation measure. No longer would stay-in-the-country wives of foreign men forfeit their U.S. citizenship.

As described by historian Candice Bredbenner, the State Department opposed the Cable Act, "alarmed by the prospect of a rise in the number of dual nationals."[68] But the act did not eliminate marriage expatriation altogether. Women who married aliens ineligible for citizenship (read: Asians) continued to forfeit their nationality, a reflection of a heavy racial streak in the U.S. naturalization regime (not fully abandoned until 1952). The 1922 legislation also transferred the 1907 act's presumption respecting naturalized citizens to native-born women who married foreigners. "If during the continuance of the marital status," the Cable Act provided, "she resides continuously for two years in a foreign State of which her husband is a citizen or subject, or for five years continuously outside the United States, she shall thereafter be subject to the same presumption" of expatriation. In other words, a woman married to a foreigner was expatriated after living abroad for a relatively short period in the same way as a naturalized citizen who returned home.

The qualification mitigated State Department concerns respecting the retreat from the bright-line expatriation ground. It would have reduced the number of difficult cases that might otherwise have added to their onerous docket of diplomatic protection disputes. There was also the backstop of the 1907 act's provision for expatriation upon naturalization in another country. A woman who acquired the citizenship of her husband's country of nationality by any affirmative act would be subject to the discrete ground of expatriation for naturalizing in a foreign state. To the extent that marital unity persisted by tradition, women's citizenship would remain at risk.

Congress eliminated the foreign-residency presumption in 1931; women who lived with their foreign husbands outside the United States no longer faced a special risk of forfeiting their citizenship by virtue of the marriage alone. The fall of the discriminatory expatriation regime tracked developments at the international level. Attempts to eliminate involuntary nationality mechanisms applying only to women were hampered by concerns relating to dual nationality. So long as most states provided for both automatic naturalization and expatriation of women upon marriage to men of other nationality, dual citizenship was suppressed. Jurists involved in early-twentieth-century efforts to harmonize nationality laws were chary to relinquish that symmetry, even at the expense of sex inequality, and saw efforts to secure sex equality as a threat to broader nationality reform initiatives.[69] Efforts to adopt a nondiscrimination principle in the 1930 Hague Convention on Nationality failed. But mirroring the evolution of U.S. practice, other states stepped away from the marital unity approach. In 1934, western hemisphere states concluded the Montevideo Convention on the Nationality of Women in whose simple operative part parties agreed that "[t]here shall be no distinction based on sex as regards nationality, in their legislation or in their practice."[70] The United States ratified the treaty almost immediately.

As other states moved away from automatic marital naturalization, the increase in dual nationals may not have been dramatic. An American woman marrying a foreigner would in many cases simply have kept her U.S. citizenship while not acquiring that of her husband. To the extent that the non-discriminatory regime increased the incidence of dual citizenship, it does not appear to have compounded diplomatic fractures triggered by the status. This may have been the consequence of other, more persistently discriminatory aspects of the international system through the middle of the twentieth century. Women were not subject to conscription. That eliminated the most common source of disputes relating to diplomatic protection. There were no women who faced P. A. Lelong's quandary in traveling to France, no women who after having had their nationality forcibly transferred by marriage ended up being pressed into uniform against their will. Bilateral disputes relating to dual national women were rare, reflecting women's subjugated status in other areas of the law.

Disputes regarding male dual nationals had been reduced by the decline of perpetual allegiance, election mechanisms, bilateral treaty arrangements, and the 1907 act, which otherwise remained in force. But dual citizenship still presented an irritant to foreign relations if only because expatriation mechanisms remained imperfect. In the meantime, the moral disfavor associated with the status would have been as effective as any legal constraint in policing dual nationality. The intense opprobrium aimed at "double allegiance" might be explained, in part, by the law's failure to stamp it out. So threatening was dual nationality to the national interest and the international order that it required the backstop of formidable social norms, reflected in the common understanding of dual nationality as something like bigamy or TR's "self-evident absurdity." These norms wouldn't suffice to keep the boundaries of community clear enough as states moved into the more dangerously competitive environment of the mid-twentieth century.

# Congress, the Courts, and the World against Dual Citizenship

Tomoya Kawakita was not a nice person. As an interpreter for a Japanese metals company using POW labor in mines on frigid Honshu Island during the Second World War, he was known among prisoners as "The Efficiency Expert" and "The Meat Ball" for his brutal treatment of American prisoners of war. In one case, he forced a detainee to kneel on bamboo for hours while holding a bucket of water over his head. When the prisoner's elbows bent and the water sloshed out, Kawakita would strike him and refill the container. In other incidents he pushed and poked U.S. service members thrown in cesspools for stealing Red Cross medical supplies.[1]

The son of a Calexico grocer, Kawakita had U.S. citizenship by birth and Japanese nationality by parentage. "Tom" grew up in Calexico and won a letter on his high school football team. He had been studying in Japan at the war's beginning, unable to return to the United States. After the war, Kawakita made his way back to the States, enrolling as a student at the University of Southern California. A dumbfounded former POW recognized Kawakita while shopping at a Sears department store and reported his presence in the United States to the FBI. Kawakita was convicted of treason and sentenced to death.[2]

Only citizens can be charged with treason committed abroad. Kawakita's conviction, upheld on appeal by the U.S. Supreme Court in a 1952 decision,[3] has sometimes been held out as cautionary tale for those holding dual nationality.[4]

In fact it was a freak case. Kawakita wasn't the only Japanese national born in the United States who "levied war" against the United States or gave the enemy "aid and comfort." Thousands of so-called Nisei either found themselves (like Kawakita) in Japan at the war's outbreak or chose to return in the service of the Emperor.[5] But Kawakita was one of only a small handful who faced treason charges in U.S. federal court. Almost all others had lost their citizenship through expatriating conduct. Very few had acted against the United States while not at the same time losing citizenship. (Tokyo Rose, an American-born radio announcer who broadcast propaganda to U.S. GIs during the war, was another.) Under the 1940 Nationality Act, individuals entering into the armed services of another state automatically lost their U.S. citizenship.[6] Thousands of dual Japanese and American, German and American, and Italian and American citizens who served in Axis militaries lost their U.S. citizenship upon enlistment in foreign forces. As a result, none could be prosecuted for treason, a charge that can be leveled only against those owing allegiance to the United States.

By contrast, Kawakita had acted against Americans as an employee of a private Japanese company. Kawakita claimed his role at what amounted to a POW camp was equivalent to "service" in the Japanese army; he was claiming expatriation by way of a defense to treason.[7] Rejecting the claim, the U.S. Supreme Court found his citizenship to have persisted and upheld the conviction. (President Eisenhower commuted the death sentence to life in prison, and Kawakita was jailed at Alcatraz until released to Japan by President Kennedy in 1963 on the condition that he never return to the United States.)[8] But the case was the exception that proved the rule. The Kawakita case demonstrated the breadth of the mid-century expatriation regime in delimiting the boundaries of citizenship and minimizing the incidence of dual citizenship.

That regime included major nationality-related legislation in 1940 and 1952. These measures proved an American high-water mark for the dictates of exclusivity. While not barring outright the retention of dual nationality, the 1940 and 1952 acts set a standard by which evidence of any political identification with another state triggered expatriation. Although dual citizenship has never been prohibited under U.S. law, during the mid-twentieth century it was difficult in any active way to maintain an alternate nationality without putting one's U.S. citizenship at risk. This severe legislative scheme eclipsed the administrative discretion that had been central to the nineteenth-century practice.

The legal scheme was an extension of the moral opprobrium that had attached to dual nationality during the prior century. The status now was not just intolerable before God, it was also unsustainable before the law. (Before domestic law, that is, as states had failed to eradicate the status at the international level through multilateral efforts.) Loyalty and allegiance assumed a new meaning through wars hot and cold. Dual citizenship was readily situated into "fifth column" narratives. There was not a single major case of espionage involving a dual citizen—the spy would be the last to maintain outward evidence of attachment to adversary states. But the high stakes of twentieth-century conflict compounded the incentives for suppressing the status. The practice of other states tracked that of the United States. Dual citizenship was highly disfavored the world over.

At the same time, there were an increasing number of cases in which individuals might want to maintain dual citizenship. During the nineteenth century, dual citizenship threatened state interests to the extent it provoked conflict with other states. It had also been a bane to individuals insofar as it created duplicative obligations. In an era in which compulsory military service was the norm, those obligations were substantial—hence the articulation of a right to expatriate. But the twentieth century saw states looking to rationalize the system of citizen obligations, especially among friendly states. There arose more cases in which individuals affirmatively sought to maintain the status. As one commentator observed in 1955, if given the choice, "most [dual nationals] would elect to retain the double benefits and protections of dual citizenship."[9]

Where those cases bumped up against the expatriation regime, the courts came into play. The expatriation power was a frequent constitutional target. Through the middle decades of the twentieth century, the Supreme Court sustained the breadth of the legislative scheme, though its constitutionality was intensely contested. Nation-states held the line on dual citizenship even as multilateral initiatives to combat the status fell short. U.S. efforts to suppress dual citizenship were consistent with the practice of other countries, who in some cases assumed a more aggressive posture on the question, effectively policing against the status.

## Legislative Gap-Plugging

As dual nationals continued to provoke conflict between states, Congress faced pressure to expand the 1907 expatriation measure. In 1933, President Roosevelt chartered an inter-agency committee to review the entirety of U.S. nationality practices with the goal of their legislative consolidation and codification.[10] The effort took five years to complete. The committee's proposal for legislative action, delivered to Congress over the signatures of Secretary of State Cordell Hull, Attorney General Homer Cummings, and Secretary of Labor Frances Perkins, highlighted the problematic interplay of U.S. and foreign nationality practices and the large number of dual nationals that it produced. The proposal covered the full range of nationality issues, including naturalization procedures, but the committee highlighted provisions relating to loss of nationality as "of special importance."[11] The committee's proposal looked to "deprive persons of American nationality when such persons, by their own acts, or inaction, show that their real attachment is to [a] foreign country and not to the United States."[12] Existing law, the committee observed, had "proven inadequate" in preventing the transmission of citizenship to "foreign-born children having little or no connection to the United States and embroiling this Government in controversies which they may have with the governments of the foreign countries in which they reside."

Congress adopted most of the Roosevelt administration proposal verbatim. The 1940 Nationality Act set a low bar to expatriation in an attempt to reduce the incidence of dual citizenship. The law reinscribed the 1907 act's provision for loss of citizenship upon naturalization in a foreign state, the reasonableness of which, "based upon the singleness of allegiance, will hardly be questioned."[13] For native-born Americans, there was no possibility of acquiring another nationality after birth without forfeiting one's U.S. citizenship.

The 1940 act expressly provided for loss of citizenship for entering into the armed forces of a foreign state where an individual possessed the nationality of that state. (The act thus did not expatriate mercenaries serving in such units as the French Foreign Legion, for which French nationality is a disqualification.) The provision built on expatriation under the 1907 act for the taking of a foreign oath; to the extent military service in other countries was contingent on such an oath, many had lost their citizenship as a result. This had applied even to service in the armed forces of friendly states. An estimated 15–20,000 Americans had lost their citizenship for enlisting in Canadian and British forces, most before the entry of the United States into the First World War. Their citizenship was later restored by special legislation.[14] The 1940 act carved out foreign enlistment where permitted by treaty with friendly states. But it was under this provision that thousands of dual citizens lost their U.S. citizenship by serving in Axis militaries during the Second World War. In addition to service in a foreign armed force, the 1940 act also provided for loss of citizenship for accepting government employment in a foreign state for which only nationals of such state were eligible.

These expatriation grounds were perhaps to be expected insofar as they involved direct service to a foreign sovereign and the "loyalty" that would go with it. Somewhat bizarrely, the statute assumed that any dual national returning to his homeland for more than six months had joined its military or government service.[15] The measure was intended to check the activities of putative "fifth columnists."[16] Although it was never enforced, the provision evidenced the new framing of dual citizenship in security-related terms.[17]

Less obviously situated in a loyalty discourse was the 1940 act's mandate that citizenship be forfeited for voting in a foreign political election. The measure was prompted by the spectacle of U.S. citizens of German descent, many with dual citizenship, who voted in a 1935 plebiscite to return the Saarland to Germany. The Hitler regime had paid expenses for several hundred German immigrants to the United States, many of them naturalized U.S. citizens, to travel home to cast ballots in the referendum.[18] "I know we have had a lot of Nazis, so-called American citizens, go to Europe who have voted in the Saar for the annexation of territory to Germany, and Germany says that they have the right to participate and to vote, and yet they are American citizens," observed Representative Samuel Dickstein, chairman of the House Committee on Immigration and Naturalization. "There might well be circumstances where an American shown to have voted at the behest of a foreign government to advance its territorial interests would compromise his native allegiance."[19] This echoed the Roosevelt committee's characterization of "taking an active part in the political affairs of a foreign state . . . [as involving] a political attachment and practical allegiance thereto which is inconsistent with continued allegiance to the United States."[20]

The 1940 act also tightened up the 1907 Expatriation Act with respect to naturalized citizens who returned to their homelands. No longer was expatriation merely presumed upon reestablished residence in the country of origin. It was automatic after three years (two years where the nationality of the country of return was reacquired by operation of law).[21] The new measure included broad exceptions, where, for example, naturalized citizens resided abroad as employees of the U.S. government or U.S. commercial, educational, or religious entities, or for reasons of ill health. Elderly naturalized citizens who had lived in the United States for twenty-five years or longer before returning home were also exempted. But many thousands lost their citizenship under the measure. So, too, did their children, even if they had citizenship by virtue of birth in the United States, so long as permanent residence was not reestablished in the United States before the age of twenty-three.

More still faced expatriation under the 1952 act, which went a step further by expatriating birthright U.S. citizens (not only naturalized ones) who moved to or stayed in their other country of nationality. Section 350 of the statute, entitled "Dual Nationals; Divestiture of Nationality," terminated the U.S. citizenship of any individual born with dual nationality "who has voluntarily sought or claimed benefits of the nationality of any state" after residing continuously for three years after the age of twenty-two in the other state of nationality. The provision included the same broad exceptions included in the 1940 measure, the benefit of which could only be claimed upon the taking of an oath of allegiance to the United States before a U.S. consular or diplomatic official. The State Department warned traveling dual nationals of section 350's requirement.[22] Thus did Congress attempt to more effectively resolve the chronic problems associated with the presence of dual nationals in their other state of nationality.

Congress rejected only one of the Roosevelt committee's proposals, that the use of a foreign passport result in loss of nationality, and this only because some states that refused to recognize the transfer of nationality—holdouts in a perpetual allegiance approach—required their birthright nationals to use the passport of that country of origin for return visits.[23] The Department of State nonetheless continued to "discourage" U.S. citizens from obtaining foreign passports.[24] Obtaining a passport apparently qualified as a "benefit," risking expatriation under section 350.[25]

In short, an American could participate in another state's polity only at risk of sacrificing her citizenship. As one congressman asserted, overconfidently, the 1940 expatriation measure "would put an end to dual citizenship and relieve this country of those who reside in foreign lands and only claim citizenship when it serves their purpose."[26] As one federal judge observed in 1953, Congress had moved to eliminate "the plague of 'dual nationality' . . . to every degree possible."[27] Even passive dual nationals risked denationalization. The statutory enactments ramped up expatriation in ways that departed from prior administrative practice, which had taken a more holistic, less categoric approach to expatriation decisions. They added up to an almost complete prohibition on active dual nationality.

## The Courts Back Congress

These legislative efforts were mostly validated by the courts. Nineteenth-century practice—almost entirely out of the executive branch—was too variable to supply much of a judicial target. Decisions relating to diplomatic protection were not justiciable; the courts would not entertain challenges regarding the denial of protection. (Denial of diplomatic protection did not clearly deprive an individual of citizenship, though it did deny him its most valuable benefit outside the United States.) Once that practice was codified, however, the expatriation regime was fair judicial game.

The key threshold question was whether an individual could be deprived of citizenship against her will. Suffragette Ethel Mackenzie challenged the marital expatriation provision of the 1907 on the grounds that Congress had no power to expatriate citizens against their will. The Supreme Court gave the challenge a sympathetic hearing. "It may be conceded," Justice Joseph McKenna allowed in his opinion for the Court, "that a change of citizenship cannot be arbitrarily imposed, that is, imposed without the concurrence of the citizen."[28] But McKenna denied that to be the case with Mackenzie, since she had voluntarily entered into the marriage with a foreigner "with notice of the consequences." In other words, because Ethel Mackenzie knew that the marriage would result in loss of citizenship, the expatriation was neither without her consent nor arbitrary. The Court noted that the measure involved "conditions of national moment" with respect to foreign relations. *Mackenzie* set down a voluntariness test for the exercise of an expatriation power. So long as a citizen undertook the triggering activity on a voluntary basis, the termination of citizenship trumped the individual's desire to keep it.

The voluntariness standard constrained expatriation in two significant contexts. The first involved the expatriation of children by virtue of the acts of their parents. The 1939 decision in *Perkins v. Elg* involved a woman born in the United States to Swedish immigrants.[29] Her father had naturalized as an American but thereafter returned permanently to Sweden with his wife and child, where he formally renounced his U.S. citizenship. Marie Elg returned to the United States as a twenty-one-year-old, only to have the government subsequently declare her an illegal alien on the theory that she had lost her citizenship via naturalization as a Swede. Chief Justice Charles Evans Hughes rejected this argument on the grounds that her Swedish naturalization was "wholly involuntary and merely derivative." The Court instead validated the concept of election, as established by practice, under which children born with dual nationality would have the opportunity to choose U.S. over another nationality upon coming of age. By returning to the United States, the Court held, Elg had elected to retain her U.S. citizenship. In line with the decision, the 1940 and 1952 acts were careful to insulate minors from the expatriating acts of their parents.[30]

The courts also nullified expatriation where an individual established that the expatriating act itself was undertaken under duress. Scores of citizens who served in Axis militaries during the Second World War pressed this argument after the war's end. The typical claim involved a dual U.S. citizen temporarily present in Germany, Italy, or Japan when the war broke out who was conscripted to serve in the enemy forces. As described above, the 1940 act mandated automatic loss of citizenship for service in foreign armed forces. The courts found the ground inapplicable where the service was compelled.[31] Courts were most sympathetic where individuals had notified U.S. consular authorities contemporaneously that they were serving under protest. In some cases, however, courts sympathized with the futility of resisting conscription in the fascist Axis states, and accepted claims of duress based on societal factors rather than individual ones.[32]

Congress was otherwise unconstrained in setting categoric conditions for the retention of citizenship if the conditions themselves allowed for the exercise of individual will. The "voluntariness" sometimes seemed more fictional than real; as one writer noted, the approach "required a profound change in the meaning of 'voluntary.'"[33] In its 1950 decision in *Savorgnan v. United States*, the Supreme Court upheld the expatriation of Rosette Savorgnan, who had acquired Italian citizenship in the course of marrying an Italian diplomat in the United States in 1940.[34] In 1922, the marriage ground for expatriation (upheld in *Mackenzie*) had been eliminated by Congress,[35] but naturalization in another state remained a basis for termination of citizenship. Savorgnan's naturalization ceremony, oath, and accompanying documents were all in Italian, a language she did not understand. She assumed that the signing of the documents was but a step in obtaining consent of the Italian government to her marriage. According to the trial court, she "relied on her husband's statement and assurance, that . . . she merely acquired a technical Italian citizenship, which status would in no way endanger her American citizenship."[36] Savorgnan claimed, in effect, that she didn't know she was naturalizing as an Italian, a claim sustained by the trial court. The Supreme Court, however, found her actions to satisfy the voluntariness threshold; as a "competent adult," Savorgnan had expatriated herself by naturalizing in a foreign state.[37] The Court justified its decision in part on the ground that the "United States has long recognized the general undesirability of dual allegiances."

The Supreme Court also upheld the breadth of conduct giving rise to expatriation. In *Perez v. Brownell*, the Court took up foreign voting as the basis for loss of citizenship.[38] Clemente Martin Perez had been born in the United States in 1909, but had been taken to Mexico by his Mexican national parents in his youth. He had returned to the United States several times, representing himself as a Mexican citizen so that he could avoid military service obligations. Only upon facing deportation from the United States in 1953 did he play the citizenship card. The government claimed that Perez had expatriated himself by remaining outside the United States for purposes of evading the draft, which had been added to the grounds for expatriation by the 1940 act. It also claimed expatriation on the grounds that Perez had voted in a Mexican political election in 1946.

The Supreme Court upheld Perez's expatriation on the foreign voting ground. Perez was hardly a sympathetic claimant, and the voting ground supplied the cleanest basis for stripping his citizenship.[39] Writing for the Court, Justice Felix Frankfurter echoed by-then standard arguments against dual citizenship: "no man should be permitted deliberately to place himself in a position where his services may be claimed by more than one government and his allegiance be due to more than one." The voting ground was intended "to deprive of citizenship those persons who had shown that their real attachment is to the foreign country and not to the United States."[40] Frankfurter stressed the government's need to "be able to reduce to a minimum the frictions that are unavoidable in a world of sovereigns sensitive in matters touching their dignity and interests," and the Court's duty to give Congress "ample scope in selecting appropriate modes for accomplishing its purpose." The political activity of U.S. citizens abroad might be taken to represent the foreign policy of the United States. Other states might "regard [a national's] action to be the action of his government" or even "as a reflection if not an expression of its policy."[41] Foreign voting, Frankfurter observed, might also rationally evidence "elements of an allegiance to another country in some measure, at least, inconsistent with American citizenship." Frankfurter saw only loose constraints on the executive branch in putting expatriation to work as a foreign relations imperative. "Of course, Congress can attach loss of citizenship only as a consequence of conduct engaged in voluntarily," Frankfurter conceded with a nod to the *Mackenzie* ruling. "But it would be a mockery of this Court's decisions to suggest that a person, in order to lose his citizenship, must intend or desire to do so."

*Perez* drew a passionate dissent from Chief Justice Earl Warren, vaunting the citizenry as the ultimate source of all governmental power. Under this logic, in Warren's view, the government "is without power to sever the relationship that gives rise to its existence." For Warren, the stakes were high. In a line often quoted as exemplifying citizenship's worth, he trumpeted: "Citizenship *is* man's basic right for it is nothing less than the right to have rights."[42]

But even Warren did not mean to limit expatriation to cases involving formal, express renunciation of U.S. citizenship. "It has long been recognized that citizenship may not only be voluntarily renounced through exercise of the right of expatriation," the chief justice acknowledged, "but also by other actions in derogation of undivided allegiance to this country." Those actions included naturalization in another country, which "ordinarily shows a renunciation of citizenship." Warren acknowledged that "[d]oubtless, under some circumstances, a vote in a foreign election" would suffice to show a voluntary abandonment of citizenship. "For example, abandonment of citizenship might result if the person desiring to vote had to become a foreign national or represent himself to be one." His objection to the majority's position was more that foreign voting would not "invariably involve[] . . . a dilution of undivided allegiance sufficient to show a voluntary abandonment of citizenship."[43] In other words, Warren's objection was to the categoric application of the voting ground. The same lens was apparent in Warren's majority opinion in *Trop v. Dulles*. Decided the same day as *Perez*, *Trop* struck down military desertion as a ground for loss of citizenship. "Desertion in wartime, though it may merit the ultimate penalty, does not necessarily signify allegiance to a foreign state."[44] Warren had no truck with dual citizenship or divided allegiance.

The *Perez* decision marked the zenith of efforts to combat dual nationality. The mere act of voting in a foreign country would suffice to establish expatriation. That would have, at least in theory, taken care of many cases in which persistent dual nationality presented complications of foreign relations (and some that would not: one individual lost her citizenship for voting in a Canadian town's referendum to allow the sale of beer and wine.)[45] As Frankfurter put it, "the termination of citizenship terminates the problem." More than 25,000 individuals lost their citizenship on the voting ground alone between 1949 and 1965.[46] *Perez* further legitimated U.S. efforts to limit the incidence of dual nationality among American citizens.

## Universal Opprobrium

Judicial lamentations of dual nationality were echoed by the commentators. As early as 1887, one scholar complained of "interminable dissertations on the accumulation of nationalities."[47] The likes of Yale Law School's Edwin Borchard and Richard Flournoy (a State Department official and prolific writer on citizenship issues) strongly supported efforts to stamp it out.[48] Nissim Bar-Yaacov prefaced his major 1961 study of the issue by observing that "[i]t is a widely held opinion that dual nationality is an undesirable phenomenon detrimental both to the friendly relations between nations and the well-being of the individuals concerned," and concluded by affirming that "in the absence of closer universal or regional cooperation which would virtually create a common citizenship, the status of dual nationality is undesirable and should be abolished."[49] For all the ink that was spent on the question in the early part of this century, it appears that no one suggested any possible advantage from the phenomenon, at least not from the state's perspective. As of 1930, the view of dual nationality "as a damaging evil . . . seems to have been undisputed."[50]

International legal elites also took aim at the status. In the early twentieth century, nationality law was widely understood as the source of major difficulties in international relations, largely the result of disputes in the arena of diplomatic protection. The difficulties owed to state discretion in the area. If nationality laws could be harmonized, in theory at least the conflicts could be avoided. In an emotional, self-styled "plea" to confront the problem, longtime editor of the *American Journal of International Law* James Brown Scott observed that the "confusion" in this area was "so great, so universal, and so embarrassing, not to say exasperating," that it could be remedied only through an international treaty.[51] He called for all states to follow a rule of jus soli only, which would eliminate birthright dual citizenship—an individual would have the citizenship of the country in which he was born and no other. As John Wesley McWilliams wrote in 1920 in the *American Bar Association Journal*:

> The time is now ripe for the solution of these perplexing and dangerous international disputes arising from the application of the so-called principle of dual nationality. We are on the threshold of a new world; the League of Nations bids fair to become a reality; international problems and conflicting views of rights and obligations are in a state of flux; a new code of International Law is about to be formulated, and if this question of dual allegiance is to be eliminated as a source of misunderstanding and ill will between nations, the conflicting views of sovereignty and citizenship must be definitely and finally reconciled.[52]

In the late nineteenth and early twentieth centuries, nationality was the subject of discussion in various international law associations.[53] As early as 1925, one commentator could observe that the "the desirability of international agreement, with a view to securing uniformity of legislation and practice, has long occupied the attention of international jurists."[54] In 1924, the International Law Association proposed a model statute with the aim of reducing "the evils" of dual nationality and statelessness.[55]

Nationality was one of only three issues (the others relating to territorial waters and to state responsibility for violations of international law) selected in 1927 for systematic consideration at the 1930 Hague Conference on the Codification of International Law.[56] As part of the lead-up to the Hague meeting, the three subjects were taken up by a committee of highly prominent academics, practitioners, and policymakers under the sponsorship of Harvard Law School and funded by John D. Rockefeller, Jr. The effort was equivalent to a modern-day blue-ribbon commission. Billed as "The Harvard Research in International Law," the project set out to devise draft conventions for the Hague topics.[57] Among those included on the project's advisory committee were soon-to-be U.S. Supreme Court justice Benjamin Cardozo, former secretary of state Elihu Root, and American Law Institute president George Wickersham, along with academics from Harvard, Yale, and Columbia law schools, among others. Those on the nationality subcommittee included Manley O. Hudson and Philip Jessup, both of whom would later serve on the World Court. The State Department's Flournoy served as the subcommittee's reporter.

The resulting report and draft nationality treaty set its sights "to prevent[], so far as possible, cases of double nationality."[58] The report concluded that complete eradication of the status was improbable; "it is necessary to realize the fact that dual nationality does exist and will continue to exist unless all states will agree to adopt a single rule for nationality at birth," an unlikely prospect given the entrenchment of both jus soli and jus sanguinis approaches to birth citizenship.[59] In looking to control dual nationality, the Harvard group proposed that birth dual nationals retain only the nationality of country of habitual residence as of age twenty-three, a twist on the election mechanism. Its draft treaty would also have mandated loss of original nationality upon naturalization in another state. The draft sought to bar nationality through descent beyond the second generation of persons born and resident abroad, by way of precluding the "indefinite condition of dual nationality" that could result from an unbounded rule of jus sanguinis as applied to emigrant populations.[60]

The League of Nations, meanwhile, had been working on its own track. In 1926, a committee of experts drew up a more modest draft convention on nationality.[61] The League group was also top-drawer, chaired by former Swedish prime minister Hjalmar Hammarskjöld (father of the future UN secretary-general Dag Hammarskjöld). The group's report deplored "double nationality" as representing "an absolutely abnormal phase in international life." Although it acknowledged that it "would certainly be an advantage" if states were to permit expatriation, require election, and forebear from extending citizenship by descent beyond the first externally resident generation, the report concluded that prospects for such an agreement were "premature."[62] The draft agreement addressed problems of nationality relating to women and children. As for dual nationality, in contrast to the Harvard product, the League experts did not aim to reduce incidence of the status; instead, they looked to manage associated conflicts through constraints on the exercise of diplomatic protection.[63] Preparatory talks among government delegates at the Hague conference, meanwhile, were "unanimously of the opinion . . . that States should, in the exercise of their power of regulating questions of nationality, make every effort to reduce so far as possible cases of dual nationality."

At the Hague Codification Conference, the resulting Convention on Certain Questions Relating to the Conflict of Nationality Laws fell well short of eliminating nationality practices as a source of international conflict. While recognizing the virtue of an international agreement to settle nationality issues, the convention's preamble acknowledged the prematurity of reaching a uniform solution to problems of double nationality and statelessness. The instrument worked from a clear premise of state discretion: "It is for each State to determine under its own law who are its nationals. . . . Any question as to whether a person possesses the nationality of a particular State shall be determined in accordance with the law of that State."[64] Failing to follow the lead of the Harvard Research group, the treaty contained no provision for mandatory election for dual nationals at an age in majority, and it did not limit extending nationality by descent.[65] Nor did the treaty require states to recognize expatriation except when an individual possessed two nationalities "without any voluntary act on his part," and then only upon the satisfaction of conditions imposed by the state whose nationality the individual desired to renounce;[66] in other words, expatriation would be available to those who acquired dual nationality at birth but not to those coming to that status through naturalization. Scott lamented that "the caption" itself was "illuminating"; the convention considered the problem as one of conflicts and not of international law.[67] Even in the face of this light touch, it was not widely adopted, garnering only twelve ratifications. As one study notes, "Criticism of the Convention and characterization of it as a failure was widespread."[68] The Hague Convention evidenced the international community's continuing distaste for dual nationality, but the effort was largely ineffectual at combatting the status.

Regional efforts met with more success. A 1933 Inter-American Convention on Nationality provided for loss of original nationality in a party to the convention upon naturalization in another. To help enforce the mechanism, the state bestowing naturalization was obligated to communicate the fact to the state of origin.[69] In 1963, the major European states agreed to a Convention on Reduction of Cases of Multiple Nationality, whose solutions to the problem "were not radically different from those of 1930 [and the Hague Convention]."[70] Recognizing that "cases of multiple nationality are liable to cause difficulties," the European accord afforded birthright dual nationals a right to renounce citizenship of a state in which she was not resident for the prior ten years. As with the inter-American convention, it provided for automatic expatriation of original nationality in the case of naturalization.

More bilateral accords were reached, providing, for instance, for election as between two particular nationalities.[71] Other initiatives were stillborn. Two 1954 reports commissioned by the semi-official United Nations International Law Commission "endeavoured to show the origin and its magnitude of the problem of plural nationality, and to indicate remedial action which might be taken by agreement between States to remove this cause of friction from the international scene."[72] The ILC proposed a package of measures resembling those put forth by the Harvard group twenty-five years before. "Basis 1" for the accompanying proposals remained a world in which "[a]ll persons are entitled to possess one nationality, but one nationality only."[73]

The posture assumed by other states was similarly dour. As the German Federal Constitutional Court noted as late as 1974, "It is accurate to say that dual or multiple nationality is regarded, both domestically and internationally, as an evil that should be avoided or eliminated in the interest of states as well as the interests of the affected citizen." In articulating what became known as the "*Übel-Doktrin*" ("evil doctrine") with respect to dual nationality,[74] the German court justified its conclusion in familiar terms:

> States seek to achieve exclusivity of their respective nationalities in order to set clear boundaries for their sovereignty over persons; they want to be secure in the duty of loyalty of their citizens—which extends if necessary as far as risking one's life—and do not want to see it endangered by possible conflicts of loyalty owed to a foreign states.[75]

Most countries continued to terminate nationality upon naturalization in another state. Many insisted on proof of expatriation by country of origin as a predicate to naturalization. Some required election of birthright dual nationals, tolerating not even nominal dual nationality, while others adopted denationalization triggers along the lines of the 1940 American regime.

This disfavor ultimately reflected the primacy of nation-states in the world system, as well as the precarious nature of their interaction. The ebb of toleration for dual nationals, marked by the 1940 and 1952 U.S. nationality acts, as well as the Supreme Court's 1958 decision in *Perez*, coincided in the middle decades of the century with perhaps the most dangerously unstable situation the world has ever faced. No doubt, earlier eras had been riven by chronic and often bloody international conflict, but unlike in those earlier eras, the conflict was now as between peoples and not merely sovereigns. In that equation, individuals mattered in a way that they had not before. On the one hand, dual nationals represented a potential spark in the tinderbox as issues relating to their protection or responsibility for their actions could readily escalate into interstate conflict. On the other hand, in a world premised on the fact of some level of interstate conflict, dual nationals could only be presumed to do an adversary's bidding from within. As the Supreme Court once observed, "every individual of the one nation must acknowledge every individual of the other nation as his own enemy. . . . The alien enemy is bound by allegiance which commits him to lose no opportunity to forward the cause of our enemy."[76]

These twin harms amplified state efforts against dual citizenship. To hold another citizenship was to put one's American citizenship at serious risk. The law made it difficult to spread formal national identity. One had to pick sides or those sides would be picked for you. The mid-twentieth century marked the zenith of the dual citizenship anti-norm.

4

Turning the Corner on Dual Citizenship

Born Ephraim Bernstein in 1893 in Riki, Poland, Beys Afroyim had immigrated to the United States in 1912 and naturalized as a U.S. citizen in 1926. Described as a "radical modernist," he studied at the Art Institute of Chicago and National Academy of Design; was commissioned for portraits of George Bernard Shaw, Theodore Dreiser, and Arnold Schoenberg, among others, and counted Alfred Steiglitz as a patron; and directed his own "experimental" art school from 1927 until 1946. In 1949, he and his wife (who had been his student) left the United States, traveled through Europe, and settled in Israel. The marriage did not last, and desiring to return to the United States, in 1960 Afroyim applied to the U.S. consulate in Haifa for a new passport. Instead, the consulate issued him a certificate of loss of nationality. As part of his passport application, Afroyim had submitted an Israeli identification booklet which noted his voting in Israeli national elections in November 1951; this triggered the "foreign voting" ground for expatriation upheld in *Perez v. Brownell*. Afroyim challenged the revocation of citizenship in administrative proceedings, claiming that he had entered into the polls not to vote but rather sketch the voters as they cast their ballots. The State Department's Board of Review on the Loss of Nationality affirmed the consul's decision in May 1965. Afroyim thereafter retained an able attorney, Nanette Dembitz, a Justice Department veteran and second cousin of Louis Brandeis, who shifted the case to present a head-on constitutional challenge to the expatriation power before the Supreme Court.[1]

Justice Hugo Black's opinion in the Court's 1967 decision in *Afroyim v. Rusk* reversed outright the *Perez* decision less than a decade after it had been handed down, a rare about-face by an institution whose very identity hinges on the sanctity of precedent.[2] Black categorically rejected the premise that "Congress has any general power, express or implied, to take away an American citizen's citizenship without his assent." Working from his tendency to textual absolutism, Black found in the Citizenship

Clause of the Fourteenth Amendment "no indication . . . of a fleeting citizenship, good at the moment it is acquired but subject to destruction by the government at any time." He denied that Congress had any power to "rob the citizen of his citizenship." The opinion echoed the philosophical underpinnings of Chief Justice Warren's dissent in *Perez*. "Citizenship in this Nation is a part of a co-operative affair. Its citizenry is the country and the country is the citizenry," Black pronounced. "The very nature of our free government makes it completely incongruous to have a rule of law under which a group of citizens temporarily in office can deprive another group of citizens of their citizenship."

The Supreme Court had already started to pivot away from the expatriation regime before the *Afroyim* ruling. In the 1964 decision in *Schneider v. Rusk*,[3] the Court struck down the 1940 act's presumption of expatriation where a naturalized citizen had returned to her country of origin for more than three years (a presumption that had made its first appearance in the 1907 statute).[4] The case involved a woman who had immigrated from Germany as a girl, naturalized with her parents, grew up in the United States and graduated from Smith College, returning to (West) Germany after marrying a German lawyer. Justice William O. Douglas rejected the government's claim, rooted in the nineteenth-century experience, that such individuals tended to "embroil" the United States in disputes with their homelands upon return. The Court ultimately rested its decision on the measure's "impermissible assumption that naturalized citizens as a class are less reliable, and bear less allegiance to this country than do the native born. This is an assumption that is impossible for us to make."[5]

As a practical matter, it was unlikely that a dual citizen returning to West Germany in the 1960s was going to provoke the kind of disputes that the United States had with Prussia a century before. Ditto for Beys Afroyim, whose sin was to vote in an election for the Israeli Knesset. At the time of the case, Israel was America's most reliable ally outside of the North Atlantic alliance. The historical difficulties associated with dual citizenship were unlikely to draw these two countries into diplomatic conflict. As a Jew in Israel, Afroyim was unlikely to seek U.S. diplomatic protection. Afroyim only later became a citizen of the Israeli state, which did not formally exist at the time of his ballot misstep. If he had been considered a dual citizen for purposes of the case (he lived out his days as one), it might have been formally "in derogation of undivided allegiance" to the United States, to use Frankfurter's framing in *Perez*.[6] Query whether a contemporaneous loyalty to the United States and Israel would have been "divided" in any real sense. Certainly not with respect to the struggle with the Soviet Union; it was clear on whose side Israel was. Even allowing for the fact that friends sometimes spy on friends (as the Jonathan Pollard case would later demonstrate),[7] the notion of some sort of Israeli "fifth column" in its more menacing, Cold War sense was not a credible one.

Nor would the U.S. foreign policy apparatus necessarily have had anything to fear from the ostensible constraints of *Afroyim*. First, the danger of formal dual loyalties split between the U.S. and the real enemies, behind the Iron Curtain, was slight. The incidence of dual citizenship has always been contingent on migration, and migration between the East and West blocs had slowed to a trickle. Hardly anyone was getting out of the East, stymied by strict exit controls, while very few were looking to go in the other direction. (Lee Harvey Oswald presented the most famous example, but even Oswald at no time held Soviet citizenship.)[8] Those who did escape the East Bloc could be trusted to transfer both paper and sentimental loyalties, at the same time that those who might have in fact entertained allegiances to adversaries were not likely to advertise them with formal affiliations. Meanwhile, as armed conflict within the free world became increasingly implausible, the prospect of sharing nationals came to pose risks of a much lower order.[9]

## Managing Duplicative Burdens

The sorts of serious disputes between states that were once routinely triggered by dual nationals were by that time on the wane. Beneath all the loyalty verbiage, the real problem with dual citizenship was not the putative security threat. It was, rather, the way in which they confounded otherwise clear sovereign jurisdiction—a violation of the rule that good fences make good neighbors. By far the most significant source of these turf battles involved military service. The standard case involved the naturalized American male citizen who temporarily returned to his homeland only to find himself subject to military conscription. In that event, U.S. diplomatic representatives would typically intercede with homeland officials, not always with success. The phenomenon was a persistent irritant to U.S. bilateral relations during the nineteenth and early-twentieth centuries.

The 1930 Hague codification conference had addressed the issue in the Protocol Relating to Military Obligations in Certain Cases of Double Nationality.[10] The protocol pegged military service obligations to the country of habitual residence: "A person possessing two or more nationalities who habitually resides in one of the countries whose nationality he possesses, and who is in fact most closely connected with that country, shall be exempt from all military obligations in the other country or countries." The Hague effort was overly ambitious. The main convention was undersubscribed and suppressed dual nationality only at the margins. The protocol on military service obligations was also sparsely ratified. But unlike the main convention, the protocol did garner the accession of the United States. It also reflected a norm that was being assimilated into state practice.

Much of this practice took the form of bilateral agreements regarding the military service obligations of dual nationals. A handful of such agreements dated to the mid-nineteenth century, as part of the Bancroft treaties recognizing the effectiveness of naturalization, for instance, 1868 agreements between the United States and the Grand Duchy of Baden, in which the latter agreed not to hold emigrants who had naturalized as Americans for military service upon return to Baden.[11] An almost identical provision was included in an 1870 treaty with Austria-Hungary.[12] Other countries had also begun to conclude agreements to resolve conflicting or duplicative military obligations. The number of these agreements grew during the early and mid-twentieth century. Congress had adopted a resolution calling on the president to negotiate treaties with other countries shielding the U.S.-born children of their nationals from being held for military service during temporary visits home.[13] During the inter-war period, the United States concluded agreements with Sweden, Switzerland, Czechoslovakia, and Latvia on the subject.

Some states adopted domestic laws that limited the exposure of external citizens to military service. France had long conditioned expatriation on the satisfaction of military service requirements, even for nationals born abroad—hence the P. A. Lelong episode that had so agitated Theodore Roosevelt. In 1928, it enacted a law under which French nationals born abroad were released from military service upon establishing compliance with the military law of the foreign country of which they were also a national.[14] Other countries appear to have desisted from imposing service requirements on nationals habitually resident in other jurisdictions. In a 1938 cable to the U.S. consul general in Naples, the Department of State highlighted the Hague Protocol use of habitual residence as determining where a dual national would satisfy military service obligations. Although Italy was not a party to that agreement, the Department noted Italy's adoption of a policy consistent with the Hague approach. So long as the U.S. citizen was present in Italy for less than two years, Italy does not appear to have attempted conscription. Those who stayed for more than two years were presumed to have lost their citizenship in the United States under the 1907 expatriation act. (Italian cooperation ended with the outbreak of the Second World War, during which many U.S.-Italian dual citizens were conscripted.) John Bassett Moore's compendium of nineteenth-century U.S. diplomatic practice, published in 1906, is littered with accounts of European sovereigns attempting to press U.S. citizens into military service. The successor collection, compiled by Green Haywood Hackworth in 1942, contains few.

The postwar period saw an increased velocity in the pace of bilateral agreements. The practice was dense on a regional basis within Europe and between European and Latin American states. There was variation in the specifics of these bilateral arrangements, but they were all broadly consistent with the Hague Protocol approach.[15] In 1963, states under the auspices of the Council of Europe concluded a multilateral agreement to address the military obligations of dual nationals. The convention provided that individuals holding the nationality of two or more state parties should be subject to military obligations in only one, as a matter of default in the country in which the person was "ordinarily resident."[16] The convention was ratified by core European states—the United Kingdom, Germany, Italy, France, and Spain, along with a number of others. An earlier nationality treaty among Latin American states had addressed the issue by implication. To the extent that these regimes were effective, they eliminated a major downside of the status from the individual's perspective. More importantly, they mitigated what had been a major downside for states. As states stopped fighting over dual nationals, there was much less incentive to combat the status. It would take several more decades to overcome the consensus opprobrium attached to dual citizenship, which had been essentialized by marriage metaphors and loyalty talk, but the seeds for a tolerant posture were being laid.

## Pragmatism in International Courts

International tribunals, meanwhile, were also grappling with problems associated with dual nationality. Issues relating to the right of a state to exercise diplomatic protection of behalf of dual nationals increasingly found their way to court-like bodies charged with reviewing expropriation and other property-related claims. These cases typically related to the standing of a state to press a citizen's claim against a state in which the individual also held nationality. States had tried to set down a bright-line rule barring the exercise of protection by one state of nationality against another, including in the 1930 Hague Convention. Some states internalized the rule as a matter of domestic law. British passports, for example, at one time warned dual citizens that the United Kingdom would not exercise protection against another state of nationality ("United Kingdom nationals who are also nationals of another country cannot be protected by Her Majesty's representatives against the authorities of that country").[17] But the rule secured nothing better than minority adherence, with the United States counted among non-subscribers. Many states continued to press claims on behalf of dual nationals, including in formal dispute resolution procedures.

The result was a jurisprudence that accepted the fact of dual citizenship and attempted to minimize the ways in which it disrupted the international system. First, international tribunals sought to police against purely instrumental uses of nationality, requiring evidence of a "genuine link" between an individual and the state interceding on his behalf. This rule crystallized in the 1954 decision of the International Court of Justice in the *Nottebohm* case, by far the most famous decision from an international tribunal on citizenship.[18] Frederich Nottebohm had been born in Hamburg in 1881 with German nationality. In 1905, he moved to Guatemala, where he established himself in a successful family business, but he did not acquire Guatemalan nationality. A month after the outbreak of the Second World War, he acquired citizenship in the principality of Liechtenstein following a few brief visits and the payment of 40,000

Swiss francs ($8,800 at contemporary exchange rates; around $150,000 today, adjusted for inflation). Liechtenstein nationality in hand, he returned to Guatemala. In 1943, Guatemalan authorities arrested him as a German and an alien enemy, deporting him to the United States where he was detained until 1946. In 1949, the Guatemalans confiscated his properties in Guatemala, again on the premise that he was a German national. Liechtenstein brought a claim on his behalf in the World Court, alleging wrongful expropriation and other mistreatment of its national.

The ICJ denied Liechtenstein's capacity to bring the claim on the grounds that it lacked "a genuine connection of existence, interests and sentiments, together with the existence of reciprocal rights and duties." In the Court's view, Nottebohm's naturalization had "the sole aim of . . . coming within the protection of Liechtenstein but not of becoming wedded to its traditions, its interests, [or] its way of life." The Court was at pains to note that Liechtenstein could treat Nottebohm as a citizen for purposes of its own domestic law. "It is for Liechtenstein," the Court observed, "as it is for every sovereign State, to settle by its own legislation the rules relating to the acquisition of its nationality." But it refused to recognize Liechtenstein's standing to use that designation as the basis for constraining another state's exercise of its own sovereign prerogatives.

The *Nottebohm* decision was highly controversial at the time it was decided, in part because Nottebohm in fact enjoyed some attributes of organic membership in the Liechtenstein national community.[19] (His brother had lived there since 1931, and Nottebohm himself lived there from 1946 on.) The case was not from any angle about dual citizenship; if Nottebohm had dual citizenship, it was between Liechtenstein and Germany, not Liechtenstein and Guatemala. But the decision set down a test with clear application to cases involving dual citizens. A person holding only nominal citizenship in one country could not deploy that country as a shield against the actions of another country of nationality. The case would have come out the same if Nottebohm had in fact held Guatemalan citizenship. The rule protected against citizenship shopping—of an individual acquiring paper citizenship to put to work against his or her state of "effective" nationality.

But that would have taken care only of a subset of claims involving dual nationals. The approach mimicked that taken by diplomats outside of formal proceedings, in which nominal nationality was not enough to garner protection. (The background to *Nottebohm* was unusual in this respect, insofar as Liechtenstein was willing to press the claim, perhaps because Nottebohm had literally bought Liechtenstein's protection. The strategy presaged the phenomenon of "investor citizenship," a rarity then, increasingly common today.) More significant were a series of lower-profile rulings from arbitration commissions applying a "dominant" nationality test in cases where one state of citizenship attempted to espouse a claim against another state of citizenship. Where a claimant had genuine ties to more than one state, tribunals undertook fact-intensive inquiries to determine with which state the individual was more closely identified.

The questions was most frequently asked in the context of ad hoc arbitral tribunals established to resolve a group of claims between two countries in which one state espoused the claim of one of its citizens against a country whose citizenship the person also held. In the *Mergé Case*, the U.S.-Italian Conciliation Commission established to resolve property disputes arising out of the Second World War considered an individual's standing to bring a claim as a U.S. national. Florence Strunsky-Mergé was a native-born U.S. citizen who had married an Italian national in 1933 in New York, where he worked as an Italian government translator, automatically acquiring Italian nationality as a result. The claimant and her husband lived thereafter in Rome, then Tokyo, then back in Rome. The claimant was careful to maintain her U.S. citizenship by registering with U.S. consular authorities in Rome and Tokyo. She had renewed her U.S. passport as recently as 1950, on which she listed New York as her legal residence. The efficacy of her citizenship was not challenged by the United States (the United States was pressing her claim) nor by the tribunal itself, which took her dual nationality as a given. Applying the principle of dominant nationality, the tribunal denied Strunsky-Mergé's standing to bring the claim. While noting that "the conduct of the individual in his economic, social, political, civic and family life, as well as the closer and more effective bond with one of the two States must also be considered," the tribunal emphasized the factor of habitual residence in determining dominant nationality. Given Strunsky-Mergé's residence outside the United States for more than twenty years, the tribunal found that she could not qualify as a U.S. national for purposes of the claims process.[20] The *Mergé* approach was followed by the Iran-United States

Claims Tribunal, established by the 1980 Algiers Accords to resolve property disputes arising from the Iranian revolution in 1978.[21]

As with military service obligations, the approach of these tribunals confronted the fact of dual citizenship, looking to manage it rather than try to wish it away. By deciding which of two nationalities loomed larger in the individual's identity composite, the tribunals were in effect cancelling out one nationality in favor of the other. The result was to treat the dual citizen as if he were a mono-national. The tribunals were hardly celebrating dual nationality. But they were able to devise a workaround that reduced the disruptive aspects of the status for purposes of resolving international disputes.

## America Learns to Live with Dual Citizenship

The U.S. Supreme Court was almost certainly blind to these international developments, or at least it showed no evidence of taking them into account in deciding the *Afroyim* case. The Court was looking at U.S. citizenship from a constitutional rights perspective. That represented an important shift in judicial framing. Justice Frankfurter's opinion in *Perez v. Brownell* had stressed the "embarrassments in the conduct of foreign relations" that had motivated the 1940 expatriation regime, with not even a nod to individual rights. As those embarrassments faded, the Court could normalize its approach to citizenship-related disputes.

In any case, *Afroyim* was more symbolic than real in terms of immediate impact. The Court may have sacralized citizenship, but it had no particular solicitude for dual citizenship. *Afroyim* did not allude to the status, nor did it have to, since Beys Afroyim did not have citizenship in Israel when he voted there. Chief Justice Warren's dissent in *Perez*, which presaged the about-face in *Afroyim*, had allowed for expatriation where a citizen engaged in conduct "in derogation of undivided allegiance to this country." *Afroyim* brought expatriation under judicial scrutiny, but it took more than twenty years for its absolutist language to take full hold on the ground.

Though more closely scrutinized, involuntary expatriation remained an option in some cases. As a formal matter, conduct alone could not supply a categoric basis for the termination of citizenship; the government was now also required to establish that the conduct evidenced intent to relinquish citizenship. As a practical matter, in many cases—especially those involving naturalization in a foreign state—conduct continued to give the government all it needed to sustain expatriation.

In early 1969, Attorney General Ramsey Clark concluded that "voluntary relinquishment" was "not confined to a written renunciation" of citizenship, but could "also be manifested by other actions declared expatriative" under the Nationality Act.[22] The opinion sustained the government's power to expatriate a citizen by virtue of conduct indicating an intention to abandon citizenship, even where the individual did not consciously intend that result. The approach gave rise to a rebuttable presumption of intent to expatriate upon the undertaking of specified conduct, including naturalization in another country, the taking of an oath of allegiance to another country, and service in foreign armed forces or foreign government employment. Intent thereafter became a primary point of contention in expatriation cases. In a 1969 decision, for instance, an administrative board upheld the expatriation of an individual who had naturalized as a Canadian citizen. "When one voluntarily takes the nationality of another country and takes an oath of allegiance to that country, whether or not it contains a renunciation of former allegiance," its opinion suggested, "the normal inference is that there has been a transfer of allegiance from the old country to the new."[23] In 1977, by contrast, the same board reversed an expatriation order notwithstanding Canadian naturalization where an individual had inquired with and been reassured by U.S. authorities that his U.S. citizenship would not be jeopardized.[24] In practice, the threat of involuntary expatriation appears to have remained very real. The violinist Yehudi Menuhin, for instance, was threatened with the loss of U.S. citizenship after accepting merely honorary Swiss citizenship in 1970.[25]

The Supreme Court itself appeared to step back from *Afroyim* with its 1971 decision in *Rogers v. Bellei*.[26] Aldo Mario Bellei had been born in Italy in 1939, acquiring Italian citizenship under that nation's jus soli rules. Bellei also had U.S. citizenship at birth by descent through his mother, who had been born in Philadelphia and lived in the United States into her twenties. For citizenship to descend under the statutory regime in place at the time—adopted in 1934 to help combat dual nationality among those living abroad—a parent had to have resided in the United States for ten years, five of which had to be after the age of fourteen, a requirement Bellei's mother satisfied. But the regime also required the child himself to spend at least five years in the United States between the ages of fourteen and twenty-eight, failing which he would lose his citizenship.[27] Bellei had visited the United States five times for periods of some months each, but he fell well short of the five-year threshold and was deemed to have lost his citizenship upon turning twenty-eight. Bellei challenged the statute as inconsistent with the *Afroyim* ruling.

Rejecting the challenge, the Supreme Court highlighted the statute's purpose to reduce the incidence of dual citizenship. Justice Harry Blackmun credited Congress's "appropriate concern with problems attendant on dual nationality." Blackmun chauvinistically found that these "problems are particularly acute when it is the father who is the child's alien parent and the father chooses to have his family reside in the country of his own nationality. The child is reared, at best, in an atmosphere of divided loyalty. We cannot say that a concern that the child's own primary allegiance is to the country of his birth and of his father's allegiance is either misplaced or arbitrary." The residency condition, in the Court's view, was a reasonable solution to "the dual nationality dilemma."[28]

As a matter of formal legal analysis, Blackmun distinguished *Afroyim* on the grounds that the citizenship there at issue was constitutionally grounded (born in the United States, Afroyim had citizenship under the Fourteenth Amendment) whereas Bellei's was extended by statute only. In Justice Blackmun's infelicitous phrasing, Bellei "simply [was] not a Fourteenth-Amendment-first-sentence citizen."[29] Where Congress had no power to modify constitutional requirements, it could do as it pleased on the statutory side. Bellei's loss of citizenship was not in formal terms an "expatriation"; it was, rather, a matter of his having failed to satisfy a "condition subsequent" to the granting of citizenship at birth. However it was framed, *Bellei* sustained the government's power to terminate an individual's citizenship against his will as part of efforts to suppress dual citizenship.

Further refining the bounds of expatriation with its 1980 decision in *Vance v. Terrazas*, the Court considered expatriation for affirming allegiance to a foreign state.[30] Terrazas, who had been born a dual Mexican and American national, had at age twenty-two executed an application with Mexican authorities not only swearing allegiance to Mexico but also "expressly renounc[ing] United States citizenship, as well as any submission, obedience, and loyalty to any foreign government, especially to that of the United States of America." Although the Court left open the door to Terrazas's expatriation, it made clear that expatriation could only be undertaken where conduct evidenced a specific intent on the individual's part to relinquish citizenship. Mere voluntariness of conduct would not suffice; the voluntary conduct must have been accompanied by a specific intent to shed U.S. citizenship. On the one hand, formal renunciation was not a necessary predicate to expatriation. On the other hand, no category of conduct would by itself suffice to justify the involuntary termination of citizenship; in all cases, the government would also have to plead the requisite intent regarding citizenship status. "In the last analysis," wrote Justice Byron White, "expatriation depends on the will of the citizen rather than on the will of Congress and its assessment of his conduct."[31]

The specific intent requirement still left room for the government to police against dual citizenship. Naturalization oaths before other sovereigns often included renunciatory language that, taken on its face, evidenced a specific intent to relinquish original citizenship. Without evidence of contrary intent, such conduct justified expatriation. American citizens failing to document intent to retain citizenship still risked expatriation. In the *Terrazas* case itself, for example, expatriation was ultimately upheld by a lower court on the grounds that the foreign renunciation oath evidenced the requisite intent in the absence of other evidence indicating an intention to retain U.S. citizenship on the taking of such an oath.[32] The State Department's Foreign Affairs Manual—a sort of how-to for American diplomats—continued to flag activity "potentially" giving rise to the loss of nationality. Even as of the late 1980s, the Department of State was initiating an average of 4,500 potential loss of citizenship cases annually, of which 600 resulted in involuntary expatriation.

But *Terrazas* did not prove an equilibrium point. Although the opinion ostensibly put to rest *Afroyim's* lofty denials of any governmental capacity to terminate citizenship, administrative practice narrowed *Terrazas's* allowance for involuntary expatriation. Expatriation was defeated where an individual established intent to retain citizenship. In guidance issued to consular posts in the wake of *Terrazas*, the Department of State broadly itemized actions evidencing an intention to retain citizenship, including payment of U.S. taxes, voting in American elections, and continued use of a U.S. passport after the potentially expatriating conduct. The department also thereafter accepted contemporaneous statements regarding intent; as one leaflet advised, "a written statement submitted to the Embassy or Consulate in advance, expressing an intent to maintain U.S. citizenship and to continue to respect the obligations of U.S. citizenship, despite one's plans to obtain naturalization in a foreign country, would be accorded substantial weight in a loss of nationality proceeding."[33] This gave rise to a practice under which an individual naturalizing elsewhere or undertaking other conduct specified in the expatriation regime would execute a memo to the files attesting to the lack of intent to relinquish citizenship, even where words uttered would have indicated otherwise. Congress finally amended the Nationality Act in 1986 to conform with *Afroyim* and *Terrazas*, requiring that specified expatriating acts be undertaken "with the intention of relinquishing United States nationality" as a predicate to the loss of citizenship.[34]

In 1978, meanwhile, Congress had eliminated the residency requirement that had deprived the foreign-born Aldo Bellei of his U.S. citizenship, even though the provision had survived constitutional scrutiny.[35] The Department of Justice supported the repeal, noting that it caused hardship in some cases and that it was difficult to administer.[36] No one seemed to care that the action would open up another channel for dual nationals to retain the status. Those born with citizenship outside the United States would be able to retain it for a lifetime, without ever setting foot in the United States, while they would in almost all cases maintain the citizenship of their place of birth and/or residence. The 1978 measure also repealed section 350 of the 1952 nationality act, which had terminated the citizenship of birthright dual nationals who lived in their other country for more than three years, a dead letter in the wake of the *Afroyim* line.

With a 1990 policy statement, the Department of State followed suit by reversing its former presumption of expatriating intent upon a person's naturalization in another state. The new policy adopted "a uniform administrative standard of evidence based on the premise that U.S. nationals intend to retain United States nationality when they obtain naturalization in a foreign state, declare their allegiance to a foreign state, serve in the armed forces of a foreign state not engaged in hostilities with the United States, or accept non-policy level employment with a foreign government." As a result, a citizen engaging in these acts who "in so doing wishes to retain U.S. nationality need not submit prior to the commission of a potentially expatriating act a statement or evidence of his or her intent to retain U.S. nationality since such an intent will be presumed."[37] The new policy, in other words, eliminated the need to write the memo for the file regarding intent to retain U.S. citizenship in most cases. The State Department in effect gave up the fight against dual citizenship with a 1995 opinion concluding that "[i]t is no longer possible to terminate an American's citizenship without the citizen's co-operation."[38] The standard allows a U.S. citizen to undertake any activity in another polity without risk of loss of citizenship.

## The World Follows Suit

These changes in U.S. practice did not immediately generate a sharp increase in the number of dual nationals. The intense historical oppro-brium trained on the status was not going to be canceled out by some obscure bureaucratic guidance. The disapproval had been as much cultural as legal. In the popular understanding, dual citizenship remained problematic under U.S. law. Although a sense of hard, exclusive loyal-ties to the state began to dissipate with the end of the Cold War, dual citizenship remained an anomalous status at best, the kind of thing that one might hold but not advertise. There remained a vestigial on-the-street understanding that it was somehow illegal. The State Department did not actively dispel this misperception. To this day, a cautious State Department holds that the "U.S. Government does not encourage dual nationality. While recognizing the existence of dual nationality and per-mitting its existence, the U.S. Government also recognizes the problems it may cause."[39]

More importantly, for so long as the overwhelming majority of other countries continued to terminate the citizenship of those who natural-ized in the United States, the incidence of dual citizenship in the United States continued to be suppressed. Reflecting the general rule (as had been true under U.S. law before the Supreme Court dismantled it), most other states continued to denationalize individuals upon the acquisition of another nationality. When a Mexican immigrant to the United States naturalized as an American, for example, she automatically lost her Mexican citizenship as a matter of Mexican law. Dual citizenship is a two-way street. As long as other countries rejected the status, U.S. acceptance did not result in any sort of spike in the number of dual nationals.

But other countries had been moving in the same direction. The United Kingdom had dropped restrictions on dual nationality in 1948. France amended its nationality regime in 1973 to allow retention of French nationality upon naturalization in another state, as did Canada in 1976. By the 1990s, high-immigrant-sending states were relaxing their ideological stance against the status. It was this shift, perhaps more than the shift in U.S. law and practice, that generated a dramatic increase in the numbers of dual citizens in the United States. In 1998, Mexico changed its nationality law to allow its nationals naturalizing in other countries to retain their Mexican citizenship. The default position thereafter was to assume the retention of Mexican nationality except where an individual affirmatively applied to renounce it. Almost all Mexicans from that point forward would become dual citizens upon naturalizing as Americans. The more than 200,000 Mexican nationals who naturalized as Americans in 1999 automatically became dual citizens. Since then, more than 1.5 million have followed.

During the 1990s and into the early 2000s, other countries also moved to permit the retention of nationality after naturalizing in a foreign state, with Italy, the Dominican Republic, Turkey, the Philippines, and South Korea joining the likes of Ireland, Israel, and El Salvador. (The shift in the approach of other states to dual citizenship is described at length in chapter 6.) According to one study, the proportion of states automatically terminating citizenship upon naturalization in another country dropped from 55% in 1960 to 30% in 2013.[40] Nineteen out of the top twenty source states for immigrants to the United States either accept dual citizenship or do nothing to police against it. Almost all new naturalizing citizens become dual citizens at the moment they become American citizens. It's almost always costless to retain original citizenship. Taxes are now mostly accrued on the basis of residency, not citizenship. (The United States is the only exception, but that is a problem for emigrants from the United States, not immigrants to the United States.) The same is true of military service, already in many cases the subject of bilateral treaties aimed at eliminating duplicative obligations. These agreements aside, only a handful of states continue to maintain compulsory military service in any case. As one recent commentary notes, military service for dual nationals is "not even on today's radar screen."[41]

Never mind the mere act of voting, there have been many recent instances of Americans retaining their citizenship at the same time as they have assumed high political office in foreign governments. Examples have included American citizens who served as the foreign ministers of Armenia and Bosnia, and as the chief of the Estonian army.[42] The current finance minister of Ukraine is a citizen of both the United States and Ukraine. Joanna Shields, a dual U.S.-UK citizen and former head of Facebook Europe, is serving as under-secretary of state for internet safety and security in David Cameron's Conservative Party government. In 2010–11, a U.S. citizen served as prime minister of Somalia. (One report estimates that 70% of Somali parliamentarians are dual citizens.)[43] Under the old regime of exclusivity, the retention of citizenship in such circumstances would have been inconceivable. In practice, the only expatriating act which is now subsequently enforceable against an individual seeking to retain citizenship is formal renunciation before a U.S. diplomatic or consular officer overseas.[44] Even then, there may be defenses to denationalization.[45] These developments add up to a complete toleration of dual citizenship, at least for birthright U.S. citizens who acquire or retain additional nationality. Naturalization in a foreign state will no longer result in the loss of U.S. nationality.

So dual citizenship will now be the incidental result of naturalization, when an immigrant naturalizes as an American or when an American acquires another citizenship. Add to those sources the many who will now be born with the status. Birth dual citizens result from the interplay of jus soli and jus sanguinis. The children of the many recent immigrants to the United States will often be born with two citizenships: U.S. citizenship by birth in the territory of the United States and another citizenship by birth to parents of that nationality. That will almost always be the case with respect to the children of several million non-immigrants, present in the United States temporarily for study or work. This will also often be true of those born to the more than seven million U.S. citizens residing outside the United States, who will usually have U.S. citizenship by descent and may be extended citizenship of the country in which they are born. Children whose parents have different nationalities will (again, typically) have the citizenship of each parent at birth. Mixed nationality parentage will generate a non-trivial number of children born with three nationalities where the birth occurs in a third country with jus soli rules. The child of a British father and Italian mother born in the United States will be born a tri-national. Some smaller but growing number could have four or more citizenships at birth where one or both parents themselves have plural nationality, something that will become more common as this generation of dual citizens mixes with others in an increasingly mobile global context.

Birthright dual citizenship also inevitably resulted from earlier waves of migration. But that was the target of the election requirements and expatriation triggers described above. Those mechanisms are now rarely in play. Very few countries persist in requiring birth dual citizens to choose when they come of age. Once one has dual citizenship, by birth or otherwise, it is unlikely to get taken away. No national or international statistical surveys of the incidence of dual citizenship have been conducted to date. But there can be little doubt that the number of dual citizens is trending upward. As migration increases, there will be more individuals who are either born with or become eligible for more than one nationality. States, meanwhile, have largely given up the fight.

5

## Acceptance and Embrace

If there was going to be a flashpoint relating to the rise of dual citizenship, it would have been the 1998 change in Mexico's law allowing for the retention of Mexican nationality after naturalization in the United States. Immigration from Mexico was as controversial in the 1990s as it is today. Coupled with immigration debates, rancorous even then, one might have expected the prospect of millions of dual Mexican and American citizens to provoke renewed opposition to dual citizenship.

Some did try to use the change in Mexico's law to rally opposition against the status. "Never before has the United States had to face a problem of dual loyalties among its citizens of such great magnitude and proximity," Reagan protégé Linda Chavez argued. "For the first time, millions of U.S. citizens could declare their allegiance to a neighboring country."[1] Deploying the old marriage analogy, columnist Georgie Anne Geyer suggested that dual citizenship "introduces into the lifeblood of the nation a kind of dangerous civic polygamy. What are the principles under which you live and act? Those of America—or those of Colombia, of Mexico, of India?" She suggested that dual citizenship could "easily" be stopped: "by law, by regulation, perhaps merely by a ruling of the Immigration and Naturalization Service. If we do not, I guess we deserve the divided loyalties that this country increasingly evokes."[2] Political scientist Samuel P. Huntington highlighted the putative loyalty issue with an episode in which Mexican American fans dominated a 1998 Los Angeles soccer match between the United States and Mexico in which "The Star-Spangled Banner" was loudly booed. Decrying the rise of dual citizenship, Huntington lamented that "bigamy is now acceptable."[3]

In the end, the Mexican nationality reform came and went without much notice, on Capitol Hill or elsewhere. That presents something of a puzzle. With the Mexican focal point, dual citizenship seemed ripe for political reaction on the coattails of intense immigration restrictionist sentiment. The plug-and-play framing of dual citizenship as a breach of loyalty and allegiance should have been an easy sell to conservative constituencies.

But dual citizenship had already become too pervasive an American phenomenon to fit into these other tropes. In 1997 I participated in a conference on immigration and citizenship in the twenty-first century at the Sanford School of Public Policy at Duke University. Held in the wake of the report of the U.S. Commission on Immigration Reform (known as the Jordan Commission, after its chairwoman, former congresswoman Barbara Jordan), the event brought together leading policymakers and scholars.[4] There was a sense that citizenship policy was at an inflection point. At dinner on Halloween night, I sat next to the Republican chief counsel of the House Immigration Subcommittee. This was a key adviser to Lamar Smith, the subcommittee chair at the time, an outspoken restrictionist legislator. I asked him what we could expect by way of a legislative response to the prospective surge in dual nationals. His response: "You know, I have nephews and nieces who have dual Irish and American citizenship, and they're good kids." Even as of the late 1990s, Americans were sharing citizenship not just with Mexico but with such countries as Ireland, Italy, and Israel. This created a mismatch between political incentives on immigration policy and political incentives on citizenship policy. Dual citizenship cut across the political spectrum. It had come to implicate powerful ethnic constituencies, ones hardly worth antagonizing on an issue whose valence was now largely symbolic.

The encounter goes a long way to explaining why dual citizenship failed to ignite a political firestorm. By the time of the Mexican shift, dual citizenship was already too mainstream a phenomenon to be walked back. It has been accepted without a fight. Dual citizenship managed to stay under the political radar screen on the way to becoming a common condition. But those political contingencies beg the question of whether dual citizenship should have been accepted, whether it is a benign or even constructive feature of American society at its intersection with globalization. How did it morph from a status so often compared to bigamy to being one held by classmates, neighbors, and relatives, from a status that was uniformly abhorred to one that is proudly or casually advertised?

Geyer was correct that, in theory, dual citizenship arising through U.S. naturalization could legally have been blocked. The Supreme Court's decision in *Afroyim* involved only the taking, not the giving, of U.S. citizenship. The United States could have moved to enforce the renunciation oath, under which naturalizing citizens "renounce and abjure absolutely and entirely all allegiance and fidelity to any foreign prince, potentate, state, or sovereignty of whom or which the applicant was before a subject or citizen."[5] Though an enduring statutory prerequisite to naturalization and ostensible bar to the retention of the prior nationality, the oath has never been enforced. Applicants for naturalization have never been required to demonstrate that they have taken steps to make good on their renunciation. Historically, this non-enforcement resulted from the imposition of perpetual allegiance by other states, as a result of which naturalizing individuals had no power to terminate their original nationality.

Facing the prospect of a large dual Mexican-U.S. population, some suggested that the oath be given teeth. As John Fonte argued, "To retain allegiance to another constitution after promising sole allegiance to the American constitution, by definition, violates the spirit of our constitutional morality."[6] The American Legion passed a resolution encouraging Congress "to enact measures to enforce the Oath of Renunciation and Allegiance and reject dual allegiance in principle and restrict and narrow its application in practice."[7] But no serious steps were taken in that direction. There was a subsequent effort to enact criminal sanctions for violations of the oath of renunciation. The proposal would have attached fines and jail time for activities resulting in loss of citizenship under the pre-*Afroyim* regimes (service in armed forces, taking an oath of allegiance to another state, holding foreign government office) as undertaken by naturalized citizens. The law would have directed the secretary of state to "return to the traditional policy of the Department of State of viewing dual/multiple citizenship as problematic and as something to be discouraged not encouraged."[8] The bill was introduced and a hearing was held. (I was among the witnesses testifying before the House subcommittee, speaking to two or three members of the committee and many empty seats.)[9] The proposal was promptly forgotten. Dual citizenship proved a non-issue.

## The Myth of the Dual-Citizen Security Risk

Dual citizenship now poses little threat to the polity in security terms, if it ever did. On the contrary, any attempt to preclude the naturalization of those who would keep their original nationality will result in a net detriment to the national community by perpetuating a large population of resident aliens unable to participate in the political process, to perfect their inclusion in the community of Americans, or to enjoy the rights of citizenship. It is on that basis at least in the U.S. and other receiving states, that the dual citizens among us should not simply be tolerated but embraced.

The security risks posed by dual citizenship have always been exaggerated. There is no notable case of a dual citizen engaging in spying for his other country of nationality. Dual nationals were not much of a problem even in the context of declared war between nations. When such conflict occurred, the dual national was often forced to choose sides. But the choice itself, under the regime established under U.S. law in 1940, typically eliminated the status and one or the other citizenship was terminated. That's how the putative problem of dual citizenship was solved during the Second World War. The dual citizen who enlisted in the armed forces of another state automatically lost his U.S. citizenship. Former citizenship in the United States by itself did not render that individual a greater threat than any other enemy alien soldier. Nor was the "fifth column" specter of the Cold War any more substantial. Those who would do the bidding of the East Bloc were not well advised to retain the citizenship tie to the American adversary (and they did not). Dual citizenship shared with other states would have been even harder to spin as a security threat. To the extent that loyalty and allegiance were ever consequential to conduct, security conflicts between the United States and its Cold War allies were minimal.

Today, this kind of traditional security concern—situated in the context of inter-state conflict—is increasingly far-fetched. If large dual national populations weren't a threat during the Second World War, they aren't a threat today. The prospect of war between major states is now as remote as at any time since the Peace of Westphalia. It's hard to frame the large dual Mexican and American population as a fifth column. Extreme anti-immigration activists speak of a "reconquista" in which

Mexico takes back its ceded lands through immigration and dual citizenship. Even outspoken restrictionist Dan Stein has difficulty playing out such a scenario. In 1996 congressional hearings, he condemned the increase in dual nationals that would result from then-proposed changes in Mexican laws. "If Mexico sought in the future to re-occupy parts of the southern U.S.," he asked, "whose side would these dual nationals be on?" But he had to follow his own query with a tepid, "maybe this danger is not realistic, but it should be considered."[10] Most other pairings are similarly implausible.

To the extent that the United States does find itself engaging in military operations against other states, it is against states that are undemocratic, unrepresentative of their citizens, and thus less likely to instill any real loyalties on the part of dual nationals. The son of Somali warlord Mohammed Aidid (a nominal if not formal enemy of U.S. and United Nations forces) was put on active duty in the U.S. Marines during the mid-1990s peacekeeping operation in Somalia, and returned there afterward to take his dead father's place.[11] The United States would hardly have had to fret about the loyalty of dual Iraqi-U.S. citizens in either of the Gulf conflicts; those individuals would have held themselves out as loyal to Iraq the country and nonetheless have supported military action against Saddam Hussein's regime.

## Dual-Citizen Terrorists

Today, of course, the primary security threat comes from non-state actors in the form of terrorist organizations. Post-9/11, "loyalty" has returned to political discourse. But counter-terror cultures do not map well onto a dual citizenship frame. One doesn't hold citizenship in a terrorist group. Many terrorists have citizenship in nations allied with the United States (Saudi Arabia, for example). To the extent that loyalties are divided or transferred, it is not along a citizenship axis. The adversaries are asymmetric; it's no longer a question of being on one side or another.

A handful of Americans have been implicated in terrorist operations against the United States. Some have been dual citizens. Some, like Yaser Hamdi, have been nominal U.S. citizens; born to Saudi parents in Louisiana while his father worked on an oil rig there, relocated to Saudi Arabia in infancy, Hamdi didn't even know he was a U.S. citizen when apprehended on the battlefield in Afghanistan in late 2001. Others have had more substantial ties. Anwar al-Awlaki was born in New Mexico in 1971 and lived in the United States until he was seven, when he moved with his parents to Yemen. Al-Awlaki returned at nineteen for college, earning a B.S. at Colorado State and remaining in the country until he was thirty. His son was born in Denver in 1995.

There have been calls to strip these individuals of their U.S. citizenship. But terrorist activity doesn't fit into the 1940 statutory loss-of-nationality provisions. Enacted in the old world, they provided for termination of citizenship for "entering, or serving in, the armed forces of a foreign state." In 2010, Senator Joe Lieberman introduced the Enemy Expatriation Act, which would have amended the statute to include engaging in hostilities against the United States in the context of an international conflict as expatriating conduct.[12] One might have expected legislative acclamation for the proposal, a no-cost addition to the counter-terror arsenal.

The bill ended up going nowhere, prompting not even a committee hearing, much less serious legislative consideration.[13] It wouldn't have been worth the trouble in any case. Court-imposed constitutional constraints on expatriation raise the bar on terminating citizenship on the basis of terrorist activity; under the Supreme Court's rulings in *Afroyim* and *Terrazas*, the government would need to prove that the terrorist conduct was undertaken with the specific intent to relinquish citizenship. In other words, the government would have to prove not just that an individual engaged in the hostilities against the United States but also produce evidence establishing the desire to expatriate. That would be difficult in most cases.

It might have worked to expatriate Adam Gadahn (not a dual citizen), who shredded his U.S. passport in a YouTube video.[14] It would not have applied, or at least not obviously applied, to al-Awlaki, who was implicated in the so-called underwear bomber plot and other planned attacks against the United States. Al-Awlaki may have participated in hostilities against the United States, but that by itself did not demonstrate an intention to forfeit U.S. citizenship. Even if the Lieberman bill had passed, it would have taken years of litigation with an uncertain result to secure the termination of al-Awlaki's citizenship. That couldn't have been very attractive relative to other options. The standard for undertaking a drone strike is lower than for expatriation; in the end, it was easier (and more effective) to kill al-Awlaki than to expatriate him.

In any case, the fact that al-Awlaki and other terrorists have dual citizenship doesn't make them more of a threat. With the rise of the Islamic State and the growing number of "foreign fighters," Senator Ted Cruz and others revived the terrorist expatriation measure.[15] Again it fell flat. Cruz justified the measure as protecting Americans from returning ISIS agents. "Would anyone of good conscience in either party want that person," asked Cruz, "to be able to come back and land in LaGuardia airport with a U.S. passport and walk unmolested onto our streets?"[16] Never mind LaGuardia as an unlikely port of entry from the caliphate. If the government knew enough about a U.S. citizen's complicity with ISIS to strip him of his citizenship, it would know enough not to allow him to "walk unmolested." If it didn't have evidence of the connection, it wouldn't be able to satisfy the evidentiary requirement of intent to relinquish citizenship. Even if one accepts the continuing exigency of the terror threat, dual citizenship does not compound the vulnerability. In short, dual citizenship poses no extra costs in the counter-terror context.[17]

Security concerns and loyalty tropes have always oriented an accessible takedown of dual citizenship—one that fortified social norms against the status—where highlighting more prosaic difficulties were unlikely to do the trick. Historically, it was the costs associated with the diplomatic protection of dual nationals that made the status so dangerous. Even though these costs implicated conniving dual nationals (at worst) rather than malign ones, these costs were equally dramatic (including the possibility of war). But diplomatic protection has been largely subsumed by the umbrella of international human rights, under which the international community protects the abused regardless of nationality. The intersection of diplomatic protection and dual nationality was far more uncomfortable in a world in which states could treat their own nationals as they pleased.

There are some cases in which states still stick their necks out on behalf of their citizens. A more literal form of protection comes with the evacuation of citizens from global hot spots. Citizens caught in foreign crossfire have historically been able to turn to their home country as rescuer. That poses a resource burden on the state. Evacuation operations can be expensive. To the extent that individuals retain U.S. citizenship after permanently relocating outside the United States (many to their country of origin), that might be a justification for continuing to suppress the status. This sparked a major debate in Canada surrounding the evacuation of 15,000 Canadians from Lebanon during the 2006 Israeli-Hezbollah conflict.[18] The operation cost $75–100 million. Some questioned the operation given that many of the evacuees were dual citizens who had relocated permanently to Lebanon—"Canadians of convenience." The problem resembles that faced by nineteenth-century U.S. authorities asked to expend diplomatic capital in defense of citizens who had long ago left the United States.

But this is only a problem when states undertake to evacuate citizens. The trend seems to be away from such guarantees. The U.S. operation out of Lebanon was shoestring compared with the Canadian, which may explain why no one complained in the United States. Elite universities and employers had contracted evacuation services out to private providers like International SOS, who got their clients out more quickly and efficiently than did the government.[19] Those evacuated by the government were required by law to sign promissory notes in which they undertake to reimburse the U.S. government for transportation costs equivalent to full-fare economy airfare. Evacuees who fail to repay the loan are ineligible for passport renewals.[20] On other occasions, evacuation services have not been offered at all. When disorder overtook Yemen in the spring of 2015, the State Department shut down its embassy and left an estimated 4,000–5,000 U.S. citizens to fend for themselves.[21] No rescue, no costs, no additional burden posed by dual citizens.

## We're All Democrats Now

Thus the historically more significant difficulties of dual citizenship—real or imagined—are no longer of particular moment. Dual citizenship no longer poses a threat. At the same time, attempting to police the status will have costs of its own. Fewer non-citizens will naturalize if they are not permitted to maintain their citizenship of origin, as many aliens will be unwilling for either sentimental or economic reasons to cut their ties to their homelands.

Depressed naturalization rates are a social ill from the perspective of the existing community's self-interest. This is especially true to the extent that one hews to a political conception of citizenship. If citizenship is about self-governance in an enclosed territorial space, the more residents who become citizens, the more inclusive the deliberative process will be, and more likely the general good will be furthered. As Peter Schuck observes, higher naturalization rates will improve "the quality of both the governmental process and policy outcomes that it generates." If large numbers of territorial residents remain non-citizens, lacking the franchise, political actors cannot be held accountable and policymaking becomes "seriously deformed."[22]

Some naturalization qualifications are easily justified. It is difficult to challenge the requirement that new citizens affirm adherence to the political tenets of the country of naturalization. Applicants for U.S. citizenship are required to take an oath to support the Constitution of the United States.[23] The costs of allowing participation of those who reject the oath would outweigh any benefit from their inclusion. More problematic are language qualifications.[24] Some argue that proficiency in English is necessary to meaningful political participation, that, in other words, a person who does not share the language of the polity cannot be a part of it.[25] On the other hand, language differentials can be addressed at a practical level. The Voting Rights Act requires that ballots be printed in languages other than English in jurisdictions with high immigrant concentrations.[26]

Retaining original citizenship does not detract from participation in a newly adopted polity. Political engagement in one country doesn't preclude similar commitment in another. Georgie Anne Geyer may ask of dual citizens, "What are the principles under which you live and act? Those of America—or those of Colombia, of Mexico, of India?" But naturalizing aliens have undertaken to adhere to American principles separately from their undertaking to renounce other allegiances. In a world of enlarging democracy, the likelihood of foundational conflict between our constitutional principles and the political orientation of other states has significantly diminished as international norms move toward notions of democratic entitlement.[27] Outliers aside, basic principles of governance don't differ much state to state. Political convergence at the global level allows for multiple channels of political membership and participation. Dual nationality no longer implicates the kind of ideological conflicts that it did in a world of more diverse political systems. It's

hard to be both a monarchist and a democrat, but that presents a historical problem, not a contemporary one.

Perhaps the most serious objection to the acceptance of dual nationality (from a participation-centered conception of citizenship) hinges on
the question of individual independence. Independence is central to traditional understandings of civic virtue; dependence corrupts the process
by putting personal interests ahead of the common good. The principle
was thought to justify eighteenth-century landownership qualifications
for voting, for example. The individual who retains foreign nationality,
the argument would run, remains beholden to a foreign state that will
hardly share the common good of the country of naturalization.

This is a "marching orders" argument against dual citizenship in
which the other country of allegiance expresses its preferences on a
certain political position in this country with an expectation that those
holding the other citizenship will act in line with those preferences in
this one. The prime minister of Thailand once admonished the dual-
citizen children of Thais born in the United States to "always think of
themselves as Thais first."[28] Say, for instance, that the government of
Mexico starts to endorse candidates in U.S. elections with an expectation that those holding Mexican and American citizenship would vote
those endorsements. Dual Mexican-U.S. nationals would no doubt in
that context be charged with disloyalty, at least by those who stood opposed to Mexican interests. Indeed, they already have been. One 1990s-
era opponent of dual citizenship explained it as a "way to cut down on
the number of Mexican citizens who apply for citizenship with the purpose of influencing our elections."[29] Geyer decried the Mexican switch
to accept dual citizenship as an attempt "to create a kind of political
lobby of newly enfranchised citizens of Mexican descent whose cultural
allegiance would remain with Mexico."[30]

That greatly exaggerates the extent to which states can muscle their
citizens, especially citizens who live in other countries. Governments
can't count on their nationals as reliable instruments of policy. Citizens
are no longer pliable pawns, if they ever were. Mexico and other countries have few tools to push their dual citizens resident in the United
States to do their bidding within the American political process. Nor
is there much indication that foreign countries have tried to exploit
dual nationals to their national advantage. The Mexican government

was careful to justify in apolitical terms its revised constitution permitting dual nationality. As one Mexican diplomat wrote, Mexico's move to allow dual citizenship was aimed at maintaining "cultural and symbolic links" with Mexicans abroad while accepting that those who emigrate to the United States "are expected to respect and revere the civic obligations that come with naturalization and citizenship."[31] To the extent that Mexico sees its citizens as a political resource, it's more in the way that non-governmental advocates will try to mobilize their members on agenda items.

In any case, if U.S. citizens are politically motivated to act in the interests of their country of origin, it's not contingent on the continuing formal attachment of citizenship. Americans have long voted their ethnic affiliation even where they have not maintained their original nationality. They have sometimes been accused of acting for "unpatriotic" reasons. So long as the interests of the United States and the other nation are not unalterably opposed—and there are few relationships or issues in which that remains the case—it's not clear why those motivations should deform the process. It's part of the aggregation of preferences that is central to the democratic process.

## Cementing New Ties

Nor does dual citizenship undermine citizenship framed in communitarian terms. Communitarians also mistrust substantial hurdles to naturalization. The political theorist Michael Walzer argues that "once people are admitted as residents and participants in the economy, they must be entitled to acquire citizenship, if they wish."[32] Citizenship can play an important role in cementing cultural, emotional, and spiritual ties among Americans, and thus enhance and reflect their identification as a community.[33] There may have been a time when certain alternate national loyalties were inconsistent with that cementing function. Additional allegiances might be interpreted as representing diminished commitment to the American community, attaching oneself with temporary cement, thus diluting the bond that citizenship is meant to reflect and/or facilitate. In Schuck's terms, permitting the retention of prior nationality would "lower the price" of citizenship but might also lower its value.

But sacrifices should not be demanded without cause. Higher prices translate into fewer customers. All individuals hold concurrent institutional attachments in their private capacity. The attachments of civil society—to families, schools, ethnic communities, religions, and other non-state associations of almost infinite variety—involve very real loyalties, sometimes higher than that to the state. For family, most would die; religious affiliation, at least in the abstract, can represent an allegiance more important than that to nation. As Sanford Levinson observes, "anyone who takes religion seriously poses an alternate sovereign against the claims of the state."[34] Loyalties to state and non-state attachments often conflict, in the sense that the national interest may be defined against the interest of the non-state entity. Loyalty to non-state groupings may also detract from the social cohesion of the greater community, to the extent energy devoted to one may subtract from energy devoted to the other. And yet few would suggest that these non-state identities are inconsistent with one's status as a citizen, or that the citizenship oath requires the renunciation or even subordination of such attachments. (In the early modern period, Catholic naturalization applicants for British nationality were once required to renounce the doctrine of transubstantiation.)[35] As Levinson notes, "most of us would condemn as totalitarian an explicit requirement by the United States (or any other country) that one affirm primary loyalty to *it* over the competing loyalties to family and religion."[36] Membership in such non-national communities does not necessarily dilute identity as an American. On the contrary, it is a part of it.

The same can now be said of attachments to other states as well. There is no longer any respect in which holding additional citizenship precludes full identification with the community. On average, immigrants are less assimilated in established communities than the native-born. But retention of former nationality will not in itself retard the process by which the new citizen deepens his identification with the community of his naturalized homeland. At the same time, denying the possibility of naturalization (or raising its price too high, by requiring renunciation) *will* retard that process and weaken the bonds of community, at least as delimited in territorial terms.

One can frame the issue in a cost-benefit accounting, in terms of the interests of the existing community. (We will consider the possibility that it should be protected as a right from the individual's perspective in chapter 7.) Gerald Neuman explores the question through the relative values of a resident alien who has not naturalized ("A"), a naturalized citizen who has terminated prior citizenship ("R", as in "renounced"), and a naturalized citizen who has retained that citizenship ("DC," as in "dual citizen").[37] Assuming that R > DC > A, the key question is whether the benefit posed by renunciation outweighs the societal loss posed by those who do not naturalize because of the renunciation requirement (and thus remain "A"). The inquiry is highly context dependent. But the context-dependency no longer turns on identification of the dual citizen's other allegiance. Global developments relating to the nature of the nation-state and the individual's connection to it have significantly diminished the magnitude of R > DC. From the existing community's position, it doesn't much matter whether a new citizen has or has not retained her original citizenship. To the extent that a renunciation requirement deters naturalization, society's loss from a reduced rate of naturalization plainly overshadows the benefits of enforced renunciation.

The retention of prior nationality might even be considered a plus, at least in some cases, with the result that DC > R > A. Maintaining ties to the country of origin has always been seen to enrich the community as a whole, as is much activity in the realm of civil society. A dual national brings something distinctive to the American table. To the extent that a citizen is more likely to be inculcated with American constitutional values, she may put those values to work not only in the United States but also in the country of origin. Barred from political participation in the United States, a permanent resident alien who does not naturalize will be less grounded in those values, while one who terminates his birth citizenship upon naturalization will be unable to export those values back home. Dual nationality resolves the difficulty. Its encouragement becomes a ground-level part of the U.S. strategy to enlarge global democracy. The prominence of naturalized Americans in leadership roles among transitional democracies proves the point.

In short, there is no longer any danger associated with dual national status, little possibility for forced betrayal or scenarios of entanglement. A dual Mexican and American who advocates policies that benefit Mexico is little different from a Catholic who advocates policies endorsed by the Church or a member of Amnesty International who writes his congressman at the organization's behest. It's not about disloyalty. It's about interests and identities and different modes of social contribution. As for commitment, it may be difficult fully to engage in the civic activity of more than one polity. But that should not disqualify those who might devote their energies to their new country, even while they maintain formal ties to others. As one observer notes of Mexican and American dual citizens, they "consider themselves true contributors to their adopted homeland [at the same time as] they feel a deep connection to their country of origin in their language, their cultural traditions and a heartfelt *cario* (love) that they are unwilling to leave behind."[38] The baseball player Mariano Duncan naturalized as an American because he "loves this country"; he was also "relieved" to be able to maintain his Dominican citizenship.[39]

These perspectives help explain why the explosion in the number of dual citizens has provoked so little controversy in the United States, and why barriers to the status are falling elsewhere as well. One might have expected the wave of dual Mexican-U.S. citizens to have become a part of anti-immigration tropes. It hasn't. That owes to the distinctive politics of dual citizenship and the fact that the status now implicates a broad range of ethnic constituencies. This kind of broad entrenchment couldn't have happened in the historical context in which dual citizenship threatened the system of sovereign states. By eliminating an obstacle to naturalization, acceptance of dual citizenship will facilitate the political and social integration of recent immigrants. For states, dual citizenship is not just a neutral quantity, something to be tolerated. From a cost/benefit perspective, it represents a valuable, even necessary, tool to facilitate immigrant inclusion. Dual citizenship isn't something the United States should just put up with, in a hold-your-nose kind of way. Dual citizenship makes sense from a policy perspective. It should be embraced, not resisted. Dual citizenship is good for America.

6

# Dual Citizenship and the Rise of Diaspora

Andrés Bermudez was born and reared in the poor highlands of the Mexican state of Zacatecas, a major source of immigrants to the United States. In 1974, at the age of twenty-three, Bermudez was smuggled into the United States in the trunk of a Cutlass Supreme. As with many undocumented Mexican immigrants, then and now, Bermudez came to the United States to work as a farm laborer. Unlike most undocumented Mexican immigrants, he got very rich from a patent on a tomato planting machine. He regularized his status and naturalized as a U.S. citizen, living in a mansion in the Central Valley town of Winters, California.

Bermudez kept closely connected to his Zacatecan homeland, sending money back home to support not just family but also public works projects. Bermudez had lost his Mexican citizenship when he naturalized as an American but was able to recover it under the 1998 Mexican nationality law reforms. Disgusted with the corrupt local one-party rule of the PRI and Zacatecas's failure to grow economically, Bermudez decided to run for mayor of the city of Jerez in 2001. Emigrants streamed down from California to cast ballots for the "Tomato King." Bermudez won in a landslide. Though the Mexican courts nullified the result for his failure to satisfy a one-year residency requirement, Bermudez repeated the victory in a 2004 contest. In that year, at least three other Mexican immigrants to the United States ran in municipal elections back home in Mexico.[1]

In the end, Bermudez may not have been a very good mayor. A colorful rustic character who had not cast a vote in any election on either side of the border before voting for himself, he had no real qualifications for holding office. But his story reflects the growing political role of citizens who have left their homelands, many of whom are dual citizens. Prior chapters have considered dual citizenship through the lens of immigrant-receiving states, with a focus on the most important among them, the United States. After a history of aggressive rejection, destination states have become accepting of dual citizenship. That acceptance is both explained and justified by the reduced costs posed by dual citizens and by the need to lower barriers to naturalization.

This chapter considers dual citizenship from the perspective of sending states. (The dichotomy between immigrant sending and receiving may become less meaningful in the future as migration patterns become more complex, but as a matter of historical trajectory, cultural orientations, and empirical realities, the categories hold.) Sending states traditionally rejected dual citizenship among emigrant populations, terminating citizenship upon naturalization in another state. Parallel to receiving states, source countries have also shifted to accept, even embrace, dual citizenship among their diasporas. This shift is driven by distinct political dynamics and presents distinct normative challenges. Dual citizenship in the diaspora context shakes up the geography of human community. Considered from the perspective of the state in which an individual does not reside, dual citizenship decouples the conventional conception of territory and citizenry as coextensive.

## The New Landscapes of Migration

Migration during the nineteenth century was dominated by North-North movement. After abandoning the regime of perpetual allegiance, the source states of Europe moved to a model under which naturalization in another state (often the United States) would result in loss of original citizenship. This model was adopted as South-North migration became prevalent during the twentieth century. The near-uniform approach of developing-world states was to terminate the citizenship of those who naturalized in destination states. In the South-North context, this approach was integrated into perceptions of imperial power. Those who emigrated were considered not simply to have transferred allegiance as part of an instrumental calculation but to have affirmatively turned their backs on their homelands. "Brain drain" was the concern of states (some newly independent) that were looking to put colonial economies on independent footing. In many cases artificial constructs of colonial line drawing, these states had a fragile sense of nationhood. Emigrants who adopted the citizenship of their new countries of residence were sometimes depicted as traitors in homeland cultures. Authoritarian and one-party regimes often had reason to demonize emigrants to the extent that diaspora communities hosted political opponents. External communities were more easily forgotten in a world in which, technologically speaking, out of sight translated into out of mind. Until recently, for example, many Mexicans believed that Mexican citizens were required to spit and stomp on a Mexican flag as part of the U.S. naturalization formalities. Mexicans "scorned their paisanos who had become U.S. citizens, leading naturalized migrants to hide their new status while they were in Mexico."[2]

That began to change in the 1990s. As neoliberal regimes took hold in the global South, economic strategies shifted to trade-based approaches. Developing states no longer aimed for economic autarky. Markets and foreign exchange revenues were central to the shift. Emigrant communities came to be viewed as economic footholds in developed economies. Unskilled citizens presented an economic burden at home. From abroad, they contributed to homeland economies by sending money home, now hailed under the label of foreign remittances. Though this may always have been true, economists began to aggregate remittances as a major source of foreign exchange. Emigrants were reconceived as a kind of natural resource. Along with oil or metals, they were pumping money into the economies of the South.

This phenomenon was significant even with respect to unskilled labor, whose remittances, however small on an individual level, represented large transfers on an aggregated basis. Some emigrants did much better than that. In some cases, those who made fortunes abroad did more than support family members left behind. They put money into public infrastructure, funding schools, roads, and churches. Far from traitors, they visited home as heroes. The logic has motivated acceptance of dual citizenship in traditional diasporas as well. As one Armenian parliamentarian said of that country's prosperous diaspora in the wake of Armenia's validation of dual citizenship in 2007, "It is one thing to make investments in Armenia out of a feeling of moral obligation toward the homeland. It is an entirely different thing to be a citizen and a full participant of the civic life of the nation, whether in politics, in the social sphere, or in other spheres."[3]

This economic trajectory was reinforced by material aspects of globalization. The costs of travel and communication plummeted. Emigrants could stay connected with homeland communities on a sustained basis. Cheap phone cards and charter flights kept everyone in touch. Those who stayed behind became more comfortable with developed-world sensibilities, not just through contact with their compatriot emigrants but also through increasingly saturated exposure to a global popular culture. The world to which their countrymen had migrated was no longer some sort of mystical unknown. It was a place splashed across movie screens and advertisements. These developments were already in train before the ubiquity of the internet. Now there are Skype, Facebook, and Instagram to keep members of transnational communities in the continual loop.

Cultural and economic forces pointed to inevitable political recognition of diaspora communities. Emigrants had left the territorial fold, but they remained connected to their homelands. Sending states now had reason to help maintain the connection. Citizenship became a way of cementing the tie, hence the move to allow emigrants to retain their homeland citizenship even as they naturalized in the destination state.[4] The move to acceptance, and in some cases encouragement, advanced other political interests. Only as naturalized citizens can immigrant communities exercise full political power in their new country of residence. In theory, at least, the diaspora community can advance homeland interests at the ballot box in the country of naturalization.

Finally, recognition of dual citizenship satisfied a major demand of the diaspora community itself. Diaspora constituents had various incentives to acquire citizenship in their destination countries: full political rights, full rights to social benefits, absolute freedom of entry, full immunity from deportation. In the U.S. case, citizens have advantages over lawful permanent residents for purposes of securing the admission of family members. In many countries, some kinds of public sector employment are limited to citizens. At the same time, members of diaspora communities often have reasons to retain the citizenship of their country of origin. Without citizenship, those who have left their countries of origin often require visas to return. Property ownership by non-citizens has in many countries been historically limited. For many, finally, the sentimental aspects of relinquishing one's birth citizenship is too steep a price to pay to naturalize in one's adopted country. As Peter Schuck notes, original citizenship is "like first love."[5] Comparative empirical studies have demonstrated that acceptance of dual citizenship in a sending state increases the rate of naturalization in the receiving state. One analysis using changes during the 1990s in the nationality practice of various Latin American states, controlling for other factors, found a 10% bump in naturalization rates in the United States of immigrants from countries allowing the retention of original citizenship. In other words, if immigrants don't have to give up their original citizenship, they are more likely to naturalize.[6]

For diaspora communities, dual citizenship became a top agenda item. Backed by accumulating economic heft, diaspora communities began to exercise political muscle. Emigrants maintained strong social connections to homeland communities, which became a channel of political influence. Many countries allow political campaign contributions from external citizens. As emigrants rose in stature back home, they flexed political muscle to match economic influence. Emigrants and countries of origin end up bargaining over the terms of citizenship. As David FitzGerald writes, "The leviathan becomes a supplicant."[7] Maarten Vink speaks of the phenomenon of "emulation" among states in moving to accept dual citizenship—more particularly, emulation among diasporas. As more states accept the status, with no obvious negative consequences, it becomes more difficult for homeland countries to reject change.

## Global Turnaround

The shift among sending states towards acceptance of the status has been dramatic. Along with Mexico's 1998 shift, many Central and South American states have amended their nationality laws to allow retention of citizenship after naturalization elsewhere, including Brazil, Costa Rica, Ecuador, and Colombia. According to one survey, only 8% of South American states now automatically terminate citizenship on the ground of foreign naturalization.[8] The Dominican Republic changed its law to accept dual citizenship in 1994; Haiti amended its constitution in 2012 to allow the status. Smaller Caribbean states have been at the forefront of the investor citizenship phenomenon (which I will describe in chapter 8), which necessarily requires toleration of the status. Turkey, with a major diaspora in Europe, has recognized dual citizenship since 1981.

Acceptance of dual citizenship for emigrants has been coupled with relaxed thresholds to citizenship for co-ethnics abroad, who will typically have citizenship in their place of residence. In 2010, for example, Hungary opened naturalization to any descendant of a person who was a citizen of Hungary before 1920 or between 1941 and 1945 and who can demonstrate a knowledge of the Hungarian language. More than 500,000 have applied, the vast majority while holding another citizenship.[9] Other states have similarly loosened rules for acquisition of citizenship by descent.

Cracks have shown in the edifice of East Asia's resistance to the status. In 2003, the Philippines amended its law to allow dual citizenship. In 2010, South Korea moved to allow retention in many cases.[10] China formally refuses to recognize dual citizenship but does not police the ban in any respect. Dual citizenship is increasingly common among Chinese elites.[11] (When I gave a lecture overview of immigration law to a group of Chinese judges and prosecutors, the first question related to the U.S. rule of absolute birthright citizenship, and birth tourism is increasingly popular among wealthy Chinese who are retaining Chinese nationality while acquiring another one.)[12]

India remains a holdout, pressure from an economic powerhouse diaspora notwithstanding, because the Indian constitution expressly prohibits the status. The government has developed intermediate designations for diaspora members: Persons of Indian Origin, Non-Resident Indians, and, more recently, Overseas Citizens of India. (It also has a special day on the calendar, Pravasi Bharatiya Divas, to celebrate the contribution of diaspora Indians to the country's development.) Though the last is not citizenship as a formal legal matter, the label evidences the country's move toward eventual recognition of the status; its benefits include visa-free travel to India.[13] Indonesia is beginning to feel heat from its diaspora to accept dual citizenship on a transparent strategy of emulation—it has worked for other countries, it should work for us.[14] In part because it is not a sending state with a powerful diaspora, Japan remains staunchly resistant to dual citizenship, though even it faces increasingly vocal calls for citizenship reforms.[15] It enforces the ban through background checks for passport renewals abroad. The country is apparently less successful in enforcing an election requirement for the increasing number of children with mixed parentage.[16]

A similar story can be told of African states. Many African states barred dual citizenship at independence out of a perhaps understandable fear that dual citizenship held by a sizable rump of the population with a colonial power would pose genuine issues of loyalty. Resistance to dual citizenship may also have reflected the insecurity of these states as such, enjoying no rationale beyond lines drawn on a map in Berlin. Although African states have lagged in the trend toward accepting dual citizenship, many have changed their laws on the status, since 1995 including Angola, Ghana, Kenya, and Rwanda.[17] South Africa allows those who naturalize elsewhere to retain South African citizenship, but only with prior governmental permission, and it does not allow those naturalizing in South Africa to retain citizenship in country of origin. As of 2010, one study found thirty-two African states permitting the status at least in some permutations (some for birth citizens only, Nigeria and Senegal, for example), with twenty-one totally prohibiting it.[18] Zimbabwe has since rewritten its constitution to allow the status. Diaspora pressure is mounting in such states as Zambia, Liberia, and Tanzania.

There are similar trends among receiving states, because receiving states are sending states, too. As an incident of economic globalization, all states have increasing external populations to which they have reason to remain connected. Though it is difficult to speak of a German or American "diaspora" in the way it describes the transnational Indian, Jamaican, Korean, or Turkish community, developed states see at least the possibility of economic returns from their external citizens (more so among second-tier developed countries such as Italy or Greece). There may also be cultural drivers. Christian Joppke speaks of a re-ethnicization of European citizenries, under which citizenship is more liberally extended on the basis of descent. Relationships with its emigrant population was a major factor in the acceptance of dual citizenship by Italy in 1992, for example.[19] Once these states (mostly European) have recognized dual citizenship among their emigrant populations, it becomes more difficult to deny it to those who have immigrated to their countries and are now habitual residents.[20] Such disparities have been condemned as discriminatory in the wrong direction—it is more important, for example, that German citizenship be facilitated for Turkish immigrants in Germany, not for German immigrants and their descendants in (say) Canada.

Nor, finally, do sending and receiving states act in isolation. Instrumentalist sending-state acceptance of dual citizenship is ineffective to the extent dual citizenship is rejected by receiving states. Receiving state insistence on the termination of homeland citizenship trumps sending-state policy. That has led sending states who have embraced dual citizenship to press reticent receiving states to liberalize their policies on the issue. The Turkish government has aggressively pressed the government of Germany through diplomatic and public channels to broaden its acceptance of dual citizenship, for example; Germany's recent softening of restrictions on dual citizenship removed a major thorn in bilateral relations between the two states.[21] The contrast to the nineteenth-century practice is clear. Countries used to lobby each other to remove the causes of dual citizenship; now they do the opposite.

## Political Rights and the External Citizen

Dual citizenship insures full or near-full political rights in a state of residence. In a few states there remain some legacy restrictions on office holding (a phenomenon I will discuss in chapter 7), but dual citizens enjoy the franchise in their state of habitual residence, as citizens and residents of that state. That vindicates the foundational premise of democratic self-governance: individuals should have a say in their governance, assumed to be organized on a territorial basis. The self-governance principle has fueled calls for extending the vote for non-citizens in their place of residence, on the grounds that all residents, citizens or not, are affected by government. Many countries now permit non-citizen voting on the local level.[22] Citizens of one EU member state resident in another have the right to vote in local elections in their country of residence. A few countries (New Zealand is an example) have extended the vote to longer-term non-citizen residents in national elections.

The political status of citizens living outside their country of citizenship has attracted less attention. Historically, most states denied the enjoyment of political rights to non-resident citizens during the period of absence (beyond diplomatic and military personnel stationed abroad), much less after permanent relocation. This practice worked from an unexamined corollary to the self-governance paradigm: that absent citizens, even in large numbers, simply do not have much of a claim on or need for the full bundle of rights accorded residents. If government is largely a territorial enterprise, the argument runs, then the absent citizen does not need to be protected from or participate in it.

But this runs smack into another understanding of democratic citizenship: that political rights are enjoyed by all citizens, on a formally equal basis. The dominant practice under which absent citizens were denied political rights is dissipating. External citizens more often carry political rights with them even as they relocate in—and become citizens of—other countries.

Most states now afford full voting rights to external citizens in national elections. Countries that allow absentee voting by mail include the United States, Spain, and Italy. Countries that provide for polling places at embassies and consulates abroad include Poland, Lithuania, Ukraine, Colombia, Venezuela, the Dominican Republic, Peru, France, Russia, Sweden, the Philippines, and Spain. Switzerland, France, and the Philippines have adopted e-voting for external citizens, and more are sure to follow.[23]

A handful of countries, including the United Kingdom, Canada, and New Zealand, have disqualified citizens after a certain period of non-residence: fifteen years in the case of the United Kingdom, five in the case of Canada, and three for New Zealand, although in the latter two cases the period runs from the last presence of any duration. In 2012, a German court struck down a similar disqualification applicable after a twenty-five-year absence.[24] In May 2014, a Canadian court struck down that country's residency condition as "arbitrary."[25] The Philippines used to disqualify legal permanent residents of other countries unless they executed an affidavit declaring an intention to resume residency in the Philippines within three years of voter registration; the return affidavit requirement was eliminated in 2013.[26] Some states allow all nonresidents to vote on the condition that they return home to cast ballots. Israel and Taiwan are examples. Ireland restricts the eligibility of external citizens to those non-resident for less than eighteen months, and then only if they return to vote. Others, including key sending-states Mexico and Turkey, have abandoned the presence requirement.

Blanket franchise ineligibility for non-resident citizens is now the minority practice. Some countries continue as a default rule to deprive external citizens of voting privileges during the period of non-residency.

These holdout countries include Denmark, India, and Nepal. Even among these, however, most include exceptions for those abroad in government service (Denmark, for example) and, in some cases, for those on overseas assignment with a home-based corporation and those studying abroad. Hungary, South Africa, and El Salvador are among states that have recently abandoned residency requirements for the franchise.[27]

Most countries that permit non-resident voting (including those that require non-residents to return home to cast ballots) do not provide separate representation in national legislatures for non-resident communities. Instead, non-resident voters are assimilated into the electorate on some other basis. Typically, assimilated approaches count the external voter through her last place of residence in the country. External citizens of Germany, Spain, and the United States, for example, vote through their last place of in-country residence. Hungary's external citizens vote for national party lists. In direct elections for national presidencies, external votes will in most cases be counted on the same one person, one vote basis as their resident co-nationals.

But other countries provide discrete representation for non-resident communities in national legislatures. Recent developments suggest that others will follow suit. External citizens of France and Columbia have a constitutionally protected right to separate representation in the upper chamber of their national legislatures. Six delegates of the seventy-two-member national assembly of Cape Verde are selected by non-resident voters, as are eight out of 380 Algerian parliamentarians. Ten seats in the 217-member Tunisian parliament are reserved for those citizens resident in France. In 2001, Italy allocated six upper-house and twelve lower-house seats for external citizens as part of legislation extending them the right to vote. In 2012, the Dominican Republic established seven seats in its parliament for external citizens. Until 2003, non-resident citizens of Croatia were discretely represented according to the level of their turnout—in other words, the number of seats allocated to non-residents depending on how many voted (this has since been changed to allocate a fixed number of three parliamentary seats to external citizens).[28] Separate representation has also been proposed in Ireland (as part of a general proposal extending franchise rights to some non-resident citizens) and Mexico. In Switzerland, a proposal has been floated to create a twenty-seventh canton to represent non-resident citizens.[29]

Anecdotal evidence suggests that turnout among eligible non-resident voting populations is growing more robust. Only 3,000 of 200,000 Colombian citizens resident in the United States cast ballots in 1990 elections for the Colombian presidency.[30] Only 14,000 non-resident British citizens voted in 1997 parliamentary elections, a small fraction of the hundreds of thousands who were eligible. A 1999 Council of Europe report concluded that "in countries which allow their expatriates to vote, the actual participation rate is so low as to have little effect on the outcome."[31] But there are examples of higher participation. In 1994 Swedish parliamentary elections, for example, approximately 25,000 out of 80,000 eligible non-residents cast ballots; France and Austria report turnout rates around 25% of total eligible non-resident voters; and in the first election in which Belgians abroad were permitted to participate in 2003, participation was more than 60% of eligible voters. An estimated 90% of eligible Eritreans abroad voted in a 1993 referendum on independence. And though it is clearly an anomalous case, in the 2005 post-invasion elections in Iraq, 265,000 non-resident Iraqis cast ballots, 93% of those registered (though many fewer than those who would have been eligible to vote).[32] In 2006, an estimated 40% of external Italians voted in parliamentary elections.[33] More than a million overseas Filipinos are already registered for 2016 presidential elections.[34] As more countries allow for balloting by mail and, inevitably, the internet as opposed to requiring non-resident voters to make sometimes distant trips to diplomatic facilities, the transaction costs of external voting will diminish and participation rates may increase correspondingly. That said, turnout among external citizens appears invariably lower than turnout in-country. (As *The Economist* puts it, "some emigrants are homesick. Others are sick of home.")[35]

In any case, the trend toward a more generous external citizen franchise is clear. The trend appears to be nearly unidirectional, with far more states moving to expand the franchise than to roll it back. (Among the few exceptions were the elimination of a legislative seat for external Cook Islanders and a shortening of the non-residency period—from twenty to fifteen years—after which external British citizens lose their vote.) External citizen voting is becoming a common feature of democracy after globalization. Many of these external citizens will have two or even more citizenships, in many cases also holding citizenship in their new state of residence.

## The Responsible External Voter

As with dual citizenship itself, external voting takes some getting used to. Dual citizenship breaks down what was once assumed to be an exclusive relationship between states and their members. External voting challenges the congruence of territory and polity. In the conventional imagination, governance happens within territorial boundaries that also define the society exercising its self-governance. Some number of citizens of modern states have always lived abroad. With few exceptions, they lost their rights of political participation during their absence. To the extent they took the franchise with them, it was on a permissive basis only. States felt no need to justify the denial of the vote to external populations.

As external citizen voting becomes more common, it has provoked resistance. Opponents of the practice argue that it translates into irresponsible voting, uninformed voting, and/or undisciplined voting. Residency restrictions may also be tied to the perceived challenges of large-scale out-of-country electoral logistics. These objections explain the former rarity of external voting. They once presented a principled basis for denying the franchise to those territorially absent. But the same shifts in global architecture that have undermined objections to dual citizenship also undermine the force of objections to external voting in most contexts. Nor do other objections to the non-resident franchise—that it undermines political participation in countries of residence or that it contradicts the equality norm of modern citizenship—justify denying the vote to non-residents.

The "irresponsible voter" argument assumes non-residents lack a stake in homeland election contests and will fail to exercise the franchise in a conscientious manner. Because non-residents do not live with the consequences of their vote, they will not exercise it with the care that one would expect of resident voters, who vote responsibly out of self-interest. As one resident citizen of Mexico observed in expressing opposition to the political participation of external citizens, "We're the ones who are in the trenches, on a war footing, not them. Yes, their support for our democracy is important, but we're the ones who must live with the consequences." Rainer Bauböck argues that "migrants who demand a voice in the political process at home can be accused of imposing their interests from the outside without sharing any responsibility for the outcome."[36]

The premise is increasingly tenuous in the face of globalization. Non-resident citizens often have significant interests in policymaking in their (other) country of citizenship. Non-residents own property, operate businesses, and have made other investments (including financial support for schools, road building, and other public works) either located in or involving transactions with the home country. As one advocate of non-resident voting for Salvadorans living in the United States observed, "If they are the ones carrying El Salvador's economy on their backs, then they have political rights at home and should have a say in their nation's destiny, whether they live there or not."[37] Similarly, in light of their $150 billion contribution to the homeland economy over the last ten years, "overseas Pakistanis have the right to ask: is our money good enough, but not our vote?"[38] Non-resident citizens owning real property in homelands, as is often the case, will be subject to applicable property taxes. (The United States is exceptional in imposing income taxes on external citizens.) Non-resident citizens have clear interests with respect to nationality and military service laws.

External citizens will be affected by the provision of consular services and diplomatic protection.[39] Almost 10% of all Mexican citizens live in the United States, a massive constituency for the more than fifty Mexican consulates there. These and other non-residents (especially those who retire abroad) will have an interest in social welfare policy. Many non-resident citizens return to their home country, and thus have an important interest in the future course of home country government. In justifying 1975 legislation protecting the right of non-resident citizens to vote in federal elections, the U.S. Congress stressed that they have "distinct Congressional interests. The citizen outside the country is interested, for example, in the exchange rate of the dollar, social security benefits, or the energy situation. Furthermore, the local citizen and the overseas citizen share a number of common national interests, such as Federal taxation, defense expenditures (for example, U.S. troops stationed overseas), inflation, and the integrity and competence of our National Government."[40] Americans abroad have a clear stake in the U.S. tax system. On top of ordinary filing requirements, they are now subject to an exceptional regime relating to foreign bank holdings. The Foreign Account Tax Compliance Act (FATCA) has sparked an uproar among external Americans, who shoulder a targeted set of burdens about which they should have a political say.

Thousands of citizens of Israel and Taiwan return home to vote—a kind of electoral tourism—which would seem by itself to evidence a high non-resident interest in those contests.[41] Before changes in Dominican law allowed for polling in place of foreign residence, large numbers of Dominican citizens would return home from New York to vote in elections there.[42] To the extent that non-residents lack a stake in homeland governance, they are unlikely to exercise the franchise at all, even where the costs of participation are low. Anemic non-resident participation rates in Colombian and British elections belie assertions that large numbers of uninterested non-resident voters will necessarily participate if given the opportunity.

## Voting Abroad, Normalized

Much the same goes for charges that non-resident voting will be uninformed. As a 1984 UK parliamentary report fretted, "Their use of the right will be a farce. They will not be able to meet their candidate, to question the candidate or be canvassed by someone calling on behalf of the candidate. They may not receive any election literature, and they may therefore know nothing of the candidate except his or her name and party."[43] Those who are truly uninformed are unlikely to participate. Those who want to stay or become informed regarding political developments in their home countries obviously have the means to do so. Physical location has little bearing on access to political information. Even in the pre-internet context of 1975, the U.S. Congress observed that non-residents "keep in close touch with the affairs at home, through correspondence, television and radio, and American newspapers and magazines."[44] Non-residents may be better informed to the extent their sources are less vulnerable to official manipulation. For example, Russians living outside of Russia are "better equipped than most Russians to judge the political scene since they receive unbiased information."[45] The same developments rebut charges that non-resident citizens can't engage in politically responsible citizenship, which requires "a willingness to argue, to listen, and to accept the force of better reasons," in short, "some ongoing involvement."[46] Deliberative participation has been enabled across space by the communications revolution. The concentrated nature of many emigrant communities in many cases will permit more traditional face-to-face engagement as well.

The weakest case against external citizen voting is that it is undisciplined, which is a polite way of opposing external citizen voting where it would go against you. That's why Zimbabwe's Robert Mugabe has so aggressively resisted external citizen voting, for example, because it would undermine his grip on power. Ruling parties by definition have an interest in preserving the status quo, and the political uncertainties posed by non-resident communities have sometimes proved an obstacle to regularizing their electoral participation. The non-resident community is tarred as an illegitimate "swing" bloc dictating a change in home-country government. A former attorney general of Mexico, for example, argued that in a close election where "the deciding votes might well be cast by dual citizens," candidates would need "to take care that their campaign issues and proposals not be alien to the interests of U.S. citizens nor opposed to those held by the U.S. government."[47]

This concern is also unsupportable, both empirically and normatively. In many cases, voter participation among non-residents in those countries that allow the practice have been so low as to minimize the danger that non-resident voters will command a decisive position in any given election. Moreover, to the extent that non-resident voters do influence election results that doesn't justify their exclusion. External U.S. citizens probably tipped the balance in the 2000 U.S. presidential election, providing George W. Bush's slim margin of victory in the decisive Florida balloting. Strategists for the 2004 U.S. presidential elections identified "battleground states" of an atypical description, including Iraq, South Korea, Israel, and Italy.[48] Assuming that non-resident citizens have an interest in homeland governance, and that they are no less likely to exercise the franchise in a less responsible or less informed manner than resident voters, they should enjoy facilitated rights of participation in national elections.

Where warranted by numbers and interests, external citizens should have some assurance of a voice in national policymaking. Dismissing fears of a "hypothetical mass invasion of electors from abroad," a 1999 Council of Europe report argued that "the issue has nothing to do with the number of people concerned, but is essentially a matter of fundamental, inalienable human rights. . . . The right to vote is an essential part of the democratic process, and every expatriate European should be entitled to exercise it in his/her country of origin."[49] The International Covenant on Civil and Political Rights provides that "every citizen . . . shall have the right and opportunity . . . without unreasonable restrictions . . . to vote."[50] That supplies a hook for framing the issue as one of human rights.

Politics sometimes retards adoption of external citizen voting. But politics can also advance it. Increasing global democratization has been an important part of the story. As more states engage in democratic politics, there are more opportunities for those politics to be engaged outside a state as well as within. Transitional democracies sometimes implicate diaspora communities populated by active political exiles, those oppressed by authoritarian regimes. External citizens have sometimes been extended the vote as part of the transition to democracy in recognition of their role in the transition. Non-resident Iraqi citizens were included in the first elections post-Saddam in 2005, for example.

In established democracies, political parties have looked to calculate whether they stand to win or lose by granting non-residents the vote. Where parties in power see an opposition hold on external communities, they have resisted expanding the franchise. With respect to the adoption of external voting under Mexican law, observers agreed that "a belief that none of Mexico's three major parties would automatically benefit from the new votes" facilitated by the change was "[k]ey to the move."[51] When ruling parties see an electoral advantage in external citizens voting, they will push for it. That was blatantly the case when Hungarian ultra-nationalist leader Viktor Orbán pushed through voting rights for newly minted Hungarian citizens resident in bordering Central European states in 2011.[52] Those in power do not always accurately make the calculation. Silvio Berlusconi thought that non-resident Italians would be supportive of his business-friendly regime. In fact, they tipped the balance on the way to his electoral defeat.[53] Whatever the dynamic of party politics, there is a ratchet effect: once the vote is extended to external citizens, it is unlikely to be retracted. In other words, it just takes one regime that sees a net gain from external votes for external voting to be adopted on a permanent basis.

Logistics, finally, no longer pose a serious obstacle to the political exclusion of diaspora communities. Modern electoral management techniques, along with the use of international observers, should reduce the risk of fraud even in large-scale non-resident polling. The risk of fraud may be lower with respect to external voting than with in-territory voting, especially in cases where democratic practices are better established in the country of residence relative to the homeland. New York City police officers monitoring polling places for voting in Dominican Republic elections, for example, enjoyed "a political disinterest in the election which lent them a greater legitimacy than the officers patrolling sites in the Dominican Republic."[54] Similarly, external voters for Filipino elections are "immune from rampant vote-buying and intimidation that mar Philippine elections."[55] That may not always be the case, as external voting can pose distinct challenges. External voting in 2014 Hungarian elections was riddled with irregularities, and standards appeared to discriminate among non-resident voters to favor the ruling regime (those formerly resident in the country faced a more difficult registration process than did those never resident). External voting should be subject to the same standards of integrity as resident voting. The stabilization of democratic practices in most countries has reduced the risk of disturbances that in the past may have been associated with election campaigns. That may explain why some countries, including Germany and Switzerland, have abandoned laws under which foreign residents could vote in home-country elections only by mail.[56] Canada, somewhat idiosyncratically, has officially refused to recognize or facilitate in-person foreign voting in Canada, though it appears to have backed down from taking any steps to obstruct it.[57] Moves to enable external voting through the internet should eventually address any lingering concerns.

## Voting Here, Voting There

The issue of external citizen voting has also been tied up in questions relating to the rise of dual citizenship. Some observers accept dual citizenship as a status but draw the line at dual voting, proposing that dual citizens be permitted to vote only in their country of residence.[58] The suggestion is that non-resident voting by dual nationals will divert such persons from deeper political engagement in the place that they live. As one immigrant community leader cautioned, "interest in overseas politics could divert energy from those here."[59] But that point rests on the premise that individuals have a fixed quantum of energy to devote to political participation, and that participation in one arena will inevitably subtract from participation in another. It is true that there are only so many hours in the day, but we do not always work from such zero-sum assumptions. In the United States, we don't condemn participation in state and local politics as lowering likely engagement in federal politics. Involvement with a school board, for example, would not necessarily be inconsistent with activity in other political arenas. On the contrary, the individual engaged on school issues may be more likely to maintain involvements on other civic fronts. In any case, empirical studies of transnational politics are beginning to show that multiple sites of engagement may grow participation in each. "The expanding opportunities for migrants to be involved in the electoral politics of their sending countries does appear to have an independent effect on their perceptions of long-term connection to the United States," concludes Louis DeSipio, "and, in more cases than not, speeds it."[60]

The same goes for engagement in civil society, generally considered a virtue in the republican conception of political being. However true it may be that in some instances a deep commitment to non-governmental forms of association (including international ones) may limit the depth of direct political engagement, on average rank-and-file participation would have no such consequence. On the question of dual citizenship generally, Peter Schuck supposes that "it is doubtful (although possible) that parents with two sets of children from different marriages manage to devote the same amount of time to each child as they would if they had only one set of children to raise."[61] But that exaggerates the weight of our political identities. Even intensive political engagements fall short of what is demanded in the context of the true family, and would usually allow room for parallel commitments.

This view also suggests that obstructing participation in homeland politics will inevitably channel energy into the politics of the host country. Blocked from voting back home, the logic runs, the naturalized citizen is more likely to vote in his adopted country. That also seems unlikely; the probability of casting a host-country vote wouldn't likely increase with the loss of a homeland one. People will participate in those collectivities (many or few) of which they feel a part and in which they perceive interests. Participation rights in one community will not necessarily affect the exercise of rights in another. Moreover, voting is just one form of political engagement. An immigrant who is denied the franchise in his homeland may well have other routes of participation available to him, which he will take or leave as identity and other factors determine, hence the political consequence of external citizen communities even where they do not enjoy the franchise. To the extent that diaspora communities feel more connected to their homelands than to their host states, denying them the franchise as external citizens is unlikely to energize them as resident citizens.

Finally, some attack dual voting on the ground that it violates the norm of political equality central to the modern conception of citizenship.[62] To the extent dual nationals are permitted to vote in both countries of nationality, that privileges them over their mono-national counterparts. John Fonte, for example, laments the emergence of dual citizens as "specially privileged, supra-citizens who have voting power in more than one nation."[63] But the argument overestimates the importance of the franchise as a citizenship right and measure of equality. A mono-national American might envy a dual national British-American colleague not because he can vote in UK elections, but rather because he enjoys the personal and professional advantages of EU citizenship (to live, travel, and work there without restriction). If rights other than the franchise loom large, the answer to the equality objection is to prohibit dual nationality altogether, not to limit parallel political rights that may come with the status.

Second, assuming the importance of the franchise, depriving nonresident dual nationals of their right to vote presents an equality problem of its own. In the resulting framework, some citizens (resident and nonresident mono-nationals) have full political rights, while other citizens (dual nationals) do not. To the extent that the inequality is internally generated (that is, within the citizenship regime itself, rather than the result of interplay with other regimes), the problem seems more serious than that posed by holding franchise rights in more than one polity. The non-resident dual national loses a voice in decision making implicating her interests; to deny the franchise would seem to amount to a denial of self-government. In any case, no state appears currently to make the maintenance of alternate nationality material to the extension of voting privileges. As the acceptance of dual citizenship broadens, it seems unlikely that objections to dual-citizen voting will have much traction.

## The First Congressional District for Overseas Americans

This isn't to say that voting for external citizens is as straightforward as it is for resident ones. There are competing mechanisms of representation. Under an "assimilated representation" approach, external citizens are registered and vote through their last place of in-country residence. "Discrete representation" affords non-resident citizens separate representation in national legislative institutions. Which model is more appropriate will depend on context.

Assimilated representation is more easily implemented in most countries, especially those whose territorially based districting system is constitutionally entrenched. (A congressional district for external U.S. citizens? Not going to happen.) It works best where non-resident citizens are small in number and politically unengaged, not warranting discrete representation in national legislatures. Assimilated representation has the advantage of maintaining the formal equality of non-resident voters. Their votes count as much as those of their residential counterparts.

Where feasible as a matter of constitutional structure, however, discrete representation may be the better mechanism. Non-resident citizens have distinctive interests by virtue of being non-resident. Dispersed through in-country territorial jurisdictions under the assimilated model, non-resident voters are less likely to have their distinct interests represented in national decision making. Discrete representation uses territorial districting. In that respect it deviates from ordinary, domestic districting only insofar as the territory involved is outside sovereign jurisdiction and may be non-contiguous.

Discrete representation for external citizens need not be in the same proportion as for resident ones. Non-resident citizens have interests in home-country policymaking, but that interest will typically be less intense than the interests of resident citizens, a fact reflected in lower electoral participation rates where non-residents are permitted to vote. That is the approach taken by most countries that have established overseas legislative districts. For instance, although there are twice as many diaspora Cape Verdeans as there are Cape Verdeans resident in Cape Verde, they are allocated less than 10% of the seats in the national assembly.[64] The argument for asymmetric representation seems particularly strong where citizenship is liberally extended to diaspora communities in ways that attenuate the connection of the external citizen to homeland governance. If such diaspora citizens were extended full voting privileges, their large numbers could overwhelm resident electorates even though their interests might be marginal. Although one could expect (as explained above) that external citizens with trivial interests would take a pass on voting privileges, the risk in certain cases of mobilized, largely disconnected external voters upsetting home state politics might be substantial enough to deny participation rights.

Ireland presents an example: the numbers of resident and non-resident Irish citizens are approximately equal, and large numbers of other non-residents (most of them in the United States) are eligible for the status. As one commentator notes, "This establishes a potential problem, in that the population of Irish citizens living outside Ireland would form a massive political block if they all voted together."[65] One could imagine plausible scenarios in which the non-resident vote leaned heavily away from the sentiment of resident voters—in the Irish context, on such charged social issues as abortion and same-sex marriage. This presents a legitimate normative basis for restricting external citizen voting along the lines of the "irresponsible voter" objection in cases where the proportion of external to resident citizens is high and the threshold for the acquisition of external citizenship is low. That might also militate, for instance, against the assimilated enfranchisement of large non-resident Hungarian populations in neighboring states.

But that is not an argument for cutting diaspora populations out of the electoral picture altogether. Even a citizen who has never resided in her country of citizenship is likely to have political interests in her country's governance, if only through the association of identity and perhaps through much more. In the face of those interests, it seems difficult to justify the categoric disenfranchisement of external citizens.

Some states that provide for non-resident voting, including the United States, require that the citizen have resided at some point in the home country.[66] Insofar as prior residence diminishes as a proxy for interests, the condition may lose its normative force. Similarly, some scholars have suggested that the franchise not be extended beyond the first émigré generation.[67] That would seem more problematic still, insofar as it excludes subsequent generations who evidence and accumulate homeland interests through some period of residence. Germany recently moved to allow citizens never resident in Germany to vote if they "have acquired a personal and direct familiarity with the political conditions in the Federal Republic of Germany and [are] affected by them." Perhaps that supplies a kind of middle ground, shifting presumptions in the case of the never-resident. As globalization facilitates sustained, material homeland connections into subsequent generations, there should be no blanket bar to voting among those who are born in other countries but who may still have substantial interests in the state of which they are external citizens.

Even at lower proportional levels, external citizens should still prefer discrete representation. With discrete representation comes a direct, undiluted voice in decision making. In assimilated voting systems, at least those based on territorial jurisdiction, non-resident interests are less likely to find legislative advocates. In those systems adopting discrete representation, there is a high probability of dual citizens being elected to homeland legislatures. Those seeking to represent external citizens will likely be established in their place of residence, which increases the likelihood that they will have naturalized. Such was the case with Renato Turano, twice elected to represent "North America" in the Italian parliament. A Chicago business person, one-time chair of the American Bakers Association, he has both U.S. and Italian citizenship. The Tomato King is another example, albeit as the perhaps more remarkable case of someone winning homeland elective office at the local level.

The disadvantages of any form of electoral representation—or lack thereof—are mitigated by non-electoral forms of political participation. In some countries, official or semi-official "councils" of non-residents (sometimes including non-citizens of national descent) have been established to represent non-resident interests, often through ministries of foreign affairs.[68] The Parliamentary Assembly of the Council of Europe has recommended the establishment of a "council of Europeans abroad," in the interest of "representing European expatriates at the pan-European level."[69] Many countries have cabinet-level posts to manage diaspora affairs. Haiti has a minister of Haitians living abroad; Ireland a minister of state for the diaspora; India a minister of overseas Indian affairs; Mexico an "Institute of Mexicans Abroad." In the United States, residents abroad send a voting delegation—"Democrats Abroad"—to the Democratic Party presidential nominating convention. That creates a channel of political participation for some.[70] Although the creation of a separate voting congressional district for non-resident Americans would require a constitutional amendment (a non-starter), a lesser entry point would be the addition of a non-voting "delegate" like those afforded U.S. territories such as Guam and Puerto Rico, as well as the District of Columbia.[71]

Meanwhile, few countries appear to limit political campaign contributions on the basis of residence (or status as a dual national). The wealth of emigrant communities relative to their homelands affords them significant political power, as a source for campaign funds, even when they lack the vote. It has become routine, for instance, for Latin American politicians to make campaign swings through emigrant populations resident in the United States, even where those populations cannot vote or where (in the absence of in-place voting mechanisms) they do not vote in large numbers.[72] Turkey's Recep Erdoğan led a rally before 18,000 supporters in Cologne in the run-up to July 2014 elections, the first in which Turkish citizens could vote from abroad. In addition to campaign contributions, non-residents can engage in political speech targeted at home electorates. Indirect forms of political participation by non-residents further evidence the interests of non-resident communities in home-country government, as well as the inevitability that such interests will exert themselves in available channels of influence. Supporters of one Indian political party, for example, ran phone banks remotely from the United States to get out the vote among those back in India in 2013 elections there.[73]

The political assertion of external citizens highlights the decoupling of citizenship and territory. External citizens are not just passport carriers. Some, at least, are looking for status mostly like the one they had back home. That many of these external citizens are also dual citizens adds further complexity. Political diaspora isn't just a matter of adding enclaves outside the homeland, it's about the new layering of political membership. Most countries are beyond the question of whether they will accept dual citizenship. The next question is how dual citizens will be incorporated in national communities, and how national communities will be reimagined to adapt to the new mode of membership.

7

# Dual Citizenship as Human Right

Some years back, a student of mine came to me with his father's problem. A longtime engineer at one of the large U.S. defense contractors, his security clearance was being revoked when it was discovered that he held dual citizenship with Israel. Without his security clearance, he would not be able to do his job. The revocation of the clearance was as good as a pink slip. The clearance was yanked under U.S. government rules under which dual citizenship in most circumstances will count as a "foreign preference." Under State Department guidelines, "exercise of any right, privilege or obligation of foreign citizenship" may "indicate a preference for a foreign country over the United States." For the Defense Department, the "exercise of dual citizenship" likewise raises a security concern. That includes mere possession of a foreign passport as the citizen of another country as well as "accepting educational, medical, or other benefits, such as retirement and social welfare, from a foreign country."[1]

Dual citizenship can only be mitigated for security clearance purposes in narrow circumstances. DoD adjudicative guidelines allow the presumption of foreign preference to be overcome where, for instance, the foreign passport "is destroyed and the individual expresses a willingness to renounce the foreign citizenship." In one 2014 case, a payroll consultant to a defense contractor who had held a security clearance without incident for almost a decade had the clearance revoked when it was discovered that he held dual citizenship with France. The employee testified that he "would not renounce [his] French citizenship for a job," and so the revocation was upheld on administrative appeal.[2] In another recent case, a person born in the United States with dual Japanese-U.S. citizenship was denied a clearance even though she agreed to destroy her Japanese passport. "She has close emotional ties to both nations," the administrative judge concluded. "One thing that became clear is that she has certain aspects of her personal long-term relationship between the U.S. and Japan to work out. For example, it appears that Applicant moved to the U.S. to be with her fiancé, not because she felt an overwhelming desire to be only an American citizen into the future."[3] On that basis, the judge could not find that there was little or no potential for "pressure, coercion, exploitation or duress," presumably by the government of Japan.

The rule against security clearances for dual citizens may or may not have made sense in the old era in which citizenship presented zero-sum loyalties. It also may or may not have made sense in an era in which "Top Secret" had some real meaning. Today, more than five million Americans have security clearances. There are many jobs for which it is a requirement, both in and out of government. Of course, no one has a "right" to a security clearance.[4] But even for purposes of security clearances, some forms of discrimination would be unacceptable. We would never accept a security clearance regime that disqualified individuals who belonged to the Catholic Church on the theory that they might do Rome's bidding. Might the disqualification of dual citizens represent a similarly unsustainable kind of discrimination? We have seen how, for most of modern history, dual citizenship was considered an anomaly at best and an abomination at worst. It is now a commonplace of globalization. The sequence has been from strong disfavor to toleration; some states have moved to embrace the status. Could dual citizenship now achieve the status of a right?

This chapter makes a bounded case for recognizing a right to acquire and maintain dual citizenship. It does so through the optics of freedom of association and liberal autonomy values. Citizenship comprises both a form of association and a vehicle for individual identity. The liberal state has no business obstructing alternate national ties in the absence of a compelling interest. That interest once existed, to the extent that dual nationality destabilized interstate relations, and explains the historical opprobrium attached to the status. Laws directed at reducing the incidence of dual citizenship may also unjustifiably burden the exercise of political rights. Today, the material downside risks (if any) posed by dual citizens have dissipated to the point that the state is no longer justified in suppressing the status.

As described above, dual citizenship was highly disfavored until the end of the twentieth century because of the serious threat that dual nationality once posed to world order. States engaged in the human equivalent of turf contests over individuals to whom they both laid claim. State power was correlated to control of resources, and states sought to control resources, physical and human.[5] Just as world order was undermined by competing claims to territory, so too with persons.

The historical threat posed by dual nationals was indirect rather than direct. There was nothing essentially immoral about multiple national connections, nor were dual nationals enabled by their status to harm the state. By blurring the boundaries of human community between states, the status destabilized interstate relations. The problem resulted from legal conventions. Dual nationality was the chink in the armor of sovereignty, a condition that the logic of sovereignty could not process. As Alexander Aleinikoff and Douglas Klusmeyer put it, "The fundamental rule of the international regime is that states should look after their own, and only their own."[6] Individual agency had little to do with problem; the worst that could be said of dual nationals is that they sometimes sought strategically to use their alternate nationality for purposes of diplomatic protection. The indirect nature of the threat, however, made it no less serious. Because the ultimate risk of dual nationality was to provoke the antagonism of other states, it was more serious than the prospect of "disloyalty." That explains why states were so intent on eradicating the status.

Isolating the source of disfavor for dual nationality also explains its more recent acceptance. Sovereignty, such as it is, no longer allows states full discretion in the treatment of nationals. That eliminates the architectural feature of international society that had rendered dual nationality a threat to interstate order. Other developments have incidentally further diminished the threat. The overall global setting had also become more stable. The endpoint is that dual citizenship does not pose a material social cost. This changes the balance in evaluating the justification for residual governmental interference with the status.

In short, dual citizens are no longer an exceptional source of conflict in a world in which interstate conflict has been reduced. They do not impose other direct costs on states. This is reflected in the more recent practice of states. Where dual nationality was once highly disfavored, if not outlawed, it has become widely accepted. Many states no longer pursue strategies intended to suppress dual nationality. Many have abandoned the practice under which naturalization in another country automatically resulted in loss of citizenship. Under the new majority practice, those who naturalize maintain their original citizenship as a default position. With respect to those born with dual citizenship, few states now require election at the age of majority. Both of these changes in state practice have made dual citizenship legally sustainable in many instances. As described in the previous chapter, some among so-called "sending" states have determined that dual citizenship is in their national interest.

## The Individual View

These observations frame dual citizenship in terms of state interest: previously a clear detriment, more recently a neutral quantity, and now perhaps a benefit. Historically, individual interests in the status were ignored. To the extent they were considered at all, it was by way of asserting the congruence of state and individual interests in combating the status. It is true that in many cases dual nationality translated into dual obligations, especially with respect to military service, and that individuals shared an interest in shedding one or the other of their nationalities (typically that of the state of non-residence). This individual interest in avoiding dual nationality was dressed up as resolving associated "psychological difficulties" with the status, working from the loyalty tropes described above.[7] No allowances were made in the commentary or elsewhere for the possibility that persons eligible for more than one nationality would want to maintain them.

Today, dual citizenship is a desirable status in most cases for most individuals. State acceptance of the status has often been as a result of expatriate lobbying, demonstrating the self-interest. Fewer states require military service,[8] and among those that do, bilateral arrangements have resolved duplicative military service obligations for those holding dual citizenship.[9] Taxes are now primarily assessed on criteria other than citizenship, usually on the basis of residence. (The United States is exceptional in taxing its citizens habitually resident abroad.) To the extent that duplicative tax obligations arise as a result of dual citizenship or residence, they have also been mitigated by treaty in most cases.

So additional citizenships pose few additional obligations. They may pose some added benefits, among them rights of entry and residence, some public benefits (most additionally contingent on residence, like educational benefits), eligibility for employment, and the like. Although these benefits are usually not dramatic, where the costs of securing and/or maintaining an additional citizenship are effectively zero, dual citizenship makes sense from the individual's perspective whenever it supplies a non-trivial benefit. (Sometimes a trivial one will do, as with my own initial motivation for securing German citizenship—reduced admission rates at EU museums.) That explains the higher incidence of pairings in which at least one citizenship is premium, especially in the sense of travel benefits and entry rights.

It is one thing to frame dual citizenship as an individual interest, another to frame it as an individual right. There are alternate bases for establishing a right to acquire and/maintain dual citizenship. (It should go without saying that any right to dual citizenship is premised on underlying eligibility for more than one citizenship. I am not making a case that individuals can simply decide they want dual citizenship and then claim it.) The first works from a conception of citizenship as identity and as a form of association. The other plays citizenship as necessary to perfecting political rights of self-governance. Both cases are theoretically strong and enjoy growing indirect support in practice. They still must overcome deep-seated social and cultural norms against dual nationality, the heavy mantle of immorality that long draped the status. These norms are stickier than merely legal ones, and it will take something on the order of a cognitive shift to establish dual citizenship as a right.

How would such a right be vindicated? For purposes of the rights analysis, the key is not so much how individuals secure dual citizenship but rather how they are obstructed from securing or maintaining the status. The right would constrain states from policing the status. With respect to dual citizenship acquired at birth through mixed parentage, for example, states historically attempted to combat dual nationality by requiring election at the age of majority. The right in this context would be asserted against either or both states to the extent they required election, allowing the individual to maintain the status into adulthood. With respect to dual citizenship resulting from naturalization, some states of origin (Japan, for example) persist in terminating original citizenship upon the acquisition of another citizenship (an expatriation mechanism). The right in this context would be asserted against the country of origin, to maintain original citizenship notwithstanding the acquisition of the additional citizenship. Finally, there is dual citizenship which results from naturalization but for the requirement of the naturalizing state that the applicant terminate original citizenship (an effective renunciation requirement—effective in the sense that it goes beyond "an empty verbal gesture").[10] A right to dual citizenship in that case would be asserted against the state of prospective naturalization.

## Dual Citizenship as Associative Freedom

To the extent that citizenship is taken as a form of membership, it is not clear what grounds there are to restrict it. Citizenship is like membership in other organizations, affiliations that define identity. Membership in the state is akin to membership in religions, clubs, non-governmental organizations, and political parties.[11] These memberships may have both instrumentalist and non-instrumentalist motivations. As a matter of both constitutional and international law, states may not restrict membership in non-state entities without some good reason. For instance, the International Covenant on Civil and Political Rights provides that "[e]veryone shall have the right to freedom of association with others," derogable only where "necessary . . . in the interests of national security or public safety, public order, the protection of public health or morals or the protection of the rights and freedoms of others."[12] Where one state is willing to accept an individual as a member, can another state burden that relationship? That's the proposition with respect to the election, expatriation, and renunciation requirements. The state imposing the requirement is interfering with "association with others."

That is, assuming citizenship in another state qualifies as such. It is self-evidently associational in an everyday sense, involving the coming together of individuals in a structured organization to advance material and sentimental interests. To the extent it implicates redistribution, citizenship has material ends. But it also clearly implicates an affective attachment. As Peter Schuck observes, citizenship provides a focus of "emotional energy on a scale capable of of satisfying deep human longings for solidarity, symbolic identification, and community."[13] The question then is whether the fact that the association takes place in the structure of a (foreign) state removes citizenship from the category for rights purposes, so that no heightened justification is required for obstructing the activity. Membership and participation in foreign associations, including foreign political associations, is protected activity. Without a compelling justification, the government cannot burden membership in a foreign-based human rights group or the Catholic Church, even though both might challenge home-state policies and interests. Membership in another state shouldn't be any different.

It's no excuse that would-be dual citizens might have other institutional vehicles through which to express their alternative national attachment. In the United States, there is a long tradition of homeland-oriented, non-governmental forms of association such as the Knights of Columbus and the Ancient Order of Hibernians around which immigrant communities have organized. In the era in which dual nationality was condemned, these entities supplied a sort of surrogate home for original nationality, and it might be supposed that they continue to supply an adequate outlet for the associational impulse. (For that matter, it may today in many cases be possible to join foreign political parties, which could be taken as organizational proxies for citizenship.) But that would involve judgment on the part of the state and the constraint of individual autonomy. An individual might be willing to associate with the state of Italy but not the Knights of Columbus. The same holds for associational forms of the new diasporas, such as hometown associations; they satisfy parallel but differentiated needs from membership in the homeland state. Citizenship is a distinct vehicle for identity.

Because citizenship qualifies as associational activity, expatriation as the result of naturalization in another country should require special cause. Far from the current international legal regime under which states have discretion to terminate the citizenship of those who naturalize elsewhere, states should be held to a more exacting test. In U.S. constitutional law, this test is described as "strict scrutiny," under which only a narrowly tailored, compelling governmental interest will work to sustain a restriction on associational activity.[14]

The expatriation mechanism doesn't pass this test. In most cases, the balance will be lopsided in favor of protecting an associational right to acquire membership in another state without risk of forfeiting original citizenship. As described above, dual citizens no longer pose the serious (albeit indirect) threat to stable interstate relations that explained the intense historical disfavor for the status. Why should Japan be allowed to expatriate a Japanese citizen when she acquires U.S. citizenship? There is no risk that the dual Japanese-U.S. citizen will undermine peaceful relations between the two states. To the extent that direct security threats are the (implausible) concern, they can be addressed through more surgical forms of regulation, like espionage laws.

A handful of pairings pose a closer question in what Rainer Bauböck calls "complex cases,"[15] for example in the contexts of Central and Eastern Europe and of the former Soviet republics. Moldova might justify prohibiting dual citizenship on the theory that thousands of dual Moldovan-Russian citizens in the border Transnistrian region would increase the risk of Moldovan-Russian conflict. Considered solely from a state interests perspective, Moldova could rationally adopt an expatriation mechanism, under which any citizen acquiring the citizenship of another country would lose Moldovan nationality. Bauböck argues that extending citizenship of a kin state to transborder minorities is "a different matter" to the extent that it destabilizes "clearly demarcated" territorial jurisdictions.[16] The claim highlights regional contexts in which some of the old-world justifications for suppressing dual citizenship still seem plausible.

But in today's world that justification for suppressing dual citizenship doesn't count as compelling (leaving aside the self-governance issues, discussed below, implicated by the deprivation of political rights that come with citizenship). In fact, Russia has played the citizenship card in the context of its encroachments in Georgia and the Ukraine. It has been accused of undertaking a strategy of "passportization," handing out passports en masse to Russian co-ethnics.[17] Russia then used the alleged mistreatment of these newly minted citizens as a justification for military incursions (and, in the context of Crimea, its annexation). That was putting an old-world playbook to work; during the nineteenth and early twentieth centuries, mistreatment of citizens supplied a lawful basis for the use of force (it was the basis for the American tradition of gunboat diplomacy, for example). Today, short of a UN Security Council authorization, the alleged mistreatment of citizens will no longer suffice to validate military interventions. Passportization didn't fool anyone; the international community universally rejected Russia's make-weight citizenship arguments in Georgia and Ukraine. As the Parliamentary Assembly of the Council of Europe later resolved in the context of Russia's actions, "justifying the military actions by a member State against other member States by the need to protect its own citizens is not compatible with Council of Europe standards."[18] In any case, Russia's aggressive behavior was not contingent on the citizenship status of persons in those former Soviet territories.

Better to allow Russian ethnics in these jurisdictions to maintain dual citizenship as Russians than to deny them the status and bolster Russia's claims of discrimination. Moldova amended its citizenship law to recognize dual citizenship in 2002, and now hosts a large number of dual Russian-Moldovan citizens (and an even larger contingent of dual Romanian-Moldovan citizens). That won't solve Moldova's difficulties with Russia, but it probably won't compound them, either. Contrast Moldova's approach to that of Latvia. Latvia not only refuses to recognize dual Russian-Latvian citizenship, it has obstructed the acquisition of Latvian citizenship by long-term Russian ethnic residents, extending them instead a "non-citizen" status something like permanent residence. The discrimination has drawn fire from the OSCE and the Council of Europe. In March 2014, Russia enacted a measure allowing these Latvian Russian speakers to acquire Russian citizenship. Latvia's resistance to dual citizenship won't help defuse tensions with its former occupier.

The associational frame supplies a strong argument against expatriation, where the homeland state terminates an individual's citizenship for naturalizing elsewhere. It also helps problematize the practice under which naturalizing states require an applicant to terminate original citizenship as a condition to naturalization (the effective renunciation condition). Assuming an individual who is otherwise qualified for naturalization, the imposition of a renunciation condition also burdens associational activity. In both cases the maintenance/acquisition of one state identity requires the sacrifice of the other. The rights case against the renunciation requirement may be stronger insofar as the citizenship being denied is citizenship (in most cases) in the country of new habitual residence, where the state attachment will loom larger on an everyday basis. Some observers have made justice-based arguments that access to citizenship should not be made contingent on renunciation of prior citizenship.[19]

As for the dual citizenship acquired at birth, it presents perhaps the best application for the associational analysis, especially where it results from mixed-status parentage. In the typical case, a child's identity is molded by the parents' identities. The child of parents of different citizenships is likely to identify with both. The formerly common requirement that birthright dual nationals undertake a choice at majority (the election requirement) interferes with the individual's autonomy to maintain each connection, both of which will often be central to identity. The result of imposed election is to force a choice between parents. The strength of the case for protecting the maintenance of dual citizenship in these cases is reflected in the 1997 European Convention on Nationality, which requires parties to allow the maintenance of dual citizenship acquired automatically at birth.[20]

Karen Knop argues that the relational elements of citizenship—in effect, situating citizenship in the family—requires the acceptance of dual citizenship resulting from mixed status parentage, working from the "psychological, physical, and material relevance of a common nationality for the mother-child relationship." More broadly, relational nationality acknowledges that

> [l]oyalty to our state of birth is bound up with our love for our parents and siblings, who are part of the state; it is possible that loyalty to a spouse's state is affected by our love for him or her or by our love for our children, who have ties to that state.[21]

That covers birth dual citizenship by mixed parentage. It also covers naturalization as a result of spousal relationships, which can be burdened by expatriation and effective renunciation requirements. Knop works from feminist premises and the intensity of family ties. Eligibility for dual citizenship is often generated by such ties. But even where family ties are absent, the associational optic is relational. The logic applies to dual citizenship generally, whatever the source of "loyalty" to the relevant states. In the absence of governmental interest, there is no cause to suppress the actuation of such sentiments.

## Dual Citizenship as Political Right

Dual citizenship also implicates self-governance values. Formal status as a citizen is typically necessary to the perfection of political rights. If dual citizenship is obstructed, with the result that an individual is denied a citizenship for which she would otherwise by eligible, political rights are likely to be compromised, and the acquisition and maintenance of dual citizenship thus becomes a protectable predicate status.

Self-governance values are most clearly implicated where a state requires a naturalization applicant to terminate her citizenship of origin as a condition for naturalization. Renunciation becomes a part of the price of naturalization. The magnitude of this price will vary. In some cases it may be low, for instance, in the case of a refugee who has fled persecution in his country of origin. In many cases, it will be high for material and/or sentimental reasons. By surrendering homeland citizenship, emigrants may be giving up property ownership, entry rights, and public benefits. They will also lose political leverage by which to influence homeland policies salient to emigrant interests. The sentimental costs are probably more prevalent, for all the reasons discussed above in the context of associative freedoms. The characterization of original citizenship as something like first love suggests not just an expressive but an intimate association.

Renunciation thus burdens naturalization. An individual from country A who immigrates to country B and now habitually resides there must pay for full political rights in the form of terminating his formal connection to country A. International law has traditionally afforded states full discretion to impose a renunciation requirement on naturalizing citizens. But this discretion is increasingly in tension with the liberal self-governance paradigm. Liberal theory works from the premise that that those territorially present are members of "society," are affected by governmental action, and should be able to participate in self-governance on the basis of equality. That's why liberal theory has assumed the virtue of low barriers to naturalization. Some theorists have asserted the necessity of a naturalization option after some period of residence.[22] Under that approach, the renunciation condition offends liberal values, insofar as it contributes to a disconnect between society (defined in territorial terms) and the polity (defined by citizenship status).

The expatriation and election mechanisms are more consistent with the territorial foundations of liberal governance paradigms. The expatriation mechanism reinforces the correlation of territorial location and citizenship, in the typical case by terminating the citizenship of an individual who has moved to another country on a permanent basis. Likewise the election requirement, insofar as individuals forced to choose between citizenships will choose the citizenship associated with residence. But self-governance no longer works on a territorially delimited basis. As explained in chapter 6, non-resident citizens will often have a stake in the politics of their homelands. Political rights, even external ones, shouldn't have to be sacrificed at a false altar of exclusive national attachment.

Nor would a norm protective of dual citizenship impinge on other individual rights. As suggested in the previous chapter, dual citizenship does not violate principles of political equality. (This has sometimes been deployed to obstruct acceptance of the status, most prominently in German citizenship reform debates in the late 1990s.) Dual citizens don't get extra political rights within the polities of which they are members; as Bauböck observes, "As long as these votes are not aggregated at a higher level, the principle of one person/one vote has not been infringed."[23]

True, a dual citizen might be said to have multiple channels of access to global institutions, which might be supposed to afford him greater status than those holding a single citizenship only. But global governance is not formally democratic on the basis of equality, except at the level of states. (Considered at the level of the individual, the citizen of San Marino has far greater clout than the citizen of China.) Representation through states in international institutions is highly attenuated. Moreover, the channels to global influence are multiple and include non-state vehicles. Amnesty International, the Catholic Church, and Google clearly have influence in international decision making, sometimes with formal status (many non-state actors have observer status—sometimes involving decision-making powers—in international institutions).

## Setting Dual Citizenship Right

Suggesting a right to maintain dual citizenship is novel, the normative logic notwithstanding. The ferocity of old cultural norms against the status has left little space for a rights framing, even as practice has shifted toward tolerance, at the option of the state. But there are signs that dual citizenship may come to be conceived as a protectable right. Individuals who hold or are eligible for dual citizenship are seeking the change of relevant legal regimes where states continue to obstruct the status. The fact that states increasingly accept the practice helps lay the groundwork for the assertion of a right. This is true as a matter of cultural cognition; as fewer states reject the status, the holdouts start to look out of line with prevailing practice on a matter that affects individual interests. It is also true as a matter of law; state practice is important to establishing the existence of a right.

Recent experience in Germany highlights the connection of dual citizenship and political rights. Germany had long resisted acceptance of dual citizenship. As Kay Hailbronner observes, "dual nationality has always been considered to be inconsistent with the concept of loyalty and attachment to Germany."[24] Naturalization applicants were required to prove termination of original citizenship. Opposition to dual citizenship was a major factor in Germany's longstanding rejection of jus soli (dating at least to 1913), insofar as the children of immigrants to Germany would in many cases have been born with German citizenship and the citizenship of their parents. Coupled with other restrictive naturalization policies, the result was a sizable immigrant population denied citizenship on an intergenerational basis. Even children whose grandparents had immigrated to Germany were not entitled to citizenship at birth; as of 2003, about one-fifth of all non-citizens present in Germany had been born there.[25] This largely Turkish community protested the denial of political participation rights for lack of citizenship at the same time that its members sought to maintain their Turkish nationality. International human rights NGOs condemned the restrictive aspects of the German citizenship regime.

Legislation enacted in 1999 after a bitter political fight took the important step of accepting jus soli citizenship in some cases. Although there were many factors driving the reform, "international human rights norms were omnipresent in the debate."[26] With respect to dual citizenship, the 1999 measure kicked the can down the road. Those born in Germany after 1990 to parents legally resident for at least seven years were extended German citizenship from birth. But those born with another nationality had to pick one or the other before their twenty-third birthday in what was known as the "option model," a contemporary version of the nineteenth-century election requirement. As the first cohort under the law faced the required choice in the early 2010s, it became clear that the scheme wasn't sustainable, and the debate was reengaged. The Social Democratic Party (SPD) made the issue a condition to renewing participation in the grand coalition with Angela Merkel's Christian Democrats after the 2013 parliamentary elections. The result was a 2014 law accepting dual citizenship for those born with it, so long as they have lived in Germany for at least eight years prior to the age of twenty-one. The measure was inflected with a rights discourse. As the German government's commissioner for human rights argued in advocating the reform, "if we work on the assumption that everyone should have the right to participate in the democratic process, then we have to make naturalization even easier and not make a big deal about dual citizenship."[27]

The reform was partly about political inclusion. It addressed discriminatory aspects of Germany's approach to dual citizenship. Condemned in principle, dual citizenship had already been increasingly accepted by Germany in practice—for some. Citizens of other EU member states and Switzerland have been permitted by law since 2007 to retain their citizenship of origin after naturalizing as Germans, as are citizens of states who do not permit expatriation (a few states, such as Morocco, continue to adhere to the regime of perpetual allegiance that pervaded nineteenth-century practice). The 1999 law allowed for the retention of original citizenship in other "exceptional circumstances" by bureaucratic discretion. As a result, more than 50% of those naturalized in Germany since 2008 have maintained their prior citizenship in the process.[28] Meanwhile, native-born Germans who naturalize elsewhere are able to retain their German citizenship upon a showing of any continuing ties to Germany, a possibility of which the German "expat" community is increasingly taking advantage of in the United States and other destination states.

Those pushing to scrap the option model were able to exploit the ways in which the scheme discriminated against Turkish immigrants. It still does: although many of those born in Germany with Turkish and German citizenship will now be able to retain both into adulthood, those immigrating from Turkey are not entitled to retain Turkish citizenship upon naturalization as Germans even though EU-origin applicants can. That may not be sustainable: many SPD members voiced disappointment at the 2014 compromise, as have Turkish government officials. It will be difficult for Germany to sustain a regime against charges of unjustified national-origins discrimination in the face of its now-clear willingness to accept dual citizenship in many cases. If a Greek national can retain her citizenship when naturalizing as a German, why can't a Turk?

## Unsustainable Discriminations

Germany is hardly alone among European states in moving to allow emigrants to retain citizenship as they naturalize in their states of new permanent residence, in part the result of pressure from the emigrants themselves. Most European states already accept dual citizenship among immigrants as well (Germany stands as a laggard in this respect). Those that haven't may move to broad acceptance all at once. In 2014, Denmark enacted legislation allowing dual citizenship both for external Danes naturalizing elsewhere and for immigrants naturalizing as Danes. As in Germany, a large proportion of immigrants (estimated at around 40%) were already retaining homeland citizenship through exceptions. But it was pressure from native-born Danish citizens living elsewhere that was politically crucial to the change. One external Dane framed the issue in autonomy terms: "Citizenship is such an important part of one's identity that forcing someone to choose is the same as forcing a child to choose between their mother or father or a mother to choose between her children."[29]

The Netherlands presents the most prominent example where a renunciation requirement for immigrants was eliminated (in 1991) and then reinstated (in 1997) and toughened (in 2010). By way of preempting the discrimination charge, a bill was introduced in the Dutch parliament that would have terminated the citizenship of any Dutch citizen naturalizing in another country, eliminating liberal exceptions to a general rule of expatriation.[30] The proposal provoked outrage among external Dutch citizens, who collected 25,000 signatures for a petition against the bill,[31] which was shelved. Meanwhile, many resident in the Netherlands are ending up with dual citizenship notwithstanding the renunciation requirement, from which refugees and those whose home countries do not recognize renunciation are exempted. An estimated 1.2 million in the Netherlands hold dual citizenship, 7% of the total population. The thumb can't easily be put back into the dike even where there is a will to try.

The move to apply non-discrimination principles to dual citizenship is evident elsewhere. Where states are allowing some citizens to maintain dual citizenship, they are finding it more difficult to deny it to others. In Australia, the fact that immigrants could keep their original citizenship upon naturalization in Australia (not being required to renounce their original citizenship) was an important factor in allowing native-born Australians to keep their original citizenship after naturalizing elsewhere (eliminating it as a ground for expatriation). As the leading authority on Australian citizenship observed, "there was a basic inequality in the former system. . . . [S]ome people were able to be dual citizens and others were not entitled to this privilege; it depended upon the order of obtaining the citizenship."[32] A number of African states discriminate in a reverse fashion, allowing birthright citizens to acquire dual nationality at the same time that they require renunciation of those who naturalize.[33] Current Pakistani nationality law allows dual citizenship with sixteen countries (Western European, the United States, Canada, Australia, and a few others). Latvia recently moved to allow dual citizenship with EU, NATO, and a handful of other states, but not (most notably) with Russia. That kind of discrimination will be difficult to sustain. Equality talk in this context indirectly establishes dual citizenship as a protectable interest.

States are also confronting second-order rights issues associated with dual citizenship. The constitutions of several countries bar office-holding by dual nationals—Australia, Jamaica, Bangladesh, Malawi, Nigeria, Pakistan, and Latvia, as well as in Hong Kong. Other countries do so by statute; the Philippines and Moldova are examples. In these states, politicians will occasionally hurl charges that their political enemies are secret dual citizens. The spats have a somewhat "gotcha" feel, a lighter version of anti-communist blacklisting. In a 2009–10 drama that threatened the ruling party's slim majority, four members of the Jamaican parliament were unseated when it was discovered that they held U.S. citizenship. (In another example of nationality-related discrimination, Jamaican officeholders are permitted to hold citizenship in Commonwealth countries but not others.)

Some states have considered shelving such restrictions. They have proved difficult to dislodge, as is often the case with constitutional provisions, especially those with ostensibly patriotic purposes.[34] But the debates about constraints on dual-citizen office-holding are now sometimes being framed as infringing individual rights. A recent (failed) effort in Pakistan was conceived as eliminating impermissible discrimination against dual nationals, "whose allegiance to Pakistan should not be in doubt," in the characterization of the Association of Pakistani Lawyers.[35] A Sri Lankan commentator deployed human rights arguments against a recent constitutional amendment that has been interpreted to bar dual-citizen office-holding.[36] The fact that restrictions on office-holding are being contested at all could presage an endpoint at which dual citizens are protected not only in their status but from discrimination on that basis.

In the counter-terror context, some states are discriminating against dual citizens in expatriation measures. In part to avoid the statelessness that would result from terminating the citizenship of mono-nationals, in 2014 Canada enacted legislation allowing for the expatriation of terrorists and those convicted of other security crimes but only where the individual has or could claim the citizenship of another state. The United Kingdom has had in place a broader measure allowing deprivation of citizenship where it would be "conducive to the public good" of dual nationals and naturalized citizens who could acquire another citizenship. Similar measures have been proposed in Australia, the Netherlands, and Austria. As Rayner Thwaites observes, these regimes offend equality as between citizens. Where a dual and mono-national engage in the same conduct, only the former can be stripped of his citizenship, imputing "a lesser degree of 'belonging' to dual citizens than mono-citizens."[37] The motivation to avoid statelessness is irrelevant. "What makes the conditional nature of their citizenship objectionable is how it marks them as lower in standing relative to their fellow citizens," argues Matthew Gibney. "It has nothing to do with their relationship to another, different state."[38] The Canadian measure is the subject of a constitutional challenge in the Canadian courts, a ruling on which could imply an underlying right to maintain dual citizenship.

The same goes for the other limited contexts in which dual citizens face discrimination. In the United States, private employers can't discriminate against dual citizens in hiring decisions.[39] The U.S. security clearance restrictions described at the beginning of the chapter no longer make much sense. They force a choice that shouldn't be forced: between a job and an identity. That sort of discrimination-based challenge could ripen into a claim to protect a right to maintain dual citizenship. U.S. courts were once reticent about intervening in the national security context, even when rights have been at issue. That has changed in recent years.[40] Although the current doctrine affords the executive branch tremendous discretion with respect to security clearance decisions, the judiciary's less deferential stance in foreign affairs could make the courts more receptive to a discrimination claim.

## Shifting International Law

International law shows more direct signs of validating an emerging right to dual citizenship. The nineteenth and twentieth centuries saw multiple efforts aimed at eliminating the status. Although states could not see their way to coordinating citizenship laws to that end, they agreed on the objective. Past multilateral conventions relating to nationality had uniformly condemned dual citizenship. The 1930 Hague Convention expressed "the ideal towards which the efforts of humanity should be directed in this domain is the abolition of all cases both of statelessness and of double nationality." In 1963, European states negotiated a treaty finding that "cases of multiple nationality are liable to cause difficulties" and mandating "joint action to reduce as far as possible the number of cases of multiple nationality."[41] As one commentator concludes, "Suffice to say that, for a considerable period of time, international law served to organize inter-state relations according to a basic understanding that dual or multiple nationality was considered undesirable, problematic and deviant from the ideal of 'one nationality for each and everyone.'"[42]

By contrast, the 1997 European Convention on Nationality refrains from condemning multiple nationality as a problem, instead noting "the desirability of finding appropriate solutions to consequences of multiple nationality and in particular as regards the rights and duties of multiple nationals." In its operative provisions, the convention requires states to permit dual citizenship in the case of children born with the status and in the case of persons acquiring nationality automatically by marriage. The Convention also provides that states may not make termination of original nationality a condition to naturalization where such termination is not possible or cannot be reasonably required—hence the exceptions to the renunciation requirement in such countries as the Netherlands and Germany.[43]

The 1997 European Convention may represent a watershed, creating a foundation on which to build more expansive protections under international law.[44] More recent soft-law instruments evidence increasing normative pressure on states to accept dual citizenship. The Parliamentary Assembly of the Council of Europe recently concluded that "the prohibition of multiple nationalities should no longer be an obstacle to the integration of large groups of long-term resident aliens. The renunciation of the nationality of origin should not be a necessary precondition for the acquisition of the nationality of the host country."[45] Recognizing the "reality of multiple identities," the OSCE's 2012 Ljubljana Guidelines on Integration of Diverse Societies likewise called for greater acceptance of the status: "Providing access to citizenship to long-term residents while not requiring the renunciation of a previous citizenship encourages participation and a sense of belonging and may contribute to the integration of societies." The Ljubljana Guidelines also asserted the application of non-discrimination principles in regulating access to citizenship and stressed the importance of allowing children to retain multiple citizenships acquired at birth.[46] Meanwhile, human rights organizations are starting to press holdout states to liberalize their rules on dual citizenship. The Open Society Institute, for example, has called upon African states to accept dual citizenship for both birthright and naturalized citizenship, eliminating expatriation and renunciation requirements.[47]

Dual citizenship has been normalized as an incident of globalization. Nonetheless, some states will continue to obstruct individuals from holding the status. Acceptance of the status has been conceived as a matter of policy and state interest. It is now possible to frame acquisition and maintenance of the status as a right, to the extent dual citizenship implicates individual autonomy and self-governance values. Because it no longer poses a substantial threat to state interests, these values are beginning to be vindicated in international norms. Although a hard, universal rule requiring dual citizenship is not an immediate prospect, the emergence of an articulated, protectable right to the status will act like a global nudge. States will have a harder time resisting acceptance in the face of these norms, which will reinforce other incentives. A right to dual citizenship establishes its normativity in addition to its expediency. The combination will help entrench the new place of dual citizenship in the global order.

8

# Dual Citizenship, Declining Citizenship

Interested in acquiring dual citizenship? You may be eligible. It may be a question of doing a little genealogical research, finding the grandparent or great-grandparent who held citizenship in a country with liberal rules of descent. In some cases your ethnicity or religion will be the ticket to an additional nationality. If all else fails, you can buy one.

And why might you be interested? Acquiring citizenship in some cases represents a strong statement of identity. It may also formalize a political voice in a state in which one has a self-governance interest. But there will be many cases in which acquiring another citizenship will be more instrumental than high-minded. Part of my own motivation for acquiring German citizenship was to avoid lines at European ports of entry and to exploit EU-only discounts at continental museums and other attractions. And my other citizenship is American, one of the world's best. Not all citizenships are created equal. If your citizenship of origin is not a premium one, you will have added incentives to acquire an additional nationality. Those with Russian and Chinese passports, for example, face onerous visa requirements in their global travels, even the plutocrats among them. Acquiring a better class of citizenship—in the United States or a member state of the European Union, or even a Caribbean island state—will speed them on their way.

These are not traditional incentives for acquiring citizenship. This chapter describes how dual citizenship is undermining state-based identities, reflecting and accelerating a postnational world. There's an initial paradox here, insofar as plural citizenship putatively facilitates state-based connections. But acceptance of plural citizenship is likely to lower the intensity of the citizen-state affiliation and the intensity of bonds among citizens. A citizenship regime that tolerates dual citizenship will count more members who subordinate the attachment to other national attachments. That's the inevitable corollary of the move from an exclusive to a non-exclusive relationship.

To be sure, as suggested in the preceding chapters, dual citizenship may reap short-term gains for both immigrant-sending and immigrant-receiving states. It is clearly being used as an instrument of state policy by diaspora states, as homeland governments attempt to cement ties to prosperous emigrants. Tolerating dual citizenship also serves receiving states by facilitating naturalization and political assimilation. But in both contexts state policies are defensive, aimed to shore up the increasingly leaky boundaries of national community. Whether they will in fact further state interests, even in the short term, remains to be seen. In the long term, they will almost surely contribute to the dilution of state-based identity. In a subtle, out-of-the-headlines way, dual citizenship is hollowing out the state within, and there's nothing that can be done about it.

## Dual Citizenship in the Interest of the State

One can't establish the end of the nation-state by deploying the growth of dual citizenship. Citizenship is about membership in states, dual citizenship as much as singular citizenship. Dual citizenship evidences the continuing salience of states in the world order.[1] Plural citizenship facilitates the identification of individuals with state-based communities by allowing those individuals to formalize the multiple national attachments they may have as a matter of social fact. In the world that frowned upon dual nationality, secondary national attachments were obstructed. An individual who would have liked to be associated with each of two states was forced to choose between them, diminishing the attachment to the state not chosen. Today, both attachments can be sustained and cultivated through the channels of full membership.

I described in chapter 6 how dual citizenship is thought to serve the interests of sending states. Dual citizenship has emerged as a potential tool for states to cement relations with external communities and to facilitate the repatriation (literal or figurative) of the economic, political, and cultural resources they have come to represent.

But it is not clear that dual citizenship actually serves sending-state interests according to this logic. There is nothing necessarily state-enhancing in this deployment of dual citizenship. Retention of home-country citizenship is in most cases essentially cost-free for emigrants, as few states require payment of taxes, military service, or other obligations from non-resident citizens. In many cases, retention is a passive affair. In cases involving naturalization elsewhere, maintaining original citizenship requires no affirmative act. Where action is required, the data evidences weakness in the state-based tie. When Mexico amended its citizenship law to allow retention of Mexican nationality upon naturalization elsewhere, it also established a streamlined process for the restoration of nationality for the many hundreds of thousands who had lost it under the prior, dual-citizenship-intolerant regime. Only 67,000 applied for restoration during an initial five-year application window.[2]

Dual citizenship has value to external citizen populations. Acceptance of dual citizenship by homeland states allows external populations to secure citizenship in their places of external residence without relinquishing the material and sentimental advantages of retained original citizenship. It allows immigrants to enjoy, in some sense, the best of both worlds. But dual citizenship is not a necessary predicate to maintaining transnational community ties. One doesn't need to be a dual citizen to maintain homeland connections. One doesn't need to be a dual citizen to send remittances. Dual citizenship may facilitate social and economic ties, by making it easier to travel or to own property and operate businesses. But that doesn't necessarily translate into reinforced state ties. Dual citizenship in many cases is not put to work at all. It's a passport unused in a living-room drawer. Where dual citizenship is possible at little cost, it may not correlate with affective ties at any level.

Dual citizenship can serve the interests of receiving states as well as sending states. A system of singular nationality places a high price on naturalization, where terminating original nationality is perceived as costly by the would-be naturalization applicant. For some that cost is too steep, and notwithstanding their eligibility to naturalize, they will refuse to opt in. The failure of a large proportion of immigrants to naturalize poses a challenge to receiving states. Such a denizen population may not assimilate politically, which may in turn also retard social and cultural integration into the community. At some point, the territorial presence of political non-members will undermine the liberal premises of the modern democratic state, even if the non-membership is a matter of choice.

So dual citizenship may make for good naturalization policy, but dual nationality ultimately evidences and further erodes receiving-state solidarities. Receiving states (especially the United States) were histori-cally in a position to set down naturalization and sole nationality as a take-it-or-leave proposition. Today, that receiving states might have to lower the barriers to naturalization by way of enticing applications betrays the diminishing bargaining power of receiving states vis-à-vis potential members. Receiving states can no longer dictate the terms of admission, or do so only at the peril of deterring a significant popula-tion of permanent residents from becoming full members of the polity and of corroding the representative democratic process as a result. Some political theorists advocate that naturalization be at the option of the immigrant (in other words, that naturalization be reduced to a matter of signing up).[3] Others call for the automatic naturalization of long-term residents.[4] That is improbable as a policy matter and problematic even from the perspective of political liberalism, insofar as it constrains the autonomy of individuals to define their own identities. The shift shows that immigrants can no longer be assumed to prefer citizenship in their country of resettlement, even if they are eligible for it. In this frame, the increasing difficulty of "the sale" indicates the diminished quantity that citizenship represents.

## A Nation of Second Choicers

The growing incidence of dual citizenship does more than evidence the decline of citizenship. It also contributes to that decline and the decou-pling of citizenship status from actual parameters of community. In a world that demanded singular citizenship, individuals could be assumed to opt for a particular citizenship because it was their first choice. On average, that choice would reflect a balancing of the affective and instru-mental benefits of one citizenship relative to another. These factors would often point in the same direction and reflect an actual priority of community membership. Naturalization reflected a reprioritization of identity. The acquisition of receiving-state citizenship—as accompanied by the loss of original citizenship—would (again, on average) reflect a change in the order of community ties. Even where old social and cultural ties were maintained, naturalization would evidence their sub-ordination to the new affiliation. Citizenship defined a core community because it coincided with the group for whom receiving state identity was a first choice among national identities.

Dual citizenship cancels this logic. There is no longer any implicit ranking in the citizenship choice. One can acquire citizenship in states to which one has subordinate or even nominal ties without sacrificing one's primary attachment. Some citizens will sustain a substantial tie to another polity in terms of their identity and commitments. That may not be identity-dilutive, at least to the extent that identity and commitment are non-zero-sum quantities. An individual can still be meaningfully attached to one state at the same time as she holds more (or perhaps even equally) significant attachments to others. The child of mixed parentage may be deeply and genuinely enmeshed and identified with the nationalities of each parent, each of which she holds. But the attachment is difficult to measure in the absence of forcing a choice.

Dual citizenship also shifts the dynamics of ordinary naturalization in such a way as to further detach citizenship from social membership. Because of dual citizenship, naturalization may make sense even in the absence of any love for a state of residence. It affords locational security: once a citizen, an individual is absolutely immune to deportation. Naturalization may make one eligible for certain social benefits. In the United States, non-citizens are ineligible for some forms of public relief. They are barred from some types of public-sector employment. Citizens are advantaged with respect to securing the admission of family members. A permanent resident might undertake naturalization to secure any of these advantages without becoming an American in any other sense. Dual citizenship enables the phenomenon because it doesn't force a choice.

As dual citizenship becomes more commonplace, the United States becomes a community of second choicers, with a corresponding loss of filial intensity. Acceptance of dual citizenship in the United States, observes the anthropologist Arjun Appadurai, facilitates its transformation from "being a land of immigrants [to] being one node in a postnational network of diasporas."[5] Samuel Huntington asserts more plainly that "American citizenship becomes simply an add-on to another citizenship."[6] In an increasingly common practice, some immigrants are naturalizing as part of an exit strategy. To insure absolute rights of reentry, they naturalize before returning to their homeland (often at retirement). The sequence is the opposite of historical assimilationist tropes, in which naturalization reflects the final transfer of loyalty from old sovereign to new. It couldn't happen without the acceptance of dual citizenship.

The second-choice phenomenon may be particularly evident in the U.S. context in the absence of strong non-citizenship markers of national community. The strong ethnic or religious identity of a country of origin may trump the thin American one. The United States may once have had a strong civic and cultural identity to which immigrants could "convert." But that identity has become less distinct as it is adopted by the rest of the world. It is no longer special to be a constitutional democracy, as it once was. American culture has gone global, assimilated into the cultures of other countries. Coupled with the material elements of globalization that enable sustained connections with homeland societies, the possibility of dominant, "first love" citizenship is high.

A similar phenomenon is evident in receiving states that (unlike the United States) have their own ethnic, religious, or other socio-cultural markers. A Muslim immigrant to a European state accepting dual citizenship can naturalize in the absence of any genuine identification with the new state of residence. European states are sensitive to this prospect, which explains in part why some have resisted (Germany) or even attempted to reverse (the Netherlands) acceptance of the status.

The analysis applies to sending states as well. Emigrants who transplant their primary locus of social to their new place of residence may retain their original citizenship because retention comes at no cost, the migration of actual identity notwithstanding, especially to subsequent immigrant generations. As retention becomes the default position from a legal perspective and it is renunciation that requires affirmative action on the part of the individual naturalizing elsewhere, most emigrants won't bother with the formal termination of the original tie.

## Citizenships of Convenience, Inherited or Bought

In the context of immigration, at least dual citizens will have real ties to both states. But dual citizenship is also enabling nationality on more attenuated terms. An increasing number of states offer citizenship on the basis of ancestry with no residency requirement. For example, Irish citizenship is available to any individual living anywhere in the world with one grandparent who was born in Ireland, with no requirement that the individual (or her parent) ever have resided in Ireland. It's a diaspora citizenship, broadly speaking, but removed from the emigrating generation. This kind of citizenship wouldn't have many takers if most states continued to police dual citizenship—if naturalization in another state resulted in termination of original citizenship. It wouldn't be worth it to give up citizenship in your state of birth and/or residence for this kind of affinity citizenship. Acquiring Irish citizenship this way may well reflect an important identity, but many will also be interested in the benefits of European Union citizenship that come with it.

Pursuant to a 2014 law, Sephardic Jews can claim Spanish citizenship with no residency condition even though their forbearers have not lived in Spain for more than 500 years. The program is ostensibly a form of atonement for the expulsion of Jews from Spain during the Inquisition. Many Sephardic Jews have maintained a distinctive culture, including through their own language, Ladino, so in many cases there will be a genuine identity that can be affirmed through the extension of citizenship. But others will be taking advantage of the offer primarily to secure EU rights. The program is popular among Israeli citizens who may want to live in the EU as well as Jews looking to escape Venezuela and Turkey, where they face increasing discrimination.[7] From Spain's perspective, the program may prove a low-cost way to attract economically prosperous immigrants. Tellingly, perhaps, Spain has not made a parallel offer to the descendants of Moors also expelled from Spain during the Inquisition. Some have highlighted the discrimination as revealing a cynical motivation.[8] The German law under which I secured German citizenship through my German Jewish refugee father supplies another example of atonement/affinity citizenship, though at closer temporal remove. (The German offer has also been popular among Israelis seeking a second passport.) My ties to Germany are pretty thin—I am a German who speaks no German. It goes without saying that I would not have pursued citizenship under the program if it had jeopardized my U.S. citizenship. It is only with dual citizenship that these programs take hold.

More obviously and purely instrumental are so-called "investor citizenship" programs. In these programs, individuals pay for citizenship. Several Caribbean states offer investor citizenship. Citizenship in the island nation of Dominica can be had for a mere $100,000. St. Kitts and Nevis requires a $250,000 donation to the St. Kitts and Nevis Sugar Industry Diversification Foundation.[9] In return, you get a passport good for visa-free travel to many EU countries, Switzerland, and Canada, among others. EU-member state Cyprus offered citizenship as a consolation to those who lost more than three million euros in the banking collapse there.[10]

Malta's adoption of an investor citizenship program in 2013 was a possible breakthrough moment for investor citizenship. As part not just of the EU but of the free-movement Schengen zone, a Maltese passport is a ticket to work and residence in Berlin, Paris, or London. The program originally sported a 650,000-euro price tag, with no residence requirement. Russian and Chinese nationals could buy Maltese citizenship and proceed directly to other (perhaps more attractive) European destinations. In the face of pushback from the European Commission, the price was raised to 1.15 million euros (350,000 euros in real estate investment and the purchase of at least 150,000 euros in government bonds, so the additional amount is recoupable). Spouses and children can be added for a mere 25,000 euros each. A nominal one-year residency requirement was tacked on, which can be satisfied with minimal physical presence. One broker translates the residence requirement into "a minimum of two visits within the year, or showing water and electricity bills, or having a club membership, or similar."[11] Joining a gym should do the trick.

These schemes are derided by some progressives as "cash for passports."[12] They involve the extension of citizenship without any evidence of social integration, attachment, political or other commitment. In almost all cases investor citizens will retain other nationality when they add the new one to their shopping cart. There would have few takers if dual citizenship was not permitted.

Investor citizenship would have been inconceivable fifty years ago. Most major developed countries have adopted indirect investor citizenship programs with investor residency programs, sometimes known as "golden visas." A $500,000 investment that creates twenty jobs will get you a U.S. green card. Several European states are offering permanent residence status in exchange for real estate investments—a way to prop up sagging housing markets in Portugal, Hungary, Ireland, and Spain, for as little as 160,000 euros.[13] Some of these programs fast-track visa holders to citizenship. There is a pretense, in most of the schemes, that as resident immigrants the visa holders will acquire social solidarities on the way to naturalization, but that is mostly a fiction. Foreigners who can plonk down hundreds of thousands of dollars by way of an entry fee are unlikely to be rubbing elbows with the locals at the neighborhood grocery store. It was in part out of recognition of that social detachment that Canada rescinded its investor visa program in 2014. But Canada is the exception. Investor programs generate high revenues with almost no direct costs. States see that citizenship is worth something, and they are increasingly willing to sell it.

The result is diminished intensity of citizen affiliation. "The selling of nationality," observe Aleinikoff and Klusmeyer, "unquestionably cheapens its value as a form of allegiance."[14] In a regime intolerant of dual citizenship, individuals would be forced to choose among citizenships for which they were eligible. In some cases, instrumental factors might have outweighed sentimental ones, but the calculation had to be made. Do I want the benefits of one citizenship enough that I am willing to give up the other? That balancing no longer has to be undertaken in most cases. Dual citizenship increases the strategic use of citizenship on the part of individuals. The probability that citizenship will be retained or acquired for instrumental purposes has grown with acceptance of multiple citizenship attachments.

## Blurring Borders

Dual citizenship's dilutive effect on state-based identity is also suggested in schematic terms. If one paints the question as one of human geography, the norm against dual citizenship enforced community boundaries. When dual citizenship was policed, an individual was on one side of the line or the other. There was minimal straddling or overlap between communities. Just as territorial borders created spatial disjunctures—in the days before globalization, a border was as consequential as any topographic barrier in terms of social, cultural, and political development—so too did the boundaries of citizenship. By minimizing overlap in state-based communities, the norm against dual nationality made those communities more distinct. That approach eliminated scalar possibilities, instead creating clear binary arrangements that reinforced the sense of other in cross-community perceptions. It rigidly separated the "us" and the "them." Citizenship rules suppressing the incidence of dual nationality contributed to the community identification. The rules made a difference in a world that would otherwise have seen multiple symmetrical memberships.

Acceptance of plural citizenship erodes this distinctiveness among national communities. One scholar suggests that with the acceptance of dual citizenship, "state power is not displaced but simply divided."[15] But the division dissipates the connection of state and citizen. As Samuel Huntington observed, "For a person with two or more citizenships, no one citizenship can be as important as his one citizenship is to a person who only has one."[16] As a matter of human geography, it becomes impossible to say where one community leaves off and another takes on. A graphic representation of citizenship status would now be much more complex than a territorial map, characterized by overlapping spaces rather than separated ones. It is as if territory were to come under various joint regimes, in which more than one government exercised jurisdiction over the same piece of territory. The arrangement is no longer binary. Secondary citizenship threatens the dilution—even the trivialization—of citizenship solidarities.

## Dual Citizenship at the Olympics

Olympic nationality demonstrates how dual citizenship is eating away at citizenship as an institution. Sport supplies interesting terrain on which to explore meanings of loyalty and identity. International competition unifies the state and its citizens, overcoming political, social, and cultural cleavages. The Olympic Games represents the apex of this national solidarity. At the international level, the preferences of consuming publics break down along national lines.

At one time that unity extended to competitors. Olympic athletes were all "of" the countries they represented, social members of the states for whom they played. That is less true today. Recent Olympic Games have produced a litany of stories highlighting anomalous national affiliations of various competitors.

Competitors still have to be citizens of the countries for which they compete—that's required under Rule 41 of the Olympic Charter.[17] But the requirement is as easily gamed as particular countries let it be. Countries with flexible citizenship rules are all too happy to issue passports to Olympic competitors. Some fast-track naturalization, waiving the usual requirements for those who proffer "exceptional services" to the state.[18] Russia has been a serial offender. Becky Hammon and J. R. Holden were both granted quickie citizenship on the way to playing basketball for Russia at the 2008 Beijing Games. Ditto for Victor Ahn, the short-track skater who competed for Russia at Sochi after having won medals for South Korea in 2006. Ahn openly shopped around for a new nationality after feuding with his South Korean coaches.[19] There was little pretense that Hammon, Holden, and Ahn had become Russian in any sense beyond the possession of Russian passports. As Hammon put it, "I'm absolutely still 100 percent an American."[20]

The anomalous situations often involve cases in which athletes aren't good enough for their home-country teams but are good enough for others. That was the case with Hammon and Holden. Others have exploited their ancestry in discovering eligibility for the nationality of countries glad to have them as competitors. Haley Nemra, a born-and-bred American, had never even visited the Marshall Islands before representing that country in track and field in Beijing. Chris Kaman's tenuous connection to Germany—and its Olympic basketball team—was a great-grandparent born there.[21] There is at least one case at the intersection of investor and Olympic citizenship: Gary and Angelica di Silvestri, a pair of unexceptional fortysomething cross-country skiers from Staten Island, represented cheapie-citizenship Dominica at the 2014 Sochi Winter Olympics, at their expense. (In the end, though both marched at the opening ceremonies, neither actually competed.)[22]

The trend is enabled by relaxed citizenship requirements, based on descent, state discretion, or a hefty check. But wide acceptance of dual citizenship also stands as a necessary condition. American athletes wouldn't be competing for Russia, the Marshall Islands, or Dominica if they had to sacrifice their U.S. citizenship as part of the deal. It would be far too high a price to pay, especially given the thin or non-existent ties to the country of competition. With acceptance of dual citizenship, there is no price at all. The case of figure skater Yuko Kavaguti, who renounced her Japanese citizenship in order to compete as part of a Russian pair in the 2010 Vancouver Winter Olympics, is the exception that proves the rule, necessitated by Japan's vigilant (now idiosyncratic) enforcement of rules against dual citizenship.[23] We can assume, by contrast, that Becky Hammon is back to traveling on her U.S. passport.

That wouldn't always have been the case. The phenomenon reflects a shift in norms relating to dual citizenship (and citizenship generally). In the Cold War context, especially, the Olympics supplied an arena for a kind of surrogate warfare. Individuals competing for other countries would have been derided as athletic traitors, especially across the East-West divide. Nor would states have been inclined to accept such individuals as competitors, even where it would have enhanced medal counts. The vortex of state-based loyalty and identity allowed only member-representatives on the playing fields (even more so than the battlefield, where non-citizen contributions have always been accepted). The prospect of an American competing for a Russian basketball team would have been unthinkable during the Cold War. Today, the risk of social opprobrium from the individual's perspective has been minimized, while many states seem happy to cast beyond their national communities to the end of improving their Olympic performance.

Members of the Olympic establishment have been unhappy about the flying of "flags of convenience." As former IOC president Jacques Rogge observed, "From a moral standpoint, we should avoid this transfer market in athletes."[24] Some sporting federations have pushed back with additional nationality rules that operate as an overlay on the Charter's Rule 41. In some sports, the barriers to switching sporting nationality are severe. Under the sporting federation rules of soccer (FIFA)[25] and basketball (FIBA),[26] a player who has participated in a match at the international level for one country is in most cases permanently barred from competing for another. In the name of "protect[ing] the integrity of international competition," ice hockey allows only one "final and irrevocable" transfer of sporting nationality during a player's lifetime.[27] (Though it is not competitor-specific, basketball allows teams to include only one naturalized player.)[28]

These rules may be effective at deterring instrumental nationality for country-hopping purposes in the sporting context, but they are overinclusive and unfair to competitors. Absolute prohibitions on nationality transfer harken back to the nineteenth-century regime of perpetual allegiance described in chapter 1. For soccer and basketball purposes, "once a Brazilian, always a Brazilian." The approach bars transfers even in cases in which the competitor has transferred social attachments to a new state of residence. If a Brazilian citizen plays soccer at the international level for Brazil, and thereafter permanently resettles in the United States and naturalizes as an American, and becomes an American in every other sense, he is still Brazilian as far as FIFA is concerned. That seems unfair and unsustainable in an increasingly migratory world.

Other sports add a "meaningful connection" requirement for those who seek to transfer their sporting nationality or who elect between more than one citizenship in the case of dual citizens who have not previously competed at the international level. In many sports (including archery, equestrian, field hockey, pentathlon, triathlon, and all of the ski competitions), a competitor seeking to transfer sporting nationality must establish residency in the country to which he seeks to transfer affiliation. The International Ski Federation waives the residency requirement where the competitor was born in the territory of the state to which he seeks to transfer sporting nationality or was born to a parent holding nationality in that state.[29] Soccer and ice hockey require dual nationals who have not previously competed at the international level to have a connection beyond citizenship, through place of birth, parentage, or residency.[30]

This approach mimics the approach of the International Court of Justice in its 1954 *Nottebohm* ruling, which denied the international effect of nationality in the absence of a "genuine link" between the state and the individual.[31] The Olympic nationality regime uses this "genuine link" approach to balance sovereign interests to determine nationality on the one hand and to be insulated from transparently instrumental assertions of nationality on the other. But *Nottebohm* no longer provides a workable approach. Affective attachments have become difficult to measure in an era of greater mobility. Countermoves by the Olympic movement and sporting authorities along these lines are unlikely to police instrumental citizenship in anything more than an arbitrary way. They will exclude some who have genuine attachments while including many who do not. The residency requirements adopted by several sporting federations raise barriers to instrumental naturalization, making it harder for a state simply to sign a player for purposes of Olympic competition. On the other hand, residency restrictions can be overcome during the course of training without any meaningful social integration on the athlete's part. One can satisfy a residency requirement without establishing a genuine link or even a modicum of social membership. Many who satisfy requirements by virtue of parentage or place of birth will likewise have little real connection on that basis. The five dual U.S.-German citizens who competed in the 2014 Brazil World Cup were all born in Germany to U.S. armed forces personnel stationed there. They are even less "German" than I am.

It's not only the Olympic establishment that has lamented the rise of nominal nationals among Olympic competitors. Some progressive nationalists also see a threat here. Ayelet Shachar has indicted Olympic "passport-swapping" on broadly normative grounds as undermining "the whole system of fair play and sportsmanship." In Shachar's view, states that recruit athletes from other countries are "unscrupulous" in their "drive to reach the top of the podium."[32] But the trend is unlikely to be reversed. Citizenship is too easily gamed.

The Olympics and other international sporting competitions might be better off eliminating the requirement that participants hold citizenship in the states for which they compete. Citizenship is a formality in many of these cases. It serves no purpose beyond eligibility. The individual is not being made a citizen on the expectation that she will establish or maintain a connection in any other way. There is often no pretense of social membership. The Games could still be organized along national lines. But that wouldn't require that team members have a social or even a formal connection to the state for which they are playing. Professional sports supplies a model in which teams are geographically affiliated but player eligibility is not contingent on geographic origin or attachments. The Olympic equivalent would be to allow athletes to compete for any national team willing to take them. Under this regime, athletes could compete for states of which they are not nationals. We don't require that our ball players hail from the cities they play for. Why should we require any more of our Olympic athletes?

That wouldn't spell the end of sentimental national attachments. All other things reasonably equal, an individual will prefer to compete for a country with which he has an affective attachment.[33] As among all states with which such attachment exists (including multiple states of citizenship), she is likely to prefer the state with which she has the strongest attachment. Sports fans will continue to root for their national teams, even if they are stocked with non- or nominal nationals, just as fans root for Yankee players even if they were born in Boston. But these valences are weak in historical perspective. When all things are not equal, individuals will be open to alternative affiliations. Sports fans may have strong nationally oriented preferences, but Olympic competition is no longer a form of surrogate warfare. As Hammon noted in responding to critics, "This is basketball, not World War III." The continued salience of national affiliation proves only that national association supplies a slice of individual identity composites, a distance removed from the former condition in which it was (at the global level) an identity that trumped all others.

Olympic citizenship nicely demonstrates the postnational proposition that citizenship (and with it the state) is generally in decline. You still need to be a citizen of the country you play for. But in many cases, getting that citizenship is a formality, a matter either of luck (the grandparent) or as a part of a transaction (the state recruiting competitors). Diminished thresholds to eligibility reflect diminished solidarities. Acceptance of dual citizenship is the wedge. Without dual citizenship, most would compete only for their state of dominant social attachment or not at all.

## The Progressive Problem with Dual Citizenship

Olympic citizenship is also a mirror on the surprisingly tepid attitude of progressives toward dual citizenship. One might expect progressives to support liberalized policies toward the status. To the extent that citizenship is about identity, dual citizenship validates autonomy values that are central to the liberal worldview. But to the extent that dual citizenship dilutes solidarity, it threatens the project of the liberal state. Liberal theorists are aware of this threat. Shachar has broadened "Olympic citizenship" into a concept that includes investor and affinity citizenship regimes.[34] Competition among states for money and talent is hollowing out the national community.

Progressives are especially critical of investor citizenship, which they see as the crass commodification of a sacred public good. But even in its more benign forms, dual citizenship makes them fidget. While acknowledging the positive aspect of dual citizenship in "facilitat[ing] the spread of transnational communities of descent," for example, Noah Pickus warns that if "pursued indiscriminately, dual citizenship risks exacerbating the process of alienation and fragmentation already at work within the United States."[35] Editorialist Josh Marshall may be in favor of legalizing undocumented immigrants. But he rejects dual citizenship as inconsistent with full commitment to the political community. Marshall doesn't think "there should be such a thing as dual citizenship," harkening back to Theodore Roosevelt's characterization a century ago. "In my mind it's almost a contradiction in terms."[36]

These lamentations are well founded, as this chapter hopes to demonstrate. Dual citizenship does undermine national bonds. This chapter thus supplies a strong small-"d" democratic argument for reversing the near-universal tolerance for dual citizenship. If dual citizenship were suppressed, it would strengthen the state in its constructive functions. The stronger the bonds felt among citizens, the more citizenship can serve as a platform for redistribution. Dual citizenship undermines those bonds. It loosens membership rules in a way that diminishes the meaning of membership itself. Insofar as citizenship comes to reflect less intensive communal bonds, the state is less likely to serve as a vehicle for robust redistributionist and rights-protective policies, which in turn will result in waning institutional power. The success of the state as a vehicle for vindicating justice can be built only on "communities of character."[37] Dual citizenship subtly destabilizes a state's capacity for self-definition.

If citizenship were a matter of policy within the exclusive control of states, these dilutive tendencies could be reversed. States could revert to a position of intolerance for the status. Many conservatives would agree, albeit for reasons that cater more to national chauvinism and/or anti-immigration politics. When arch-conservative congresswomen Michelle Bachmann revealed that she had acquired Swiss citizenship through her husband, she was excoriated by her political fellow travelers, and she quickly backed down.[38] Accidental dual citizen Ted Cruz renounced his happenstance Canadian citizenship. The coda to this description, the conclusion to this book, might be a call to return to past vigilance against the status. One might even expect it to draw support from across the political spectrum.

But the increasing incidence of dual citizenship cannot be stopped by the state or anyone else. It will not be legislated away. Too many important mainstream political constituencies have availed themselves of the status (powerful external citizen communities not the least of them). As described in the previous chapter, international law is moving to protect the status, which will raise the cost of attempting to suppress it. Sending states see it as a way of cementing sustained homeland ties, with corresponding economic returns. For receiving states, dual citizenship facilitates naturalization, which in turn accelerates assimilation. Whether or not such interests are actually advanced, acceptance of dual citizenship comes at little or no short-term material cost from the perspective of the state or existing citizens. Added or retained citizens do not, generally speaking, pose a drain on the public fisc or other resources by the fact of their citizenship status. Benefits forthcoming to individuals (as well as obligations owed to states) are generally determined by residence, not citizenship. Calculating interests on a short-term basis points to acceptance.

## Membership Has Its Privileges

Citizenship is still worth something. For a U.S. citizen such as myself, the added benefit of a German passport is minimal and likely to stay that way. I'm probably too old ever to move to the EU, whatever fantasies my EU citizenship might enable. For my children, there is still significant potential. If they want to take advantage of EU educational or professional opportunities, their German citizenship could make a difference, possibilities for which their mono-citizen counterparts may be ineligible. It's a plus. I have to confess on some occasions to indulging in a kind of humblebrag in telling others about my German citizenship, in the sheepish way that a colleague might let on that he is flying business class for a work trip. I've felt a little embarrassed about it with some who would like to secure EU citizenship but can't. I feel more embarrassed with one friend whose parents immigrated from Austria who would like Austrian citizenship for himself and his kids, who has (in my view) a much greater entitlement than I but has no basis for securing the status under Austria's tight citizenship law.

Considered in a global context, that's a rich kid's problem. For those in less prosperous countries, having access to the premium citizenship will be a much bigger deal. A Dominican citizen with U.S. citizenship will be significantly privileged relative to her mono-national Dominican compatriot. David Cook-Martín tells the story of hundreds of thousands of Argentines who took advantage of Italian and Spanish lineage by way of securing EU citizenship and a ticket out of the economic crisis that struck Argentina in 2000. Per capita income in Argentina fell from about $9,500 in 2000 to $3,200 in 2002 at the same time it was rising in Italy and Spain. There were no job prospects at home. There were many in the EU, but only for those with EU citizenship eligibility. Some were in luck, some not. There was a "constellation of citizenship," in Bauböck's terms, in which not everyone shared.[39] Argentine mono-nationality without the EU tie comprised a kind of second-class citizenship.

Dual citizenship results in inequality. Not political inequality—for reasons described above, dual citizenship vindicates self-governance norms. To the extent that one has interests in both countries of citizenship, one should have a voice in how each is governed. Having an "extra" vote in another country doesn't make you any more powerful in this one. Proof is in the intuition that no one would envy my having a vote in German parliamentary elections. On the other hand, friends and colleagues might raise their eyebrows just a bit at free quality graduate school programs for children. One can easily imagine the perception of inequality when the stakes are higher, as in the Dominican and Argentine examples. The inequality relates to life opportunity. Dual citizenship can open doors for some that are closed to others. As Ayelet Shachar argues, "with the marked increase in dual nationality . . . some will be in possession of more diversified bundle or shares in several membership 'corporations,' whereas others will own merely a single citizenship parcel . . . , further deepening concerns about stratification and unequal opportunity."[40]

The argument is not as straightforward as that. To the extent additional nationalities pay dividends, it could be more in the way that affiliation with non-state entities can advantage individuals relative to the state. Members of powerful institutions have advantages that others lack. Life is unfair. So framed, dual citizenship doesn't violate principles of equal citizenship—someone's extra citizenship no more violates equality principles than employment at a top company or membership in a powerful union. To the extent that dual citizenship is the product of genuine social membership, moreover, it seems natural in the way of ethnicity. There are inequalities among ethnicities, but these inequalities are critiqued at the group, not individual, level. One might challenge how whites are privileged relative to blacks in the United States, for example, but one wouldn't challenge an individual's right to identify as a member of one or the other (or, for that matter, both).

But citizenship is about membership in the state. States still have distinctive capacities—including the power to grant or deny permission to locate on huge swathes of territory—that put them in a different class. Moreover, to the extent that dual citizenship is based on attenuated or non-existent social connections, it starts to look unfair in a different way. You may be lucky enough to be born with it or acquire it in some other random way (marry into it, for instance). Otherwise it will be beyond the reach of most. It would be one thing if all dual citizens hewed to an identity-based ideal in which each affiliation represented genuine social membership. If anything, that is becoming less frequently the case. To the extent that dual citizenship becomes something that the rich can get simply by being rich, moreover, it will feed into the increasingly powerful narrative of inequality with respect to our existence beyond the state, another badge of the one-percenters. Dual citizenship becomes another way in which transnational elites are privileged relative to their mono-national counterparts.

Equality-based objections to dual citizenship need to be taken seriously. But, again, it's not clear what can be done to address them, given the improbability of states moving to suppress the status on the ground. As the incidence of dual citizenship continues to grow, people the world over may become more conscious of this new dimension in which haves are divided from have-nots. But that's true of citizenship generally. In a global perspective, what single citizenship you are born with has been among the best predictors of economic well-being. Citizenship has long been an instrument of exclusion and a vehicle for inequality. In other words, dual citizenship isn't the problem, citizenship is.

But it may be less of a problem than in the past, or, more accurately, less of a problem than other sources of inequality. Citizenship doesn't get or give much anymore. The rise of dual citizenship supplies one explanation among many. To the extent citizenship is spread thinly to include many who don't really belong, it dilutes solidarities that were formerly represented by membership in the state. One is less inclined to share with those with whom one has no special common bond. Dual citizenship enables nominal citizenship, the mere formal status of which can't shoulder the burden of redistributive undertakings. Citizenship is under assault from various internal and external forces. Dual citizenship reflects its declining value and will accelerate it. Citizenship remains an edifice on the global landscape. But it is starting to wear. Identity and power is slowly migrating to other forms of identity—some of which will not be so tolerant of multiple membership—in ways that are only starting to become legible.

In the meantime, more people will be collecting more passports. Dual citizenship is itself an anachronistic label as it becomes increasingly common for individuals to hold three or more citizenships. In some cases, each passport will have some meaning for the holder, like pictures on a family tree. In other cases, the passports will be more like credit cards, each offering different interest rates or rewards programs. In any case, the passport that an individual produces at airports and border crossings is less likely to coincide with the traveler's central identity. When I use my German passport at Frankfurt or Berlin, the inspector might start barking German at me and I won't have a clue. I'm sure it won't be the first time, and it certainly won't be the last.

# ACKNOWLEDGMENTS

Dual citizenship is a subject about which I have been writing for almost twenty years. This book draws on material that appeared in the *Emory Law Journal*, the *New York University Law Review*, and the *Journal of International Constitutional Law*. I am grateful to those who commented on that earlier work. I am also grateful to participants in a workshop at the University of Miami Law School, where I presented a draft version of this manuscript in the spring of 2015.

# NOTES

## INTRODUCTION

1  Rainer Bauböck, *Transnational Citizenship: Membership and Rights in International Migration* 29 (1994).

## CHAPTER 1. THE FEUDAL ROOTS AND MODERN EMERGENCE OF DUAL NATIONALITY

1  See *Report of the Trial of John Warren for Treason-Felony* 6–20 (1867).

2  See David Sim, *A Union Forever: The Irish Question and U.S. Foreign Policy in the Victorian Age* 111 (2013).

3  See *Report of the Trial of John Warren*, at 18.

4  See Patrick Steward & Bryan P. McGovern, *The Fenians: Irish Rebellion in the North Atlantic World, 1858–1876*, at 184 (2013).

5  See 3 John Bassett Moore, *A Digest of International Law* 580 (1906) (Secretary of State Seward to U.S. minister to England, Mar. 22, 1866).

6  See *Citizenship of the United States, Expatriation, and Protection Abroad*, H.R. Doc. No. 326, 59th Cong., 2d Sess. 11 (1906).

7  See H. Ex. Doc. No. 157, 40th Cong. (1868), at 362.

8  See, e.g., *Tunis-Morocco Nationality Decrees*, 1923 PCIJ (ser. B) No. 4, at 24 (advisory opinion of Feb. 7) (questions of nationality are "in principle" within the "reserved domain" of domestic questions not subject to international law); International Law Commission, *Survey of the Problem of Multiple Nationality*, U.N. Doc. A/CN.4/84 (1954), at ¶¶ 25–31 [*ILC Survey of Multiple Nationality*].

9  See League of Nations Committee of Experts for the Progressive Codification of International Law, Nationality, 20 *American Journal of International Law* 21, 23 (Special Supplement 1926).

10  *Calvin's Case*, 7 Coke Report 1a, 4a (1608).

11  See James Kettner, *The Development of American Citizenship, 1608–1870* at 8 (1978).

12  On the distinctions, see, e.g., Rainer Bauböck, *Transnational Citizenship* vii (1994) ("What does it mean to be a citizen? . . . First, it means the opposite of being a subject"); Thomas M. Franck, Clan and Superclan: Loyalty, Identity and Community in Law and Practice, 90 *American Journal of International Law* 359, 372 (1996) ("Citizenship repudiated and repealed the idea of the subject"); Dudley O. McGovney, American Citizenship, 11 *Columbia Law Review* 231, 234 (1911). One illuminating contrast of the terms "citizen" and "subject" used them in character-

izing American free whites and black slaves respectively. See 8 Opinions of the Attorneys General of the United States 139, 142 (1856).

13 See Peter H. Schuck & Rogers M. Smith, *Citizenship without Consent: Illegal Aliens in the American Polity* 17 (1985).

14 1 William Blackstone, *Commentaries* 369 (5th ed. 1773).

15 3 Moore, *A Digest of International Law*, at 552–53 (Lord Grenville to American minister, Mar. 27, 1797).

16 *Rex v. Macdonald*, 18 How. St. Tr. 858 (1747).

17 See John Bassett Moore, *American Diplomacy: Its Spirit and Achievements* 191 (1905).

18 See 9 Opinions of the Attorneys General 356, 362–63 (1859).

19 Aristide Zolberg, The Exit Revolution, in *Citizenship and Those Who Leave* 34 (Nancy L. Green & Francois Weil, eds. 2007).

20 *Report of the International Law Commission to the General Assembly on Multiple Nationality*, U.N. Doc. A/CN.4/83 (1954), at ¶6 [*ILC Córdova Report*]. See also Research in International Law of the Harvard Law School, The Law of Nationality, 23 *American Journal of International Law* 48 (Supp. 1929) [Harvard Research] (noting that failure of "certain countries to give more complete recognition to the 'right of expatriation' may be due in some measure to a desire to maintain their armies at full strength").

21 See I-Mien Tsiang, *The Question of Expatriation in America Prior to 1907*, at 46 (1942) (quoting royal proclamation of November 11, 1807).

22 See Henry Adams, 1 *History of the United States of America during the First Administration of Thomas Jefferson 1801–05*, at 529 (Lib. of America 1986) (1889).

23 See Moore, *American Diplomacy*, at 275–76; Tsiang, *Question of Expatriation*, at 45–48.

24 See, e.g., Nancy L. Green, Expatriation, Expatriates, and Expats: The American Transformation of a Concept, 114 *American Historical Review* 307 (2009).

25 "That a country might determine the conditions upon which its citizen could expatriate was hardly questioned." Edwin M. Borchard, Decadence of the American Doctrine of Voluntary Expatriation, 25 *American Journal of International Law* 312, 313 (1931).

26 For an extensive compilation of diplomatic correspondence relating to efforts by other states to require military service of naturalized Americans, see S. Exec. Doc. No. 38, 36th Cong., 1st Sess. (1860).

27 9 Opinions of the Attorneys General 356, 359 (1859). See also *Mandoli v. Acheson*, 344 U.S. 133, 135–36 (1952) (noting that U.S. championed right of expatriation as it "prosper[ed] from the migrant's freedom of choice"); Tsiang, *Question of Expatriation*, at 111–12.

28 See *Osborn v. Bank of the United States*, 22 U.S. (9 Wheat.) 738, 827 (1824).

29 See 3 Moore, *Digest of International Law*, at 566 (Secretary of State Buchanan to Mr. Rosset, Nov. 25, 1845).

30 See Adams, 1 *History of the United States*, at 528, 536.

31  See 3 Moore, *Digest of International Law*, at 438.

32  See Act of Mar. 2, 1907, 34 Stat. 1228, at § 2, repealed by 54 Stat. 1169 (1940).

33  Attorney General Caleb Cushing's comprehensive 1856 opinion on the issue found a "right of expatriation, under fit circumstances of time and manner." 8 Opinions of the Attorneys General 140, 166.

34  Cushing himself decried the "popular assumption" that the U.S. condemnation of perpetual allegiance translated into an unfettered right of expatriation for Americans. See id. at 163. He nonetheless highlighted the inconsistency in British practice that provided for the naturalization of foreigners at the same time as it denied its own native-born the right to naturalize elsewhere. Id. at 163–64.

35  See 3 Moore, *Digest of International Law*, at 567 (Secretary of State Everett to U.S. minister to Prussia, Jan. 14, 1853); id. at 570 (Secretary of State Marcy to U.S. minister to Sardinia, Nov. 10, 1855) ("a different view of the duties of this Government would be an invasion of the independence of nations, and could not fail to be productive of discord").

36  See 9 Opinions of the Attorneys General 357, 360–61 (1859).

37  See 3 Moore, *Digest of International Law*, at 564 (U.S. minister to Prussia to Mr. Knoche, July 29, 1840).

38  See id. at 567 (Secretary of State Webster to Mr. Nones, June 1, 1852).

39  40 *Congressional Globe* 1797 (1868).

40  Quoted in Sim, *A Union Forever*, at 98.

41  Act of July 27, 1868, 15 Stat. 223, codified at 22 U.S.C. § 1732.

42  Later dubbed the "Hostage Act," the law made an unlikely return to prominence in the context of the 1979–81 Iranian embassy hostage crisis, during which it was found to lend indirect support to the suspension of private claims against Iran in return for the hostages' release. See *Dames & Moore v. Regan*, 453 U.S. 654 (1981); see also Abner Mikva & Gerald L. Neuman, The Hostage Crisis and the "Hostage Act," 49 *University of Chicago Law Review* 292 (1982).

43  See H. Ex. Doc. No. 157, at 207 (reprinting letter from London *Times*, Dec. 11, 1867).

44  See Sim, *A Union Forever*, at 121.

45  Id. at 122.

46  33 & 34 Vict. 104, ch. 14 (1870) (Eng.).

47  See Mark DeWolfe Howe, 2 *The Life and Letters of George Bancroft* 257 (1908). On the conventions concluded between the U.S. and these states, see 3 Moore, *Digest of International Law*, at 390–400. On these and similar bilateral arrangements between other countries, see Nissim Bar-Yaacov, *Dual Nationality* 163–66 (1961).

48  Howe, 2 *George Bancroft*, at 274 (reproducing Bancroft letter of June 30, 1874).

49  See Edwin M. Borchard, Voluntary Expatriation, 25 *American Journal of International Law* 312, 315 (1931).

50  To which Wigmore emphatically responded: "A state cannot suffer a divided allegiance . . . Its claim on the loyalty of its people must be exclusive." John H.

Wigmore, Domicile, Double Allegiance, and World Citizenship, 21 *Illinois Law Review* 761, 764 (1927). See also Bar-Yaacov, *Dual Nationality*, at 66 (noting 1936 attempt of Italian government to conscript U.S. citizen of Italian descent, to which U.S. government successfully objected). The Soviet Union never abandoned tsarist adherence to perpetual allegiance, a legal nicety behind the power of its restrictions on physical exit.

51 See, e.g., Law of Aug. 10, 1927 (Fr.), reprinted in Richard W. Flournoy, Jr., & Manley O. Hudson, *A Collection of Nationality Law of Various Countries as Contained in Constitutions, Statutes and Treaties* 245 (1929).

52 See, e.g., Joint Resolution of May 28, 1928, 45 Stat. 789 (calling for treaty negotiations to resolve problem of American nationals held liable for military service in states in which they had former or jus sanguinis nationality).

53 W.E. Hall, *International Law* 239 (7th ed. 1917).

54 See, e.g., Harvard Research, *Law of Nationality*, at 100–6 (categorizing expatriation laws); *Citizenship of the United States, Expatriation, and Protection Abroad*, H.R. Doc. No. 326, at 12; Durward V. Sandifer, A Comparative Study of Laws Relating to Nationality at Birth and to Loss of Nationality, 29 *American Journal of International Law* 248, 272–73 (1935) (calculating that states recognizing unconditional right of expatriation accounted for 72% of international trade). The Harvard project's proposed draft convention on the law of nationality included a provision by which naturalization in one state would result in the loss of prior nationality. See Harvard Research, *Law of Nationality*, at 44.

55 See U.N. Declaration of Human Rights, article 15(2) ("no one shall be arbitrarily deprived of his nationality nor denied the right to change his nationality").

56 See Schuck & Smith, *Citizenship without Consent*, at 22–41.

## CHAPTER 2. INTERNATIONAL THREAT, MORAL DISGRACE

1 The essay, entitled "When Is an American Not an American," was reprinted in Theodore Roosevelt, *Fear God and Take Your Own Part* 272, 285 (1916).

2 Id. at 274.

3 Id. at 277.

4 See Sen. Ex. Doc. 38, 36th Cong., 1st Sess. 160 (1850) (Bancroft to Lord Palmerston, Jan. 26, 1849).

5 See 9 Opinions of the Attorneys General 356, 361 (1859).

6 3 Moore, *Digest of International Law*, at 518.

7 See *ILC Survey of Multiple Nationality* ¶ 220 (noting potentially "serious consequences" of dual nationality for individuals).

8 Bar-Yaacov, *Dual Nationality*, at 265; Alfred Michael Boll, *Multiple Nationality and International Law* 193 (2006) (quoting Hersch Lauterpacht).

9 See generally Edwin M. Borchard, *The Diplomatic Protection of Citizens Abroad* (1914); Emmerich de Vattel, *The Law of Nations or Principles of Natural Law* 139 (Carnegie Institution 1916) (foreign state entitled to intervene "in cases where justice has been denied or the decision [of a tribunal] is clearly and palpably

unjust, or the proper procedure has not been observed, or, finally, in cases where his subjects, or foreigners in general, have been discriminated against").

10  On "non-amicable methods" of diplomatic protection, see Borchard, *Diplomatic Protection*, at 192–97.

11  See id. at 26.

12  See Philip Jessup, *A Modern Law of Nations* 100–101 (1948).

13  Olivier W. Vonk, *Dual Nationality in the European Union* 40 (2012).

14  3 Moore, *Digest of International Law*, at 713 (annual message of President Grant, Dec. 7, 1874). Grant's call did not mark the first occasion in which the issue had attracted presidential attention. See John B. Moore, The Doctrine of Expatriation, *Harper's Magazine*, Jan. 1905, at 290 (noting that Buchanan administration State Department circular "in its sentiments and style bears Presidential earmarks"). President Buchanan had in fact during his tenure as a senator from Pennsylvania taken a keen interest in the expatriation issue, reflecting at least in part the interests of his substantial naturalized German American constituency. See Tsiang, *Question of Expatriation*, at 72–75.

15  See *Citizenship of the United States, Expatriation, and Protection Abroad*, H.R. Doc. No. 326, 59th Cong., 2d Sess. 23 (1906); see also Borchard, *Diplomatic Protection*, at 732 (such individuals have "committed a fraud both upon their native and upon their adopted country").

16  *To Revise and Codify the Nationality Laws of the United States into a Comprehensive Nationality Code, Hearings before the House Committee on Immigration and Naturalization*, 67th Cong., 1st Sess. 49 (1940) [*1940 Hearings*].

17  See Georg Schwarzenberger, *International Law* 363 (1949) (noting reservation on British naturalization certificate for dual national, "within the limits of the foreign state being his country of origin the holder of the certificate was not to be deemed to be a British subject").

18  See Hague Convention on Certain Questions Relating to the Conflict of Nationality Laws, Apr. 12, 1930, 179 L.N.T.S. 89, art. 4; see also *Case Regarding Reparation for Injuries Suffered in Service of the United Nations*, 1949 I.C.J. 174, 186 (noting "ordinary practice whereby a State does not exercise protection on behalf of one of its nationals against a State which regards him as its own national").

19  See, e.g., 3 Green H. Hackworth, *Digest of International Law* 353 (1942) (Secretary of State Lansing to Senator Lodge, June 9, 1915).

20  Borchard, *Diplomatic Protection*, at 685. See also Harvard Research, 23 *American Journal of International Law*, at 100–1 (listing 38 nations as of 1929 providing unconditionally for expatriation upon naturalization abroad).

21  *The Charming Betsy*, 6 U.S. 64, 120 (1806). See also Frederick Van Dyne, *Citizenship of the United States* 272 (1904) ("the most obvious and effective form of expatriation"); *Savorgnan v. United States*, 338 U.S. 491, 498 (1950) ("From the beginning, one of the most obvious and effective forms of expatriation has been that of naturalization under the laws of another nation").

22  14 Opinions of the Attorneys General 295 (1873).

23  See 3 Moore, *Digest of International Law*, at 714 (Secretary of State Bayard, Jan. 27, 1887).

24  Id. at 727 (Secretary of State Gresham to U.S. minister to Hawaii, Apr. 5, 1895).

25  See Act of Jan. 29, 1795, ch. 20, 1, 1 Stat. 414, currently codified at 8 U.S.C. § 1148(a).

26  *Williams' Case*, 29 F. Cas. 1330 (C.C.D. Conn. 1799).

27  9 Opinions of the Attorneys General 356, 360; see also 3 Hackworth, *Digest of International Law*, at 162 (statement of U.S. delegate to preparatory committee to the Conference for the Codification of International Law, The Hague, Mar. 24, 1930) ("We regard that oath and its result . . . as a finality and we shall always so regard it").

28  David Jayne Hill, Dual Citizenship in the German Imperial and State Citizenship Law, 12 *American Journal of International Law* 356, 361 (1914).

29  See 3 Moore, *Digest of International Law*, at 574 (Secretary of State Cass to U.S. minister to Prussia, July 8, 1859).

30  At first only by strong implication. The Bancroft treaties, while providing that naturalized citizens "shall be treated as such" by the state of original nationality, did not expressly provide for the termination of original nationality upon naturalization. See, e.g., North-German Union-U.S., Feb. 22, 1868, art. 1, reprinted in 2 *Treaties, Conventions, International Acts, Protocols, and Other Agreements between the United States of America and Other Powers 1776–1923*, at 1298. Later accords made explicit loss of nationality upon naturalization. See, e.g., Bulgaria--U.S., Nov. 23, 1923, art. 1, 43 Stat. 1759; Czechoslovakia-U.S., July 16, 1928, art. 1, U.S.T.S. 804.

31  Hill, Dual Citizenship in the German Imperial State, at 363.

32  See 3 Moore, *Digest of International Law*, at 936–37 (Secretary of State Evarts to Mr. Fish, Oct. 19, 1880).

33  See id. at 717.

34  See id. at 712 (Secretary of State Fish to Mr. Niles, Oct. 30, 1871).

35  See, e.g., id. at 765 (Secretary of State Fish to minister to Costa Rica, Mar. 16, 1875).

36  See Borchard, *Diplomatic Protection*, at 696–97.

37  Id.

38  See 3 Hackworth, *Digest of International Law*, at 505–6 (assistant secretary of state to U.S. minister in Nicaragua, Mar. 26, 1935).

39  Id. at 368 (assistant secretary of state to ambassador in China, Nov. 16, 1936).

40  Id. at 367 (Secretary of State Stimson to U.S. legation in Peiping, Oct. 11, 1929); see also id. at 360 (chief clerk to U.S. vice consul in Calcutta, Dec. 29, 1909) (residence abroad of birthright American-born dual citizen found sufficient justification to deny protection); id. at 282 (memorandum of under secretary of state, Dec. 2, 1922) ("There seems to be no reason why Americans born in the United States of American parentage should be deprived of a passport merely because they are residing abroad continually").

41 See North German Union-U.S., Feb. 22, 1868, art. 4, 2 *Treaties, Conventions, International Acts, Protocols, and Other Agreements between the United States of America and Other Powers 1776–1923*, at 1298 (providing that renewed residence in Germany of naturalized German would effect renunciation of U.S. nationality); Denmark-U.S., July 20, 1872, art. 3, id. at 384 (same); Haiti-U.S., Mar. 22, 1902, art. 2, id. at 939 (same); see also, e.g., Van Dyne, *Citizenship of the United States*, at 274–77.

42 See Tsiang, *Question of Expatriation*, at 14 & n.19.

43 Hall, *International Law*, at 234.

44 See Act of Mar. 26, 1790, 1 Stat. 103 (children of parent citizens); Act of Feb. 10, 1855, c. 71, § 1, 10 Stat. 604 (children of American citizen fathers); Act of May 24, 1934, § 1, 48 Stat. 797 (children of American citizen fathers or mothers).

45 See *United States v. Wong Kim Ark*, 169 U.S. 649 (1898).

46 See, e.g., 3 Hackworth, *Digest of International Law*, at 352 (citing jus soli/jus sanguinis interplay as "the classic example of dual nationality").

47 John Wesley McWilliams, Dual Nationality, 6 *American Bar Association Journal* 204, 216 (1920).

48 See Harvard Research, *Law of Nationality*, art. 12.

49 For a listing of national laws requiring election as of 1929, see Harvard Research, *Law of Nationality*, at 82–83; see also Richard W. Flournoy, Jr., Dual Nationality and Election, 30 *Yale Law Journal* 693 (1921).

50 John P. Roche, The Loss of American Nationality—The Development of Statutory Expatriation, 99 *University of Pennsylvania Law Review* 25, 32 (1950).

51 See 3 Moore, *Digest of International Law*, at 545–46.

52 Id. at 546–47.

53 Id. at 548 (Secretary of State Bayard to U.S. minister to France, Feb. 15, 1888); id. at 549 (Secretary of State Gresham to Lainfield, June 2, 1894) (denying passport renewal to German resident who had not fulfilled stated intention to return to the United States); Borchard, *Diplomatic Protection*, at 584 & n.3 (noting that in cases of persons born to alien parents in the United States who thereafter returned to their country of origin during the child's minority, "it has always been held by the Department of State . . . that he must, upon arriving at majority or shortly thereafter, make his election between the citizenship which is his by birth and the citizenship which is his by parentage").

54 For examples from other countries, see, e.g., Law of Dec. 12, 1892, art. 7(5) (Neth.), reprinted in Flournoy & Hudson, *Collection of Nationality Laws*, at 443 (providing for loss of nationality for those born outside Dutch territory after ten years of non-residence). See also Schuck & Smith, *Citizenship without Consent*, at 127 (arguing that no formal election should be required of those dual nationals born and residing in the United States).

55 3 Moore, *Digest of International Law*, at 545 (Acting Secretary of State Porter to U.S. minister to Switzerland, Sept. 14, 1885). To the extent that other countries also imposed election requirements having the effect of withdrawing nationality

from those remaining in the United States, those individuals did not remain dual nationals. See, e.g., Van Dyne, *Citizenship of the United States*, at 38 (asserting that conflicts questions raised in context of birthright dual nationals "is usually more apparent than real" because of "pretty general[] recogni[tion] of election requirement among nations").

56  See 3 Moore, *Digest of International Law*, at 712–13 (Grant message of Dec. 1, 1873); id. at 713 (Grant message of Dec. 7, 1874) (asserting that "importance of [defining basis for expatriation] is obvious").

57  See, e.g., 7 *Messages and Papers of the Presidents* 3382 (Richardson ed. 1897) (President Lincoln); cf. *Talbot v. Jansen*, 3 U.S. (3 Dall.) 133, 164 (1795) ("it is the duty of the legislature to make such provision" for the modes of expatriation).

58  See Act of Mar. 2, 1907, Pub. L. No. 59–193, 34 Stat. 1228 (1907).

59  34 Stat. at 1228, § 2. The presumption could be overcome with the "presentation of satisfactory evidence to a diplomatic or consular officer of the United States." Id.

60  Id. § 6.

61  See Act of May 24, 1934, § 1, 48 Stat. 797. A later version of the law was upheld as against constitutional attack in *Rogers v. Bellei*, 401 U.S. 815 (1971).

62  On the "zig-zag course" undertaken by the courts and the Departments of Justice and State with respect to the expatriation of naturalized citizens under the 1907 Act, see Roche, *Loss of American Nationality*, at 37–39.

63  John L. Cable, American Citizenship Rights of Women, reprinted in *American Citizenship Rights of Women, Hearing before a Subcommittee of the Committee on Immigration*, 72nd Cong., 2d Sess. 5, 18–19 (1933).

64  *Ruckgaber v. Moore*, 104 F. 947 (E.D.N.Y. 1900).

65  See Cable, American Citizenship Rights of Women, at 18.

66  Id. at 26.

67  See *Mackenzie v. Hare*, 239 U.S. 299 (1915). See also Candice Lewis Bredbenner, *A Nationality of Her Own: Women, Marriage, and the Law of Citizenship* 65–70 (1998).

68  Id. at 102.

69  See, e.g., League of Nations Committee of Experts for the Progressive Codification of International Law, Nationality, 20 *American Journal of International Law* 21, 38 (Special Supplement 1926).

70  Convention on the Nationality of Women, O.A.S. Treaty Series No. 4, 38 (1933).

CHAPTER 3. CONGRESS, THE COURTS, AND THE WORLD AGAINST DUAL CITIZENSHIP

1  See *Kawakita v. United States*, 190 F.2d 506 (9th Cir. 1951).

2  These facts are drawn from *New York Times* reports on Sept. 3, 1948 and June 6, 1947; and from David Rosenzweig, POW Camp Atrocities Led to Treason Trial, *Los Angeles Times*, Sept. 20, 2002.

3  *Kawakita v. United States*, 343 U.S. 717 (1952).

4  See, e.g., Bar-Yaacov, *Dual Nationality*, at 58–59; Paul Weis, *Nationality and Statelessness in International Law* 195–96 (2d ed. 1979).

5  See Eiichiro Azuma, *Between Two Empires: Race, History, and Transnationalism in Japanese America* (2005).
6  See Nationality Act of 1940, § 401(c), 54 Stat. 1137, 1170.
7  Nor did his experience in Japan result in expatriation under other provisions of the 1907 or 1940 acts. He was native-born, and was thus not subject to the presumption of expatriation that applied to naturalized citizens after a period of residence in their country of origin. See Thomas L. Blakemore, Jr., Recovery of Japanese Nationality as a Cause for Expatriation in American Law, 43 *American Journal of International Law* 441 (1949). In the end, Kawakita was stripped of his citizenship as a result of the treason conviction itself pursuant to the 1940 nationality act. His request to visit his parents' gravesite in the United States was denied by U.S. authorities in 1978. See H. Ansgar Kelly, Dual Nationality, the Myth of Election, and a Kinder, Gentler State Department, 23 *University of Miami Inter-American Law Review* 421, 431 (1991–92).
8  See *New York Times*, Nov. 3, 1953, and Dec. 13, 1963.
9  See Note, The Expatriation Act of 1954, 64 *Yale Law Journal* 1164, 1175 (1955).
10 *Nationality Laws of the United States: Message from the President Transmitting a Report Proposing a Revision and Codification of the Nationality Laws of the United States, House Committee Report*, 76th Congress, 1st Sess. (1938) [*Roosevelt Committee Report*].
11 Id. at vi.
12 Id. at vii.
13 Id. at 66.
14 Act of Oct. 5, 1917, 40 Stat. 340 (allowing those who took otherwise expatriating oath by enlisting in armed forces of "foreign state engaged in war with any country [e.g., Great Britain] with which the United States is at war [e.g., Germany] . . . to resume and acquire the character and privileges of a citizen of the United States").
15 1940 Act, § 402, 54 Stat. 1169. See Roche, *Loss of Nationality*, at 65 (section 402 "is indeed a peculiar enactment").
16 In fact, that is exactly what was intended, and feared: section 402 was adopted "upon the special recommendation of the War Department with a view to checking the activities of persons regarded as prospective 'fifth columnists,'" see 86 *Congressional Record* 11948 (1940), with some particular concern for certain Japanese-American residents of Hawaii and Alaska. See Roche, *Loss of Nationality*, at 66.
17 By 1950 it was not considered "an active part of the Nationality Law" by the Immigration and Naturalization Service. See id. at 67. See also *Kawakita v. United States*, 343 U.S. at 730 (finding section 402 inapplicable where individual was shown not to have served in foreign armed forces or government employment).
18 See 800 of 900 Eligibles Return, *New York Times*, Jan. 6, 1935.
19 See *1940 Hearings*, at 286–87.
20 *Roosevelt Committee Report*, at 67.

21  1940 Act, § 404, 54 Stat. at 1170.

22  See "Dual Citizens" Warned of Possible Loss of Citizenship, 33 *Department of State Bulletin* 658–59 (Oct. 24, 1955).

23  See *1940 Hearings*, at 372.

24  See 8 Marjorie M. Whiteman, *Digest of International Law* 78 (1963); 22 *Department of State Bulletin* 599 (Apr. 17, 1950).

25  "Dual Citizens" Warned, at 659 (stating that voluntarily obtaining a passport, identity card, or "other official document" from foreign country of nationality would prompt § 350 requirements).

26  86 *Congressional Record* 11944 (1940) (statement of Cong. Dickstein).

27  *Gaudio v. Dulles*, 110 F. Supp. 706, 709 (D.D.C. 1953).

28  *Mackenzie v. Hare*, 239 U.S. 299 (1915).

29  *Perkins v. Elg*, 307 U.S. 325 (1939).

30  See 1940 Act, § 403(b), 54 Stat., at 1170; 1950 Act, § 355, 66 Stat., at 272.

31  See, e.g., *Acheson v. Maenza*, 202 F.2d 453 (D.C. Cir. 1953); Charles Gordon, The Citizen and the State: Power of Congress to Expatriate American Citizens, 53 *Georgetown Law Journal* 315, 359 (1964–65) (listing cases).

32  See, e.g., *Morizumi v. Acheson*, 101 F. Supp. 976 (N.D. Cal. 1951).

33  The Expatriation Act of 1954, 64 *Yale Law Journal* 1164, 1175 (1955).

34  *Savorgnan v. United States*, 338 U.S. 491 (1950).

35  The Cable Act of 1922, ch. 411, 42 Stat. 1021 (1922).

36  73 F.Supp. 109 (W.D. Wis. 1947).

37  See *Savorgnan*, 338 U.S. at 496 & n.5.

38  *Perez v. Brownell*, 356 U.S. 44 (1958).

39  The desertion ground implicated a penal ground for expatriation, invalidated in *Trop v. Dulles*, 356 U.S. 86 (1958).

40  See 356 U.S. at 50 (quoting citizenship board explanation of expatriation).

41  356 U.S. at 59.

42  356 U.S. at 64. The observation echoed Hannah Arendt's famous dictum that all rights are national rights. Hannah Arendt, *The Origins of Totalitarianism* 299 (2d ed. 1973).

43  *Perez*, 356 U.S. at 68.

44  *Trop v. Dulles*, 356 U.S. 86 (1958). On the judicial drama associated with the handing down of Perez, Trop and a third case involving expatriation, see Patrick Weil, *The Sovereign Citizen: Denaturalization and the Origins of the American Republic* (2013).

45  *Perez*, 356 U.S. at 77.

46  See Weil, *Sovereign Citizen*, at 199.

47  Richard W. Flournoy, Jr., Dual Nationality and Election, 30 *Yale Law Journal* 545, 545 (1921) (quoting Pradier-Fodéré).

48  See Borchard, *Diplomatic Protection*, at 590–91; Richard W. Flournoy, Jr., Suggestions Concerning an International Code on the Law of Nationality, 35 *Yale Law Journal* 939, 947–50 (1926).

49  Bar-Yaacov, *Dual Nationality*, at 4, 266.

50  Otto Kimminich, The Conventions for the Prevention of Double Nationality and Their Meaning for Germany and Europe in an Era of Migration, 38 *German Yearbook of International Law* 224, 232 (1996).

51  James Brown Scott, *Observations on Nationality* 6 (1931).

52  John Wesley McWilliams, Dual Nationality, 6 *American Bar Association Journal* 204, 216–17 (1920).

53  See Harvard Research, *Law of Nationality*, at 39, 118–26 (reproducing bar association resolutions).

54  J. W. Garner, Uniformity of Law in Respect to Nationality, 19 *American Journal of International Law* 547, 550 (1925).

55  See Report of the Nationality and Naturalisation Committee, in International Law Association, *Report of the Thirty-Third Conference* 54, 57 (1924); see also id. at 46 (statement of Arthur Kuhn: "It seems to me that we are confronted with a very acute situation internationally.").

56  See Historical Survey of Development of International Law and Its Codification by International Conferences, UN Doc. A/AC.10/5 (1947), reprinted in 41 *American Journal of International Law* 32, 66 (Special Supp. 1947). See also id. at 105–07 (reproducing League of Nations Resolution approving codification conference).

57  See John P. Grant & J. Craig Barker, The Harvard Research: Genesis to Exodus and Beyond, in *The Harvard Research in International Law: Contemporary Analysis and Appraisal* 1 (John P. Grant & J. Craig Barker, eds. 2007).

58  Harvard Research, *Law of Nationality*, at 21.

59  Id. at 38.

60  Id. at 32.

61  See League of Nations Committee of Experts for the Progressive Codification of International Law, Nationality, 20 *American Journal of International Law* 21, 59–60 (Special Supplement 1926) [*League of Nations Experts Committee Report*].

62  Id. at 32; Richard W. Flournoy Jr., Nationality Convention, Protocols and Recommendations Adopted by the First Conference on the Codification of International Law, 24 *American Journal of International Law* 467, 471 (1930) ("agreement upon a single rule will be difficult to accomplish").

63  See *League of Nations Experts Committee Report*, at 59–60. Article 1 of the draft would have required parties to refrain from exercising protection against a state of which an individual was considered a national from "the moment of [his] birth." Article 6 provided that a state of naturalization could not exercise protection against "the State whose subject he originally was," if still considered a national of that state. See id.

64  Hague Convention on Nationality, arts. 1, 2.

65  See Ruth Donner, Nationality, in *Harvard Research: Contemporary Analysis*, at 62–65 (systematically comparing Harvard recommendations with results of Hague Convention).

66  Hague Convention on Nationality, art. 6.

67 Scott, *Observations on Nationality*, at 65–66.

68 Donner, *Nationality*, at 67.

69 See Convention on Nationality, 28 *American Journal of International Law* 63 (Supp. 1934).

70 Kimminich, *Prevention of Double Nationality*, at 240.

71 See, e.g., Convention of Sept. 20, 1917 (Italy-Nicaragua), art. 2, reprinted in Flournoy & Hudson, *Collection of Nationality Laws*, at 686; 1911 U.S.-Costa Rican accord described in Borchard, *Diplomatic Protection*, at 590.

72 See *ILC Survey of Multiple Nationality*, A/CN.4/84/1954, at ¶ 370.

73 See *ILC Córdova Report*, at 48. The ILC recommendations were delivered in response to a 1949 request for its views from the secretary-general of the United Nations.

74 See Gerald L. Neuman, Nationality Law in the United States and the Federal Republic of Germany: Structure and Current Problems, in *Paths to Inclusion: The Integration of Migrants in the United States and Germany* 247 (Peter Schuck & Rainer Munz, eds. 1998).

75 Judgment of May 21, 1974, 37 BVerfGE 217, 254–55.

76 *Johnson v. Eisentrager*, 339 U.S. 763, 772 (1950).

CHAPTER 4. TURNING THE CORNER ON DUAL CITIZENSHIP

1 For more background on the *Afroyim* case, see Peter J. Spiro, Afroyim: Vaunting Citizenship, Presaging Transnationality, in *Immigration Stories* 147 (David A. Martin & Peter H. Schuck, eds. 2005).

2 *Afroyim v. Rusk*, 387 U.S. 253 (1967).

3 *Schneider v. Rusk*, 377 U.S. 163 (1964).

4 1952 Act, § 352(a), 66 Stat., at 269.

5 377 U.S. at 168.

6 *Perez*, 356 U.S. at 68.

7 Pollard was not a dual citizen at the time of his conviction for delivering classified information to a foreign government. See Israel Grants Citizenship to American Spy, *New York Times*, Nov. 22, 1995.

8 See Norman Mailer, *Oswald's Tale: An American Mystery* 209 (1995).

9 Before the Court's decision in *Afroyim*, recognition of the unthreatening nature of activities in or associations with foreign polities that would otherwise result in expatriation could be accomplished only through ad hoc special statutory measures. See, e.g., Act of Oct. 5, 1917, 40 Stat. 340 (1917) (restoring citizenship to those who served in Allied forces prior to U.S. entry in WWI); S.J. Res. 47, H.J. Res. 30, 239, § 375, 81st Cong., 1st Sess. (proposing to suspend operation of § 401(e) of 1940 nationality act with respect to voting in certain Italian political elections).

10 Protocol Relating to Military Obligations in Certain Cases of Double Nationality, April 12, 1935, 178 L.N.T.S. 227.

11 Flournoy & Hudson, *Collection of Nationality Laws*, at 661.

12  Id. at 671.

13  H.J. Res. 268, 70th Cong. (1928).

14  Id. at 41.

15  For a detailed treatment, see Stephen H, Legomsky, Dual Nationality and Military Service: Strategy Number Two, in *Rights and Duties of Dual Nationals* 79 (David A. Martin & Kay Hailbronner, eds. 2003).

16  Convention on Reduction of Cases of Multiple Nationality and Military Obligations in Cases of Multiple Nationality, May 6, 1963, 634 U.N.T.S. 221, Europ. T.S. No. 43.

17  Weis, Nationality and Statelessness, at 190.

18  *Nottebohm* (Liechtenstein v. Guatemala), 1955 ICJ Rep. 4 (Apr. 6).

19  See, e.g., Josef L. Kunz, The Nottebohm Judgment (Second Phase), 54 *American Journal of International Law* 536, 537–39 (1960).

20  See *Mergé Case*, 14 Reports of International Arbitral Awards 236 (1955). On precedents of other tribunals relating to dual nationals and the dominant nationality test, see Weis, *Nationality and Statelessness*, at 169–197.

21  See Case No. A/18, 5 Iran-U.S. Claims Tribunal Reports 251, 23 *International Legal Materials* 489 (1984).

22  See 34 *Federal Register* 1079 (1969).

23  *Matter of Stanlake*, 13 Immigration and Nationality Decisions 517 (Board of Immigration Appeals 1969).

24  *Matter of Wayne*, 16 Immigration and Nationality Decisions 248 (BIA 1977).

25  See Tad Szulc, Menuhin Warned on Citizenship, *New York Times*, Dec. 4, 1970.

26  *Rogers v. Bellei*, 401 U.S. 815 (1971).

27  See 1952 Act, § 301(a)(7), 66 Stat. at 236.

28  *Bellei*, 401 U.S. at 832–33.

29  Id. at 827.

30  *Vance v. Terrazas*, 444 U.S. 252 (1980).

31  Id. at 260.

32  See *Terrazas v. Muskie*, 494 F. Supp. 1017 (N.D. Ill. 1980).

33  Quoted in H. Ansgar Kelly, Dual Nationality, the Myth of Election, and a Kinder, Gentler State Department, 23 *University of Miami Inter-American Law Review* 421, 441 (1991–92).

34  See Pub. L. No. 99–653, § 18, 100 Stat. 3658 (1986).

35  See Pub. L. No. 95–432, § 1, 92 Stat. 1046 (1978).

36  See H.R. Rpt. No. 95–1493, at 6 (1978).

37  See U.S. Department of State, Advice About Possible Loss of U.S. Citizenship and Dual Nationality, reprinted in 67 *Interpreter Releases* 1092 (1990).

38  Reprinted in 72 *Interpreter Releases* 1618 (1995).

39  See Advice about Possible Loss of U.S. Nationality and Dual Nationality, available at http://travel.state.gov/content/travel/english/legal-considerations/us-citizenship-laws-policies/citizenship-and-dual-nationality.html.

40 See Maarten P. Vink, Gerard-Rene de Groot & C. Luk, Global Dual Citizenship Database (Maastricht University 2013), available at https://macimide.maastrich-tuniversity.nl/dual-citizenship-database.

41 T. Alexander Aleinikoff & Douglas Klusmeyer, Plural Nationality: Facing the Future in a Migratory World, in *Citizenship Today: Global Perspectives and Practices* 79 (T. Alexander Aleinikoff & Douglas Klusmeyer, eds. 2001).

42 See Franck, *Clan and Superclan*, at 379. None appears to have been denationalized, notwithstanding some ambiguity in the State Department guidelines regarding foreign government office-holding. See 1990 Policy Statement, at 1093 (setting forth administrative standard of evidence under which "non-policy level" employment only is presumed not to indicate an intention to relinquish citizenship).

43 Somali Parliament Operations Said Hampered by MPs' Dual Citizenship, High Number, BBC Monitoring Africa, Jan. 2, 2010, available at http://www.biyokulule.com/view_content.php?articleid=4642.

44 See Alan James, Expatriation in the United States: Precept and Practice Today and Yesterday, 27 *San Diego Law Review* 853, 891 (1990) (article by chair of the State Department's Board of Appellate Review, which was responsible for administrative appeals in denationalization cases).

45 See Gary Endelman, Saying Goodbye to Uncle Sam: Formal Renunciation of U.S. Citizenship, 73 *Interpreter Releases* 709, 717–18 (1996).

CHAPTER 5. ACCEPTANCE AND EMBRACE

1 Linda Chavez, Dual Citizenship Claim by Mexico Natives Raises Questions about Loyalty to America, *Baltimore Sun*, Apr. 8, 1998.

2 Georgie Anne Geyer, Dual Nationality Not in America's Best Interests, *Chicago Tribune*, Jan. 10, 1997; see also Georgie Anne Geyer, *Americans No More* (1996).

3 Samuel P. Huntington, *Who Are We? The Challenges to America's National Identity* 5, 212 (2004).

4 For the resulting volume, see *Immigration and Citizenship in the Twenty-First Century* (Noah Pickus, ed. 1998).

5 8 U.S.C. § 1148(a).

6 See John Fonte, Dual Allegiance: A Challenge to Immigration Reform and Patriotic Assimilation, Center for Immigration Studies Backgrounder (November 2005), available at http://www.cis.org/DualAllegiance-Assimilation.

7 See *Dual Citizenship, Birthright Citizenship, and the Meaning of Sovereignty, Hearing before the Subcommittee on Immigration, Border, and Claims of the Committee on the Judiciary*, 109th Cong. 95 (2005) (reprinting resolution).

8 H.R. 3938, §§ 700–704, 109th Cong. (2005).

9 See *Dual Citizenship, Birthright Citizenship, and the Meaning of Sovereignty: Hearing before the Subcommittee on Immigration, Border Security, and Claims of the Committee on the Judiciary*, 109th Cong. (2005).

10 See Prepared Testimony of Dan Stein, Executive Director of the Federation of Americans for Immigration Reform, *Hearing before the Senate Judiciary Commit-*

*tee Subcommittee on Immigration and Refugee Affairs Concerning Naturalization Practices and American Citizenship*, 104th Cong. 287 (1996).

11  See James C. McKinley, Jr., How a U.S. Marine Became Leader of Somalia, *New York Times*, Aug. 12, 1996.

12  S. 3327, 111th Cong. (2010).

13  For reporting of the mostly negative response, see Kasie Hunt, Joe Lieberman Bill Would Strip Suspects' Citizenship, *Politico*, May 4, 2010.

14  See https://www.youtube.com/watch?v=s87cLZ5V8F8&feature=related.

15  See Expatriate Terrorist Act, S. 247, 114th Cong. (2015).

16  See David Sherfinski, Dems Block Cruz Bill to Strip U.S. Citizenship from Islamic State Defectors, *Washington Times*, Sept. 18, 2014.

17  For an elaboration of this argument, see Peter J. Spiro, Expatriating Terrorists, 82 *Fordham Law Review* 2169 (2014).

18  Peter Nyers, Dueling Designs: The Politics of Rescuing Dual Citizens, 14 *Citizenship Studies* 47 (2010); Audrey Macklin & François Crépeau, Multiple Citizenship, Identity and Entitlement in Canada, IIRP Study No. 6 (June 2010), available at http://yorkspace.library.yorku.ca/xmlui/bitstream/handle/10315/6755/Macklin-MultCit.pdf.

19  See Ivy Leaguers Leave Lebanon First and Fast through Private Security Firms, *ABC News*, July 21, 2006, at http://blogs.abcnews.com/theblotter/2006/07/ivy_leaguers_le.html.

20  See 22 U.S.C. § 2671(b)(2)(A); Department of State Form DS-5528, available at http://www.state.gov/documents/organization/211837.pdf.

21  See Josh Rogin, Americans Trapped in Yemen? U.S. Says 'Good Luck,' *Bloomberg View*, Apr. 22, 2015.

22  Peter H. Schuck, Membership in the Liberal Polity: The Devaluation of American Citizenship, 3 *Georgetown Immigration Law Journal* 1, 13 (1989).

23  See 8 U.S.C. § 1148(a)(1).

24  See 8 U.S.C. § 1423 (naturalization applicant must demonstrate "understanding of the English language").

25  See Gerald L. Neuman, Justifying U.S. Naturalization Policies, 35 *Virginia Journal of International Law* 237, 265–66 (1994).

26  See 42 U.S.C. § 1973aa-1a.

27  See, e.g., Thomas Franck, The Emerging Right to Democratic Governance, 86 *American Journal of International Law* 46 (1992).

28  See Barbara Crossette, Citizenship Is a Malleable Concept, *New York Times*, Aug. 18, 1996.

29  Michael Winters, Prop. 187 Sequel Would Narrow Door to Citizenship, *San Francisco Examiner*, Oct. 16, 1995 (quoting restrictionist Ron Prince).

30  See Georgie Anne Geyer, Mexico's Cynical Push for Adoption of Dual Nationality, *Chicago Tribune*, June 2, 1995; see also Federation of Americans for Immigration Reform, Dual Nationality (May 2002), available at http://www.fairus.org/issue/dual-nationality ("By allowing Mexicans in the United States to remain Mexicans

if they become Americans, the Mexican government would be attempting to maintain the allegiance of a huge voting bloc in U.S. elections").

31 Roberto Gamboa Mascarenas, Dual Nationality Preserves Heritage, *Austin American-Statesman*, Mar. 14, 1997 (editorial by consul general of Mexico in Austin).

32 See Michael Walzer, *Spheres of Justice* 60–61 (1983); see also Joseph H. Carens, *Immigrants and the Right to Stay* (2010).

33 See Schuck, Devaluation of American Citizenship, at 14–15; David A. Martin, The Civic Republican Ideal for Citizenship, and for Our Common Life, 35 *Virginia Journal of International Law* 301 (1994).

34 Sanford Levinson, Constituting Communities through Words That Bind: Reflections on Loyalty Oaths, 84 *Michigan Law Review* 1440, 1467 (1986).

35 See 7 Anne, ch. 5 (1709) (Eng.) (requiring naturalization applicants to disavow Catholic doctrine of transubstantiation); Kettner, *Development of American Citizenship*, at 70.

36 Levinson, *Constituting Communities*, at 1468; see also Michael Walzer, *Obligations: Essays on War, Disobedience, and Citizenship* 221–22 (1970) (noting that participation in non-state associations inevitably challenges the authority of the state).

37 See Neuman, Justifying U.S. Naturalization, at 273–74.

38 See Leticia Quezada, Mexican, American as a Single Identity, *Los Angeles Times*, Dec. 16, 1996.

39 See Bob Klapisch, Duncan Training to Become Citizen, [Bergen County] *Record*, Mar. 3, 1997.

## CHAPTER 6. DUAL CITIZENSHIP AND THE RISE OF DIASPORA

1 See Michael Peter Smith and Matt Bakker, The Transnational Politics of the To-mato King: Meaning and Impact, 5 *Global Networks* 129 (2005); Ginger Thompson, Mexico's 'Tomato King' Seeks a New Title, *New York Times*, July 5, 2004; Gustavo Arellano, Attack of the Tomato King, OrangeCountyLatino.us, July 6, 2006, at http://oclatino.wordpress.com/2006/07/09/attack-of-the-tomato-king/.

2 David FitzGerald, *A Nation of Emigrants: How Mexico Manages Its Migration* 136 (2008).

3 Khatchig Mouradian, Dual Citizenship: An Interview with Vahan Hovhannesian, *Armenian Weekly*, Aug. 11, 2007.

4 See, e.g., Joshua David Marcin, Migrant Workers' Remittances, Citizenship, and the State: The Case of El Salvador, 48 *Harvard Civil Rights-Civil Liberties Law Review* 531 (2013); David Leblang, Harnessing the Diaspora: The Political Economy of Dual Citizenship, Migration Remittances, and Return (2013), available at http://assets.csom.umn.edu/assets/160305.pdf (establishing empirical connection between dual citizenship rules and level of remittances).

5 Schuck, *Citizens, Strangers, and In-Betweens*, at 228.

6 See Michael Jones-Correa, *Between Two Nations: The Political Predicament of Latinos in New York City* ch. 8 (1998); Francesca Mazzolari, Determinants of

Naturalization: The Role of Dual Citizenship Laws, Center for Comparative Immigrations Studies Working Paper 117 (2005), available at http://ccis.ucsd.edu/wp-content/uploads/WP_117.pdf.

7  FitzGerald, *Nation of Emigrants*, at 174.

8  Maastricht Centre for Citizenship, Migration and Development, Global Dual Citizenship Database (2013), available at https://macimide.maastrichtuniversity.nl/dual-citizenship-database/.

9  See Nick Thorpe, Hungary Creating New Mass of EU Citizens, *BBC News*, at http://www.bbc.com/news/world-europe-24848361.

10  See, e.g., Nora Hui-Jung Kim, Flexible yet Inflexible: Development of Dual Citizenship in Korea, 18 *Journal of Korean Studies* 7 (2013).

11  See, e.g., Yin Pumin, Debating Dual Citizenship, *Beijing Review*, Oct. 2, 2014, at http://www.bjreview.com.cn/nation/txt/2014-09/25/content_642355.htm.

12  See Calum MacLeod, Chinese Flock to US to Give Birth to US Citizens, *USA Today*, Apr. 1, 2015.

13  See, e.g., Ishani Duttagupta, PIO and OCI Cards Provide Relief to NRIs from Visa Hassles, *Economic Times*, Mar. 11, 2012, at http://articles.economictimes.indiatimes.com/2012-03-11/news/31143355_1_oci-pio-card-overseas-citizen; *Report of the High Level Committee on the Indian Diaspora* ch. 36 (August 2000), available at http://indiandiaspora.nic.in/diasporapdf/chapter36.pdf.

14  See Indonesia Seeing "Positive" Signs on Dual Citizenship, *Jakarta Post*, Aug. 24, 2013.

15  See Mie Murazumi, Japan's Law on Dual Nationality in the Context of a Globalized World, 9 *Pacific Rim & Policy Journal* 415 (2000); Minoru Matsutani, Debate of Multiple Nationalities to Heat Up, *Japan Times*, Jan. 1, 2009.

16  Kyla Ryan, Japan's Better Hafu: Can Japan's Laws Keep Up with Its Emerging Internationalization?, *Diplomat*, July 22, 2014, at http://thediplomat.com/2014/07/japans-better-hafu/.

17  See Bronwen Manby, *Citizenship Law in Africa: A Comparative Study* 58 (2010). This is the first comprehensive survey of citizenship laws in Africa.

18  Id. at 63.

19  Tanja Brøndsted Sejersen, 'I Vow to Thee My Countries'—The Expansion of Dual Citizenship in the 21st Century, 42 *International Migration Review* 523, 535 (2008).

20  Christian Joppke, *Citizenship and Immigration* 63–67 (2010).

21  See Abdullah Bozkurt, Turkey Accuses Germany of Violating Human Rights of Turks, *Today's Zaman*, Nov. 1, 2011, available at http://www.todayszaman.com/news-261634-turkey-accuses-germany-of-violating-human-rights-of-turks.html; Turkey Welcomes Germany's Dual Citizenship Law, *Turkish Weekly*, Dec. 22, 2014, available at http://www.turkishweekly.net/2014/12/22/news/turkey-welcomes-germanys-dual-citizenship-law/.

22  See David C. Earnest, *Old Nations, New Voters: Nationalism, Transnationalism, and Democracy in the Era of Global Migration* (2008).

23 For a survey of external voting practices, see material compiled by the Administration and Costs of Elections (ACE) Project, Voting from Abroad, available at https://aceproject.org/ace-en/topics/va/onePage.

24 See European Commission, Communication Addressing the Consequences of Disenfranchisement of Union Citizens Exercising Their Right to Free Movement, COM(2014) 33, at 5, available at http://ec.europa.eu/justice/citizen/files/com_2014_33_en.pdf.

25 See Voting Rights Restored to Canadians Living Abroad Long-Term, *CBC News*, May, 4, 2014, at http://www.cbc.ca/m/touch/news/story/1.2631760.

26 See Commission on Filipinos Overseas, Office of the President of the Philippines, Overseas Voting Act of 2013, May 31, 2013, at http://www.cfo.gov.ph/.

27 See Electoral Commission of South Africa, How to Register and Vote Abroad, at http://www.elections.org.za/content/For-Voters/How-to-register-and-vote-abroad/.

28 See generally ACE Project, www.aceproject.org/ace-en/topics/va.

29 See Scattered Swiss Retain Voting Rights, swissinfo.ch, Dec. 14, 2009, at http://www.swissinfo.ch/eng/scattered-swiss-retain-voting-rights/8950.

30 See Jones-Correa, *Between Two Nations*, at 125.

31 See Council of Europe Parliamentary Assembly, Links between Europeans Living Abroad and Their Countries of Origin, Doc. 8339, para. 48 (Mar. 5, 1999).

32 See Hassan M. Fattah, Iraqis Abroad Seem Reluctant to Vote, Too, Sign-Up Shows, *New York Times*, Jan. 26, 2005 (reporting that more than one million expatriate Iraqis were eligible to register).

33 Sejersen, 'I Vow to Thee My Countries,' at 535.

34 See Philippine Information Agency, Overseas Voter Registration Breaches the One Million Mark for the First Time, July 11, 2014, at http://www.pia.gov.ph/mobile/index.php?article=1781405069575.

35 See Returning Officers: More Expatriates Are Electing Representatives at Home, *Economist*, June 2, 2012.

36 Alfredo Corchado, Double-Edged Sword: Latin American Governments Weigh Emigrants' Right to Vote in Their Native Land, *Dallas Morning News*, Sept. 21, 1997. See also Rainer Bauböck, Towards a Political Theory of Migrant Transnationalism, 37 *International Migration Review* 700, 711 (2003); David A. Martin, New Rules on Dual Nationality for a Democratizing Globe: Between Rejection and Embrace, 14 *Georgetown Immigration Law Journal* 1, 26 (1999) (rule allowing dual nationals the right to vote only in their country of residence would "help . . . promote mature deliberation and seriousness about the vote, because the voter will have to live with the consequences in the most direct way.").

37 Corchado, Double-Edged Sword; see also Marcin, *Remittances, Citizenship, and the State*.

38 Ajaz Haque, Overseas Pakistanis' Money Is Good—But Not Their Vote, *Express Tribune*, May 2, 2015, at http://tribune.com.pk/story/879299/overseas-pakistanis-money-is-good-but-not-their-vote/.

39  See Simon Montlake, Filipinos Abroad Get Vote, *Christian Science Monitor*, Mar.
    17, 2004, (reporting non-resident Filipino citizen interest in voting for the "candi-
    date that sticks up for her rights").

40  Overseas Citizens Voting Rights Act of 1975, House Report No. 94–649 (1975), at
    2.

41  Thousands of Citizens Return to Vote, *Jerusalem Post*, May 17, 1999. In 1997 Turk-
    ish elections, 87,000 out of 2.3 million eligible non-resident voters cast ballots at
    border polling stations.

42  See Sense of Duty to Homeland Compels Mass. Dominicans to Return to Vote,
    *Boston Globe*, May 13, 2000; New York Dominicans Strongly Back Candidates on
    Island, *New York Times*, Jun. 29, 1996.

43  UK Parliamentary Official Report, 27 June 1984, Vol. 62, c. 1029–31.

44  See House Report 94–649, at 2.

45  See To Russia—Politics with Love, Immigrants Vote in Duma Election, *Boston
    Globe*, Dec. 20, 1999.

46  Bauböck, Political Theory of Migrant Transnationalism, at 713.

47  Diego Valades, Constitutional Implications of Mexican Voting Abroad, available at
    http://www.unam.mx/voices/1999. See also Eva Ostergaard-Nielsen, Trans-State
    Loyalties and Politics of Turks and Kurds in Europe, *SAIS Review*, Winter–Spring
    2000, at 23. Cf. Celia Walden, Labour and the Missing Millions, *Daily Telegraph*,
    Dec. 1, 2004 (reporting charge that Labour government slowed overseas turnout
    drives "lest [overseas voters] vote the 'wrong' way"). Earlier failed attempts to
    establish absentee ballots were explained by the then-ruling party's "fear that the
    overwhelming majority of Mexicans living in the United States blamed [it] for poor
    economic conditions and a lack of opportunity at home and would therefore vote
    for the opposition." John Ward Anderson, Politicians without Borders: Mexico's
    Candidates Court Support of Migrants in U.S., *Washington Post*, May 9, 2000.

48  See Richard Boudreaux, Americans Abroad Are Itching to Get Their Hands on
    Ballots, *Los Angeles Times*, Oct. 20, 2004; Charles M. Sennott, Voter Registration
    Surges Abroad, *Boston Globe*, Oct. 28, 2004.

49  Council of Europe, Links between Europeans Living Abroad and Their Countries
    of Origin, at paras. 40, 85.

50  International Covenant on Civil and Political Rights art. 25, Dec. 16, 1966, 999
    U.N.T.S. 171.

51  Hugh Dellios & Oscar Avila, Doubts Cast on Pull of Absentee Vote in Next Elec-
    tion, *Chicago Tribune*, June 30, 2005.

52  See, e.g., Gergely Szakacs, Outside Hungary's Borders, a Growing Power Base for
    PM Orban, *Reuters*, May 30, 2013, at http://www.reuters.com/article/2013/05/30/
    us-hungary-diaspora-votes-idUSBRE94T0TE20130530.

53  See, e.g., David Cook-Martín, *The Scramble for Citizens: Dual Nationality and
    State Competition for Immigrants* 130, 146 (2013).

54  See Andrea Elliott, A New York Vote, But a Dominican Contest, *New York Times*,
    May 17, 2004.

55  Montlake, Filipino Voters Abroad Get the Vote.

56  Council of Europe, Links between Europeans Living Abroad and Their Countries of Origin, para. 80.

57  See Returning Officers, Economist; Colin Perkel, Elections Canada Stops Enforcing Voting Ban on Expats, *CTV News*, May 13, 2014, at http://www.ctvnews.ca/politics/elections-canada-stops-enforcing-voting-ban-on-expats-1.1819933.

58  See Martin, *New Rules on Dual Nationality*, at 25–31; see also T. Alexander Aleinikoff, *Between Principles and Politics: The Direction of U.S. Citizenship Policy* 36 (1998) (proposing bilateral agreements to limit voting of dual citizens to place of residence).

59  See Phuong Ly & Nurith C. Aizenman, Immigrant Voters' Split Ticket, Some U.S. Citizens Also Cast Ballots in Homeland, *Washington Post*, Oct. 30, 2003; see also Martin, *New Rules on Dual Nationality*, at 26.

60  See Louis DeSipio, Do Home-Country Political Ties Limit Latino Immigrant Pursuit of Civic Engagement and Citizenship?, in *Transforming Politics, Transforming America: The Political and Civic Incorporation of Immigrants in the United States* 123 (Taeku Lee et al., eds. 2007).

61  See Peter H. Schuck, Plural Citizenships, in *Immigration & Citizenship in the 21st Century*, at 149, 171.

62  See Martin, *New Rules for Dual Nationality*, at 15–16, 30 ("What is most fundamentally at stake is the equality that has been a key element in the basic understanding of what it means to be a citizen.").

63  John Fonte, Dual Allegiance: A Challenge to Immigration Reform and Patriotic Assimilation, Center for Immigration Studies Backgrounder (November 2005), at 8.

64  See Michele Wucker, The Perpetual Migration Machine and Political Power, *World Policy Journal*, Fall 2004, at 41, 44.

65  See Willem Maas, Extending Politics: Enfranchising Non-Resident European Citizens, Paper Presented at the 40th Annual Convention of the International Studies Association (Feb. 1999), available at http://www.ciaonet.org/isa/maw01.

66  See 42 U.S.C. § 1973ff-6 (1998) (defining overseas voter as person who either was or would be qualified to vote "in the last place in which the person was domiciled before leaving the United States").

67  See Bauböck, Political Theory of Migrant Transnationalism, at 714 ("As a general rule, extra-territorial voting rights should expire with the first generation").

68  See Council of Europe, Links between Europeans Living Abroad and Their Countries of Origin ¶¶ 55–73.

69  See Council of Europe Parliamentary Assembly, Recommendation 1650 (2004).

70  For details, see Democrats Abroad, at http://www.democratsabroad.org.

71  See U.S. General Accounting Office, *The U.S. Constitution and Insular Areas* 26–28 (1998) (describing role of non-voting delegates in House of Representatives). Of course, if external citizens were to gain a non-voting delegate they would

have to give up their capacity to vote for representatives in their last place of U.S. residence, a possibly unpalatable tradeoff.

72  See, e.g., Jones-Correa, *Between Two Nations*, at 164–66; Kathleen Newland, Voice after Exit: Diaspora Advocacy 8 (2010), available at http://www.migrationpolicy.org/research/voice-after-exit-diaspora-advocacy; Mexican Candidates Look to U.S. for Swing Votes, *Los Angeles Times*, May 5, 2000; Mexican Politicians Cross the U.S. Border in Search of Votes, *Financial Times*, May 6, 1998; Salvadoran Political Hopeful Campaigns Here among Exiles, *Los Angeles Times*, Feb. 20, 1999. In addition to campaign contributions, remittances allow non-resident communities to have substantial influence over the electoral preferences of friends and relatives back home, giving rise to a swing bloc of "Money Gram Mexicans." See Presidential Candidate Cuauhtémoc Cardenas' L.A. Campaign Stop Reflects Close Ties that Span Border, *Los Angeles Times*, May 7, 2000.

73  See Vanya Mehta, Nonresident Indians Play Major Role in Aam Aadmi Party's Delhi Campaign, *New York Times*, Dec. 3, 2013.

## CHAPTER 7. DUAL CITIZENSHIP AS HUMAN RIGHT

1  See 32 CFR § 147.5.

2  *In the Matter of: Applicant for Security Clearance*, ISCR Case No. 12–02082 (Dept. of Defense Office of Hearings & Appeals, Mar. 26, 2014), available at http://www.dod.mil/dodgc/doha/industrial/12–02082.h1.pdf.

3  *In the Matter of: Applicant for Security Clearance*, ISCR Case No. 12–05015 (Dept. of Defense Office of Hearings & Appeals, May 31, 2013), available at http://www.dod.mil/dodgc/doha/industrial/12–05015.h1.pdf.

4  The U.S. Supreme Court has so held. See *Department of the Navy v. Egan*, 484 U.S. 518 (1988).

5  John Torpey links the innovation of the concept of nationality to state interests in "holding onto" individuals, by way of a kind of human mercantilism. John Torpey, *The Invention of the Passport: Surveillance, Citizenship, and the State* (2000).

6  Aleinikoff & Klusmeyer, Plural Nationality, at 77.

7  See Nissim Bar-Yaacov, *Dual Nationality*, at 265 (1961).

8  See Triadafilos Triadafilopoulos, Dual Citizenship and Security Norms, in *Dual Citizenship in Global Perspective: From Unitary to Multiple Citizenship* 35 (Thomas Faist & Peter Kivisto, eds. 2007) (noting that decline of conscription "has removed one of the most important arguments against dual citizenship").

9  See Stephen H. Legomsky, Dual Nationality and Military Service: Strategy Number Two, in *Rights and Duties of Dual Nationals* 79 (David A. Martin & Kay Hailbronner, eds. 2003).

10  See David A. Martin, Introduction: The Trend toward Dual Nationality, in *Rights and Duties of Dual Nationals*, at 3, 6.

11  Cf. Rogers Smith, *Civic Ideals* 489–504 (1997) (analogizing American nation to political party).

12  International Covenant on Civil and Political Rights art. 22, Dec. 19, 1966, 999 U.N.T.S. 171.

13  Peter Schuck, *Citizens, Strangers, and In-Betweens* 175 (2000).

14  See, e.g., *Boy Scouts of America v. Dale*, 530 U.S. 640 (2000).

15  Rainer Bauböck, The Trade-off between Transnational Citizenship and Political Autonomy, in *Dual Citizenship in Global Perspective*, at 69, 79.

16  Id. at 86.

17  See, e.g., Paul A. Goble, Russian 'Passportization,' *New York Times*, Sept. 9, 2008.

18  Council of Europe Parliamentary Assembly Resolution 1989 (2014).

19  Bauböck, Political Theory of Migrant Transnationalism, at 711 ("after some time of legal residence immigrants acquire a right to naturalization that should not depend on renouncing their previous citizenship"); Ruth Rubio-Marin, Transnational Politics and the Democratic Nation-State: Normative Challenges of Expatriate Voting and Nationality Retention of Emigrants, 81 *NYU Law Review* 117, 142–43 (2006).

20  European Convention on Nationality art. 14, Nov. 6, 1997, C.E.T.S. No. 166.

21  Karen Knop, Relational Nationality: On Gender and Nationality in International Law, in *Citizenship Today*, at 89, 112.

22  See, e.g., Rainer Bauböck, *Transnational Citizenship* ch. 4; Ruth Rubio-Marin, *Immigration as a Democratic Challenge* (2000); Joseph Carens, Citizenship and Civil Society: What Rights for Residents?, in *Dual Nationality, Social Rights and Federal Citizenship in the United States and Europe* 100 (Randall Hansen & Patrick Weil, eds. 2002).

23  Bauböck, Political Theory of Migrant Transnationalism, at 717. See also Randall Hansen & Patrick Weil, Introduction: Dual Citizenship in a Changed World: Immigration, Gender and Social Rights, in *Dual Nationality, Social Rights and Federal Citizenship*, at 1, 8–9 (concluding that dual citizenship does not violate Walzer's principle of complex equality insofar as citizenship in one state will not advantage an individual in his state of additional citizenship).

24  Kay Hailbronner, Germany's Citizenship Law under Immigration Pressure, in *Dual Nationality, Social Rights and Federal Citizenship in the U.S. and Europe: The Reinvention of Citizenship* 123 (Patrick Weil & Randall Hansen, eds. 2002).

25  Simon Green, Between Ideology and Pragmatism: The Politics of Dual Nationality in Germany, 39 *International Migration Review* 921, 923 (2005).

26  James D. Ingram & Triadafilos Triadafilopoulos, Rights, Norms, and Politics: The Case of German Citizenship Reform, 77 *Social Research* 353, 375 (2010).

27  Germany's Disputed Dual Citizenship Law: 'Everyone Must Be Able to Participate,' Qantara.de, Feb. 27, 2013, at http://en.qantara.de/content/germanys-disputed-dual-citizenship-law-everyone-must-be-able-to-participate.

28  Barbara Pusch, Dual Citizenship in the Transnational German-Turkish Space: Notes from Germany, Istanbul Policy Center IPC-Mercator Policy Brief (Feb. 2015), available at http://ipc.sabanciuniv.edu/en/wp-content/uploads/2015/02/Barbara-push-feb_son1.pdf. See also Betty de Hart & Ricky van Oers, Eu-

ropean Trends in Nationality, in *Acquisition and Loss of Nationality: Policies and Trends in 15 European Countries* 317, 356 n.37 (Rainer Bauböck et al., eds. 2005); Christal Morehouse, Although Legally an Exception, Dual Nationality Has Become the Rule in Germany, European Union Democracy Observatory on Citizenship, Mar. 7, 2012, available at http://eudo-citizenship.eu/news/citizenship-news/606-although-legally-an-exception-dual-nationality-has-become-the-rule-in-germany.

29 See With Venstre on Board, Dual Citizenship Looks Likely, Online Post, May 21, 2013, at http://cphpost.dk/news14/politics-news14/with-venstre-on-board-dual-citizenship-looks-likely.html.

30 Dutchmen Grounded, *Economist*, Jan. 7, 2012.

31 Ricky van Oers et al., Country Report: The Netherlands 42 (EUDO Citizenship Observatory 2013), available at http://eudo-citizenship.eu/admin/?p=file&appl=countryProfiles&f=Netherlands.pdf.

32 Kim Rubenstein, *Australian Citizenship in Context* § 4.6.1.1 (2002).

33 Manby, *Citizenship Law in Africa*, at 59.

34 See, e.g., Gianni Zappala & Stephen Castles, Citizenship and Immigration in Australia, in *Citizenship Today*, at 32, 58–62 (describing debate in Australia).

35 See APL Resents Rejection of Dual Nationality Bill, *Asians*, Nov. 16, 2014, at http://www.theasians.co.uk/story/20141116_apl_rejection_bill.

36 Rashantha N. de Alwis-Seneviratne, The Dual National, Citizenship & Human Rights, *Colombo Telegraph*, May 5, 2015, at https://www.colombotelegraph.com/index.php/the-dual-national-citizenship-human-rights/.

37 Rayner Thwaites, The Security of Citizenship?: Finnis in the Context of the United Kingdom's Citizenship Stripping Provisions, in *Allegiance and Identity in a Globalised World* 243, 263 (Fiona Jenkins, ed. 2014). See also Audrey Macklin, Citizenship Revocation, the Privilege to Have Rights and the Production of the Alien, 40 *Queen's Law Journal* 1, 50 (2014).

38 Matthew J. Gibney, Should Citizenship Be Conditional? The Ethics of Denationalization, 75 *Journal of Politics* 646 (2013).

39 See, e.g., Justice Department Settles Immigration-Related Discrimination Claim Against The Data Entry Company Inc., May 8, 2015, at http://www.justice.gov/opa/pr/justice-department-settles-immigration-related-discrimination-claim-against-data-entry.

40 See, e.g., Zivotofsky v. Clinton, 132 S.Ct. 1421 (2012) (finding courts competent to reach merits of dispute relating to designation of Jerusalem on U.S. passports).

41 Convention on Reduction of Cases of Multiple Nationality and Military Obligations in Cases of Multiple Nationality, May 6, 1963, 634 U.N.T.S. 221, Europ. T.S. No. 43.

42 Lisa Pilgrim, International Law and European Nationality Laws 4 (EUDO Citizenship Observatory 2013), available at http://eudo-citizenship.eu/docs/Pilgram.pdf.

43 European Convention on Nationality, preamble, arts. 14 & 16.

44 See Kim Rubenstein, Globalization and Citizenship and Nationality, in *Jurisprudence for an Interconnected Globe* 159 (Catherine Dauvergne, ed. 2003) (predicting "increasing willingness in international treaty law to acknowledge and encourage dual and multiple nationality").

45 See Council of Europe Parliamentary Assembly Resolution 1989 (2014).

46 High Commissioner on National Minorities, Organisation for Security and Co-operation in Europe, Ljubljana Guidelines on Integration of Diverse Societies & Explanatory Note (November 2012), available at http://www.osce.org/hcnm/96883.

47 Manby, *Citizenship Law in Africa*, at 15.

## CHAPTER 8. DUAL CITIZENSHIP, DECLINING CITIZENSHIP

1 See Linda Bosniak, Multiple Nationality and the Postnational Transformation of Citizenship, 42 *Virginia Journal of International Law* 979 (2002).

2 See Gabriela Rico, Dual Nationality Threatens to Alter Electoral Influence, *Statesman Journal*, Jan. 30, 2005, available at http://archive.statesmanjournal.com/article/20050130/NEWS/501300317/Dual-nationality-threatens-alter-electoral-influence.

3 See Joseph H. Carens, *Immigrants and the Right to Stay* (2010).

4 Ruth Rubio-Marin, *Immigration as a Democratic Challenge* (2000); Helder De Schutter and Lea Ypi, The British Academy Brian Barry Prize Essay: Mandatory Citizenship for Immigrants, 45 *British Journal of Political Science* 235 (2015).

5 Arjun Appadurai, *Modernity at Large: Cultural Dimensions of Globalization* 171 (1996).

6 Huntington, *Who Are We?*, at 213.

7 See, e.g., Ilan Stevens, Repatriating Spain's Jews, *New York Times*, Apr. 1, 2014; Many Seek Spanish Citizenship Offered to Sephardic Jews, *New York Times*, Mar. 19, 2014; Isabel Kershner & Raphael Minder, Prospect of Spanish Citizenship Appeals to Descendants of Jews Expelled in 1492, *New York Times*, Feb. 13, 2014.

8 See Gil Shefler, Spanish Muslims, or Moriscos, Seek Parity with Jews Expelled from Spain, *Washington Post*, June 5, 2014.

9 See Kim Gittleson, Where Is the Cheapest Place to Buy Citizenship?, *BBC News*, June 3, 2014, at http://www.bbc.com/news/business-27674135.

10 See Denise Roland, Cyprus Offers Passport to Big Foreign Investors, *Telegraph*, Apr. 14, 2013.

11 See Zenturo Ltd., Frequently Asked Questions [about Individual Investor Program], at http://www.malta-citizenship.info/individual-investor-program-faq.html.

12 See Should Citizenship Be for Sale? (European Union Institute Working Paper, Ayelet Shachar & Rainer Bauböck, eds. 2014), available at http://cadmus.eui.eu/bitstream/handle/1814/29318/RSCAS_2014_01.pdf.

13 See, e.g., Madeleine Sumption & Kate Hooper, Selling Visas and Citizenship (Migration Policy Institute 2014), available at http://www.migrationpolicy.org/

research/selling-visas-and-citizenship-policy-questions-global-boom-investor-immigration; Henry Grabar, Buy a House, Get a Visa: Coming Soon Everywhere?, *Citylab*, Nov. 27, 2012, at http://www.citylab.com/housing/2012/11/buy-house-get-visa-coming-soon-everywhere/3959/.

14  Aleinikoff & Klusmeyer, Plural Nationality, at 84.

15  Bosniak, *Multiple Nationality*, at 998.

16  Huntington, *Who Are We?*, at 212.

17  Rule 41 provides that "Any competitor in the Olympic Games must be a national of the country of the [National Olympic Committee] which is entering such competitor." See Olympic Charter, available at http://www.olympic.org/Documents/olympic_charter_en.pdf.

18  As catalogued by the EUDO Citizenship Observatory, such naturalization provisions are common, including among most European states. See EUDO Citizenship Observatory, Comparing Citizenship Laws: Acquisition of Citizenship, at http://eudo-citizenship.eu/databases/modes-of-acquisition.

19  See Sam Borden, Rejecting the U.S. to Skate for Russia, *New York Times*, Feb. 9, 2014.

20  See Brook Larmer, The Year of the Mercenary Athlete, *Time*, Aug. 19, 2008. For other treatments of Olympic nationality, see, e.g., Peter Spiro, It's Time for Olympic Free Agency, *Slate*, Feb. 6, 2014; Hanna Kozlowska & Catherine A. Traywick, Carpetbagging the Olympics, *Foreign Policy*, Feb. 4, 2014, at http://foreignpolicy.com/2014/02/04/carpetbagging-the-olympics/; Lawrence Donegan, Holden Heads a Band of 'Traitors' Taking Different Passport to Glory: Concerns Are Growing over Numbers Who Have Changed Nationality to Be at Beijing, *Guardian*, Aug. 12, 2008; For a Wreath, a Flag—or Cash?, *Economist*, Aug. 12, 2004.

21  John Rosenthal, A New German? Olympian Chris Kaman and German Nationality, *World Politics Review*, Aug. 14, 2008, at http://www.worldpoliticsreview.com/articles/2568/a-new-german-olympian-chris-kaman-and-german-nationality.

22  See, e.g., Dave McKenna, Dominica's Fake Ski Team Scammed the Olympics and the Press, *Deadspin*, Feb. 24, 2014, at http://deadspin.com/dominicas-fake-ski-team-scammed-the-olympics-and-the-p-1529973935.

23  See Christopher Clarey, Now Skating for (Insert Country), *New York Times*, Jan. 28, 2010.

24  David Wharton, Going Away for the Gold, *Los Angeles Times*, Aug. 11, 2004.

25  See Federation Internationale de Football Association, FIFA Statutes 67 (August 2009 ed.).

26  See Federation Internationale de Basketball, Internal Regulations 2010, & H.2, at 67–69. Exceptions are available "in exceptional circumstances" and before the athlete reaches the age of 17. Id. & H.2.3.5.

27  See International Ice Hockey Federation, IIHF Statutes and Bylaws 2008–2012, at 205.1.3 (change "will be allowed only once in a player's life and is final and irrevocable").

28  See Federation Internationale de Basketball, Regulation H.2.3.3. ("A national team participating in an international competition of FIBA may have only one player on its team who has acquired the legal nationality of that country by naturalisation or by any other means after having reached the age of sixteen").

29  See Federation Internationale de Ski, International Ski Competition Rules 5 & 7 (2008) ("the competitor must have had his/her principal legal and effective place of residence in the new country for a minimum of two (2) years immediately prior to the date of the request to change registration to the new country/National Ski Association, except where the competitor is born in the territory of the new country or whose mother or father is a national of the new country."). See also Federation Equestre Internationale, art. 129.2.2.3 (same).

30  See FIFA, art. 16.1 (soccer); IIHF, supra, & 205.1.3 (ice hockey).

31  *Nottebohm* (Liechtenstein v. Guatemala), 1955 ICJ Rep. 4 (Apr. 6), described in chapter 3.

32  Ayelet Shachar, Picking Winners: Olympic Citizenship and the Global Race for Talent, 120 *Yale Law Journal* 2088, 2106 (2011).

33  See Cook-Martín, *Scramble for Citizens*, at 153 (of eleven international members of Barcelona's soccer franchise, all but one play international matches for country of origin).

34  See Ayelet Shachar & Ran Hirschl, Recruiting 'Super Talent': The New World of Selective Migration Regimes, 20 *Indiana Journal of Global Legal Studies* 71 (2013).

35  See Noah Pickus, *True Faith and Allegiance: Immigration and American Civic Nationalism* 181 (2005).

36  Josh Marshall, A Bad Idea, *Talking Points Memo*, May 9, 2013, http://talking-pointsmemo.com/edblog/a-bad-idea; Josh Marshall, Citizenship Matters, *Talking Points Memo*, May 11, 2013, http://talkingpointsmemo.com/edblog/citizenship-matters.

37  Michael Walzer, *Spheres of Justice*, at 62.

38  See Tim Mak, Michele Bachmann Blasted by Right Blogs, *Politico*, May 11, 2012, http://www.politico.com/news/stories/0512/76211.html.

39  Rainer Bauböck, Studying Citizenship Constellations, 36 *Journal of Ethnic and Migration Studies* 847 (2010).

40  Ayelet Shachar, *The Birthright Lottery: Citizenship and Global Inequality* 130–31 (2009).

# SELECTED BIBLIOGRAPHY

Aleinikoff, T. Alexander, and Douglas Klusmeyer, eds. *Citizenship Today: Global Perspectives and Practices.* Washington, DC: Carnegie Endowment for International Peace, 2001.

Bar-Yaacov, Nissim. *Dual Nationality.* London: Stevens, 1961.

Bauböck, Rainer. *Transnational Citizenship: Membership and Rights in International Migration.* Aldershot: Edward Elgar Publishing, 1994.

———. Towards a Political Theory of Migrant Transnationalism, 37 *International Migration Review* 700–723 (2003).

———. Studying Citizenship Constellations, 36 *Journal of Ethnic and Migration Studies* 847–59 (2010).

Blatter, Joachim. Dual Citizenship and Theories of Democracy, 15 *Citizenship Studies* 769–98 (2011).

Blatter, Joachim, et al. Acceptance of Dual Citizenship: Empirical Data and Political Contexts, Institute of Political Science/University of Lucerne "Global Governance and Democracy" Working Paper Series 02 (2009).

Bloemraad, Irene. Who Claims Dual Citizenship? The Limits of Postnationalism, the Possibilities of Transnationalism, and the Persistence of Traditional Citizenship, 38 *International Migration Review* 389–426 (2004).

———. *Becoming a Citizen: Incorporating Immigrants and Refugees in the United States and Canada.* Berkeley: University of California Press, 2006.

Boll, Alfred Michael. *Multiple Nationality and International Law.* Leiden: Martinus Nijhoff, 2006.

Borchard, Edwin M. *The Diplomatic Protection of Citizens Abroad, Or, The Law of International Claims.* New York: Banks Law Publishing, 1915.

Bosniak, Linda. Multiple Nationality and the Postnational Transformation of Citizenship, 42 *Virginia Journal of International Law* 979–1004 (2002).

Bredbenner, Candice Lewis. *A Nationality of Her Own: Women, Marriage, and the Law of Citizenship.* Berkeley: University of California Press, 1998.

Cook-Martín, David. *The Scramble for Citizens: Dual Nationality and State Competition for Immigrants.* Stanford, CA: Stanford University Press, 2013.

Dronkers, Jaap, and Maarten Peter Vink. Explaining Access to Citizenship in Europe: How Citizenship Policies Affect Naturalization Rates, 13 *European Union Politics* 390–412 (2012).

Earnest, David C. *Old Nations, New Voters: Nationalism, Transnationalism, and De-mocracy in the Era of Global Migration*. Albany: SUNY Press, 2008.

Faist, Thomas, ed. *Dual Citizenship in Europe: From Nationhood to Societal Integration*. Aldershot: Ashgate, 2007.

Faist, Thomas, and Peter Kivisto, eds. *Dual Citizenship in Global Perspective: From Unitary to Multiple Citizenship*. New York: Palgrave Macmillan, 2007.

FitzGerald, David. *A Nation of Emigrants: How Mexico Manages Its Migration*. Berkeley: University of California Press, 2008.

Flournoy, Richard W. Dual Nationality and Election, 30 *Yale Law Journal* 545–64 (1921).

Flournoy, Richard W., and Manley O. Hudson. *A Collection of Nationality Laws of Various Countries as Contained in Constitutions, Statutes and Treaties*. New York: Oxford University Press, 1929.

Fonte, John. Dual Allegiance: A Challenge to Immigration Reform and Patriotic Assimilation, Center for Immigration Studies Backgrounder (2005).

Franck, Thomas M. Clan and Superclan: Loyalty, Identity and Community in Law and Practice, 90 *American Journal of International Law* 359–83 (1996).

Geyer, Georgie Anne. *Americans No More*. New York: Atlantic Monthly Press, 2011.

Green, Nancy L., and Francois Weil, eds. *Citizenship and Those Who Leave: The Politics of Emigration and Expatriation*. Urbana: University of Illinois Press, 2007.

Green, Simon. Between Ideology and Pragmatism: The Politics of Dual Nationality in Germany, 39 *International Migration Review* 921–52 (2005).

———. Much Ado about Not-Very-Much? Assessing Ten Years of German Citizenship Reform, 16 *Citizenship Studies* 173–88 (2012).

Hackworth, Green Haywood. *Digest of International Law*. Washington, DC: U.S. Government Printing Office, 1940.

Harvard Law School Research in International Law. Draft Convention and Comments on the Law of Nationality, 23 *American Journal of International Law* 13 (Special Supplement 1929).

Herzog, Ben. *Revoking Citizenship: Expatriation in America from the Colonial Era to the War on Terror*. New York: NYU Press, 2015.

Howard, Marc Morjé. *The Politics of Citizenship in Europe*. Cambridge, UK: Cambridge University Press, 2009.

Huntington, Samuel P. *Who Are We?: The Challenges to America's National Identity*. New York: Simon & Schuster, 2004.

Ingram, James D., and Triadafilos Triadafilopoulos. Rights, Norms, and Politics: The Case of German Citizenship Reform, 77 *Social Research* 353–82 (2010).

Jones-Correa, Michael. *Between Two Nations: The Political Predicament of Latinos in New York City*. Ithaca, NY: Cornell University Press, 1998.

Joppke, Christian. *Selecting by Origin: Ethnic Migration in the Liberal State*. Cambridge, MA: Harvard University Press, 2005.

———. *Citizenship and Immigration*. Cambridge, UK: Polity, 2010.

Kelly, H. Ansgar. Dual Nationality, the Myth of Election, and a Kinder, Gentler State Department, 23 *University of Miami Inter-American Law Review* 421–64 (1992).

Kettner, James H. *The Development of American Citizenship, 1608–1870.* Chapel Hill: University of North Carolina Press, 1978.

Kimminich, Otto. The Conventions for the Prevention of Double Nationality and Their Meaning for Germany and Europe in an Era of Migration, 38 *German Yearbook of International Law* 224–32 (1996).

League of Nations Committee of Experts for the Progressive Codification of International Law. Nationality, 20 *American Journal of International Law* 21 (Special Supplement 1926).

Manby, Bronwen. *Citizenship Law in Africa: A Comparative Study.* New York: Open Society Foundations, 2010.

Martin, David A. New Rules on Dual Nationality for a Democratizing Globe: Between Rejection and Embrace, 14 *Georgetown Immigration Law Journal* 1–34 (1999).

Martin, David A., and Kay Hailbronner, eds. *Rights and Duties of Dual Nationals: Evolution and Prospects.* The Hague: Kluwer Law International, 2003.

Mazzolari, Francesca. Determinants and Effects of Naturalization: The Role of Dual Citizenship Laws, Center for Comparative Immigration Studies/University of California, San Diego Working Paper 117 (2005).

Moore, John Bassett. *A Digest of International Law.* Washington, DC: U.S. Government Printing Office, 1906.

Neuman, Gerald L. Justifying U.S. Naturalization Policies, 35 *Virginia Journal of International Law* 237–78 (1994).

Nyers, Peter. Dueling Designs: The Politics of Rescuing Dual Citizens. 14 *Citizenship Studies* 47–60 (2010).

Pickus, Noah. *True Faith and Allegiance: Immigration and American Civic Nationalism.* Princeton, NJ: Princeton University Press, 2005.

——, ed. *Immigration and Citizenship in the Twenty-First Century.* Lanham, MD: Rowman & Littlefield, 1998.

Renshon, Stanley. *The 50% American: Immigration and National Identity in an Age of Terror.* Washington, DC: Georgetown University Press, 2005.

Ronkainen, Jussi Kasperi. Mononationals, Hyphenationals, and Shadow-Nationals: Multiple Citizenship as Practice, 15 *Citizenship Studies* 247–63 (2011).

Rubio-Marín, Ruth. *Immigration as a Democratic Challenge: Citizenship and Inclusion in Germany and the United States.* Cambridge, UK: Cambridge University Press, 2000.

Schuck, Peter H. *Citizens, Strangers, and In-Betweens: Essays on Immigration and Citizenship.* Boulder, CO: Westview Press, 2000.

Schuck, Peter H., and Rogers M. Smith. *Citizenship without Consent: Illegal Aliens in the American Polity.* New Haven, CT: Yale University Press, 1985.

Shachar, Ayelet. *The Birthright Lottery: Citizenship and Global Inequality.* Cambridge, MA: Harvard University Press, 2009.

———. Picking Winners: Olympic Citizenship and the Global Race for Talent, 120 *Yale Law Journal* 2088–2139 (2015).

Shachar, Ayelet, and Rainer Bauböck. Should Citizenship Be for Sale? Florence: European University Institute/Robert Schuman Centre for Advanced Studies Working Paper (2014).

Sejersen, Tanja Brøndsted. 'I Vow to Thee My Countries'—The Expansion of Dual Citizenship in the 21st Century, 42 *International Migration Review* 523–49 (2008).

Spiro, Peter J. Dual Nationality and the Meaning of Citizenship, 46 *Emory Law Journal* 1411–85 (1997).

———. A New International Law of Citizenship, 105 *American Journal of International Law* 694–746 (2011).

———. Expatriating Terrorists, 82 *Fordham Law Review* 2169–87 (2014).

Tsiang, I.-Mien. *The Question of Expatriation in America Prior to 1907*. Baltimore: Johns Hopkins Press, 1942.

United Nations International Law Commission. Survey of the Problem of Multiple Nationality, U.N. Doc. A/CN.4/84 (1954), 2 *Yearbook of the International Law Commission 1954* (1960).

United States Congress. *Dual Citizenship, Birthright Citizenship, and the Meaning of Sovereignty: Hearing before the Subcommittee on Immigration, Border Security, and Claims of the Committee on the Judiciary*. Washington, DC: U.S. Government Printing Office, 2006.

Van Dyne, Frederick. *Citizenship of the United States*. Rochester, NY: Lawyers' Co-operative Publishing Company, 1904.

Vonk, Olivier. *Dual Nationality in the European Union: A Study on Changing Norms in Public and Private International Law and in the Municipal Laws of Four EU Member States*. Leiden: Martinus Nijhoff, 2012.

Walzer, Michael. *The Spheres of Justice: A Defense of Pluralism and Equality*. New York: Basic Books, 1983.

Weil, Patrick. *The Sovereign Citizen: Denaturalization and the Origins of the American Republic*. Philadelphia: University of Pennsylvania Press, 2012.

Weil, Patrick, and Randall Hansen, eds. *Dual Nationality, Social Rights and Federal Citizenship in the U.S. and Europe: The Reinvention of Citizenship*. Oxford: Berghahn Books, 2002.

Weis, Paul. *Nationality and Statelessness in International Law*. Alphen aan den Rijn: Sijthoff & Noordhoff, 1979.

Zolberg, Aristide R. *A Nation by Design: Immigration Policy in the Fashioning of America*. Cambridge, MA: Harvard University Press, 2008.

# INDEX

## ABOUT THE AUTHOR

Peter J. Spiro is Charles R. Weiner Professor of Law at Temple University. A former U.S. Supreme Court law clerk and National Security Council staff member, he has written widely on immigration and international and constitutional law issues in such publications as the *New York Times*, the *Wall Street Journal*, *Foreign Affairs*, and *Slate*.